Critical Human Geography

PUBLISHED

Recollections of a Revolution: Geography as a Spatial Science
Mark Billinge, Derek Gregory and Ron Martin (*editors*)

The Arena of Capital
Michael Dunford and Diane Perrons

Regional Transformation and Industrial Revolution:
A Geography of the Yorkshire Woollen Industry
Derek Gregory

Social Relations and Spatial Structures
Derek Gregory and John Urry (*editors*)

Geography and the State: An Essay in Political Geography
R. J. Johnston

Spatial Divisions of Labour: Social Structures and the
Geography of Production
Doreen Massey

Conceptions of Space in Social Thought: A Geographic
Perspective
Robert David Sack

The Urban Arena: Capital, State and Community in
Contemporary Britain
John R. Short

FORTHCOMING

A Cultural Geography of Industrialisation in Britain
Mark Billinge

Development Theory: A Critique of Essentialist Approaches
Stuart Corbridge and Steve Jones

Between Feudalism and Capitalism
Robert Dodgshon

Regions and the Philosophy of the Human Sciences
Nicholas Entrikin

Strategies for Geographical Enquiry
Derek Gregory and Ron Martin

De-Industrialisation and the British Space Economy
Ron Martin and Bob Rowthorn (*editors*)

Spatial Divisions of Labour

Social Structures and the Geography of Production

Doreen Massey

MACMILLAN

First published 1984
Reprinted 1985

Published by
Higher and Further Education Division
MACMILLAN PUBLISHERS LTD
Houndmills, Basingstoke, Hampshire RG21 2XS
and London
Companies and representatives
throughout the world

Printed in Hong Kong

ISBN 0–333–21498–6 (hard cover)
ISBN 0–333–34257–7 (paper cover)

FOR
NANCY AND JACK
*with many thanks
and much love*

Contents

Preface

This book has been a long time in the making. It began life as a contribution to a debate within the branch of geography known as 'industrial location theory' – as what I hoped would be a trenchant critique of all, or pretty much all, that had gone before, together with a second half which would present 'an alternative approach'. A number of things have happened in the period since then. I got bored with the critique. The second 'half' became the length of a book in itself, and it also changed its nature. From being a schematic outline it became increasingly grounded in what was going on in Britain and in other advanced capitalist countries.

But more than anything else I became increasingly convinced of the importance of the issues involved and of the fact that they should have a wider audience. My basic aim had been to link the geography of industry and employment to the wider, and underlying, structures of society. And one of the things I do in the book is present an approach which, I hope, makes that possible. The initial intention, in other words, was to start from the characteristics of economy and society, and proceed to explain their geography. But the more I got involved in the subject, the more it seemed that the process was not just one way. It is also the case – I would argue – that understanding geographical organisation is fundamental to understanding an economy and a society. The geography of a society makes a difference to the way it works.

If this is true analytically, it is also true politically. For there to be any hope of altering the fundamentally unequal geography of British economy and society (and that of other capitalist countries, too), a politics is necessary which links questions of geographical distribution to those of social and economic organisation. Effectively to confront the spatial inequality in Britain today means taking on much the same battles – and much the same social strata – as is necessary to win any wider progressive change. But it is equally true that any wider national political strategy must be sensitive to the variations in economic structure, in occupations, in political tradition and in the fabric of day-to-day life which exist between different parts of the country.

I have had a lot of help and support during the production of this book. Most of the book was written while I was the SSRC Fellow in Industrial Location Research, and I should like to thank the SSRC and its staff. The development of the ideas and arguments has been aided and stimulated by many friends and colleagues over a number of years. It would be impossible to mention everyone by name. What has been best about the process has been the gradual development of a practice which at least tries to argue without scoring points, and to criticise by being constructive. For their help, particularly in the final stages, however, I should like to thank Michael Ball and Huw Beynon, who read the manuscript, Nancy Massey for typing it magnificently, and a number of times, Richard Meegan, my co-worker for many eventful years, and Ron Martin, the series editor.

Faculty of Social Sciences   DOREEN MASSEY
The Open University
Milton Keynes, England

The idea for the front cover of this book was originated by John Hunt.

List of Tables

List of Figures

List of Figures

1
Changing Questions in Industrial Geography

The 1960s saw the beginnings of a major transformation in the industrial geography of the United Kingdom, and indeed in that of many other industrial capitalist countries. It is a transformation which is still going on. In the UK the end of the fifties had seen the re-emergence of the regional problem as a major political issue, as some of the old basic sectors – coal-mining, shipbuilding – went once again into decline. In other parts of the economy the centralising tendencies which had for decades dominated the geography of employment, the concentration in major metropolitan areas and the increasing dominance of the central regions – the south-east and the west midlands – gave way before another tendency, for long under way but now increasingly important, of decentralisation, both from the major cities towards smaller towns and from the central regions to those more peripheral. This dispersal meant, too, that old sectoral patterns of economic activity, the concentration of particular regions or areas in the production of particular goods, became less marked.

Much of this changing pattern, moreover, occurred as a result of the activities of large multi-plant firms, themselves becoming increasingly dominant within the national economy. As the problems of dependence on one or two industries became rather less of a preoccupation, the problems of 'branch-plant economies' became more and more evident. There were changes also in the industrial structure of the economy. While manufacturing industry had for long been declining in the proportion of jobs it provided, in 1966 the total number of people it employed fell in absolute terms, and has continued to do so. In part in parallel to this, the occupational structure of employment was also shifting: non-manual work grew rapidly at the expense of manual; old-fashioned engineering-type skills, for long the basis of many an area's prosperity, went into relative decline; white-collar jobs associated

with burgeoning managerial functions and with the 'new technology' increased in importance. These things, too, had their geographical effects. The combination of decline and decentralisation
destroyed the manufacturing base of many old urban areas, and
the uneven distribution of service jobs – in particular of the
increasingly important high-status white-collar element – became a
cause for concern. The lack of such job opportunities vied with the
problems of external control as the new concerns of regional
policy. Finally the social composition of the workforce was also
continuing to change. Women – particularly married women –
continued to increase in significance as a component of the
labour force and the distribution of female workers became an
issue of major importance.

Social and spatial changes were intimately interwoven, and in
some areas produced startling changes. In south Wales it was
rumoured that there were now more NALGO members than
members of the NUM. The west midlands – heartland only so
recently of boom, consumerism and militant car workers – saw its
economy devastated. The belt of country along the line between
London and Bristol was the new success story. In the decades since
the sixties the social and industrial structure, and the social and
industrial geography, of the UK have come to look very different.

It is not the first time that such a thing has happened. Indeed it
had only been a few decades since the pattern had been created
that now seemed so preordained and permanent. It was only in the
twenties that had begun the major decline of industries in the old
periphery (in industrial Wales and Scotland and the north-east of
England), and only since then that a new generation of industries,
many of them based around new technologies and new consumer
goods, had made the south-east and the west midlands the focus
of industrial growth. Prior to that, in the nineteenth century, it had
been in the north and west rather than the south and east where
the new industries had concentrated. In spite of the appalling
working conditions in these industries, it was the regions where
they were concentrated which had, on the whole, the higher levels
of employment and of income, for they contrasted with a still
relatively rural south and east of the country. In that period, and
on those measures, it had been the south which suffered some of
the worst 'regional problems' in the country.

*   *   *

At least twice, then, in a century and a half, the geography of British industry had been completely refashioned. And since the sixties – or so we are going to argue here – another such structural reorganisation has been under way.

How do such sea-changes come about? What lies behind them? It is changes such as these, shifts between what we shall call dominant spatial divisions of labour, that this book is going to explore.

Tradition has it that the academic division of labour assigns the job of trying to explain the spatial organisation of production within particular countries largely to the discipline of 'geography', and within that discipline to industrial geography and to a strand of work called 'industrial location theory'. But the changes in industry since the sixties have shaken industrial geography and industrial location theory to their foundations. Crises in theory are often a reflection of the real world in flux. In recent decades the spatial organisation of industry, and the questions and problems it has raised, have been transformed, and the old theoretical structures have lacked the flexibility to respond.

In formal terms the traditional theory had been derived from neo-classical economics. At its worst there had been a myopic focus on individual firms, in perfect competition and responding blindly, and perfectly, to market forces. The patent inapplicability of much of the formal model-building of this tradition, if one was interested in overall patterns of employment in the country at large, went along with a parallel school of cheery empiricism, based on censuses and surveys, and unconcerned with, if not actively scornful of, attention to theoretical formulation or problems of conceptualisation.

The shifts in industrial geography which in the sixties began to sweep not just Britain but many industrial capitalist economies, made the inadequacy of this position even more apparent. Above all, it was clear that the old, formal neo-classical models would not do. The increasing importance of large, multi-plant companies made imperative a greater recognition of the variety of behaviour exhibited by firms of different types, a variety with which the old models seemed incapable of coping. The complexity of the internal geographical structures of many of these firms forced an increased awareness of the importance of studying forms of spatial organisation rather than simply patterns of employment.

There were a number of different theoretical responses. One was to abdicate responsibility for 'explanation' in the sense previously understood. Concepts of probability and uncertainty were explored; stochastic models became popular. Another response was that of the behavioural school, which focused attention on the internal structures of firms, on the mechanisms of decision-making and implementation. Drawing on the more general behavioural approach developing within the social sciences, and using also concepts from studies of business organisation, large numbers of investigations produced a wealth of documentation of the behaviour of firms. Neither of these approaches was successful. While the probability school opted for prediction rather than explanation, the behavioural school came to a halt with description. This lack of success was, at least in part, due to the fact that while each was a response to acknowledged problems within the previously dominant neo-classical approaches, neither pinpointed the real issue. Neither succeeded in changing the terms of the debate. For both, the problem was to bridge the gap between individual behaviour and aggregate pattern. While one school sought to do this by resorting to probabilities, the other sought to build models which would be more complex than those of the classical school and which would incorporate a wider span of variables, but which were essentially a continuation of that tradition. For both approaches the ultimate aim of theory was still seen to be the construction, in one form or another, of a set of empirically testable general laws.

Other related theoretical issues were raised in the debate over regional inequality. Complaints about unequal levels of unemployment were no longer the only ones to be heard from 'the regions'. But the new problems – those which seemed to stem from external ownership, and those which were concerned as much about the type and quality of employment as with numbers of jobs pure and simple – these new problems in turn raised other new questions. It was again clearly necessary, for instance, to address oneself to the spatial organisation of production rather than just the geographical distribution of jobs. More particularly, it was necessary to focus on the *social* organisation of production and its consequences for regional differentiation.

But if this link was to be made it opened up a wider question: the relation in more general terms of 'the spatial' to 'the social'.

This issue was raised in other ways also, for it was hard to resist absolutely the idea that there was a connection between the well-recognised geographical changes and the equally important shifts going on in the national political economy and its relation to the wider international system. The question was how to establish this link. The problem was: how did an approach which had always seen its aim as the establishment of formal models and general laws cope with a situation when 'historical reality' itself so clearly forbade any such thing? The intractability of these problems led, on some fronts at least, to an impasse. It was difficult to disagree with the conclusion reached in the introduction to the most comprehensive and authoritative review of the empirical changes over the period in the industrial geography of the United Kingdom

> Ideally, investigation of the recent locational dynamics of manu-facturing industry in the United Kingdom would seem best approached in terms of some sort of theoretical framework.

The options are then reviewed, and the author concludes

> These various deficiencies thus unfortunately rule out adoption of any formal theoretical framework for this study (Keeble, 1976, pp. 2 and 4).

*   *   *

This book tries to contribute both to some of these theoretical issues and debates and to the interpretation of what has been happening in the United Kingdom's space-economy since the early sixties: its focus is on industrial geography. In spite of the impasse reached in traditional theory there has continued a rich vein of empirical and descriptive work, some examining the development of individual corporations, some, less satisfactorily, juggling with aggregate numbers and patterns. But the period has also seen the gradual and often collective building of a Marxist school of thought. For industrial geography is part of the social sciences and the alarming transformation of its object of study was not the only thing undermining its credibility in the sixties and seventies. It was also drawn into the revolution affecting social sciences more generally. It is within the second, Marxist, tradition that this book lies. It aims to set the changing geography of industry and employment within the wider context of the development of capitalist society and to examine the particular developments in Britain through the prism of the evolution of class and economic relations both within the country and internationally. Specifically, it aims to explore the geography of industry and of jobs through an interpretation of the spatial organisation of the social relations of capitalist production. It will be clear by the end of the book that regional problems, and spatial inequality more generally, have not been fundamentally challenged by any of the considerable variety of political strategies in force since the sixties, for none of them in the slightest degree challenged the underlying cause of that uneven development – the organisation of production on capitalist lines.

But the Marxist tradition, like others, also has its variations and its internal debates. There are versions which look at the world as if it were merely the pre-determined product of a set of laws and tendencies. Such approaches leave little scope for real conflict and struggle, still less for surprise and setback. They lead also to that same dichotomisation between formal models on the one hand and empirical description on the other which plagued traditional industrial location theory. Like it, too, this version of the Marxist tradition has a problem with particularity. Both have an urge to normalise for the specificity of outcomes – and in geographical studies this can have major repercussions, for a large part of what we are about is understanding unevenness, difference, place and locality. Finally, this version of Marxism tends to be, though it is not necessarily, economistic. For one thing 'the economic' level of society is so much easier to pin down, so much more amenable to the derivation of abstract long-run tendential developments. And so, from the actions of management to the politics of the State, explanations are frequently in terms solely of what is necessary for continued accumulation.

The approach adopted here aims not to be in that tradition. It adopts a mode of explanation which tries to break with the dichotomy between formal models and empirical description. It recognises underlying causal processes, but recognises, too, that such processes never operate in isolation. For it is precisely their operation in varying combinations which produces variety and uniqueness. The particular nature of capitalism in specific countries, the very different ways in which different parts of the economy respond to the general situation of economic recession, the very different impact which the entry of particular forms of economic activity can have on different regions and local areas: all are 'products of many determinations'. Instead of trying to normalise for such differences, or to treat them as merely deviations from a tendency, it is important to recognise their existence, to understand their construction and to appreciate their effects. British economy and society can only be understood by recognising its fundamentally capitalist nature. But it can only be changed – challenged politically – in its specific form. Both the general and the specific are essential, both to analysis and to action.

The focus of this book is fundamentally on what is traditionally called 'the economic'. It is a study of industrial location. The analyses here do not, therefore, attempt to cover the whole subject of 'regionalism' in its broad sense: little is said of cultural traditions, of the politics of regionalism and of how they vary between different parts of the United Kingdom. What is offered here are some elements of the potential contribution of industrial geography to that wider field. The discussions concern the spatial organisation of production and consider some of its ramifications. I am interested in the relation between industrial organisation and the geography of occupational structure, for instance; why different groups in society, different parts of the social structure, have particular geographical distributions. But, it is argued here, the study of industry and of production is *not* just a matter of 'the economic', and economic relations and phenomena are themselves constructed within a wider field of social, political and ideological relations. A real exploration of industrial geography takes one into historical shifts in national politics, into the vast variety of social forms of capital, into the whole area of gender relations and into many another wider field of enquiry.

The overall argument of this book is that behind major shifts between dominant spatial divisions of labour within a country lie changes in the spatial organisation of capitalist relations of production, the development and reorganisation of what we shall call spatial structures of production. Such shifts in spatial structures are a response to changes in class relations, economic and political, national and international. Their development is a social and conflictual process; the geography of industry is an object of struggle. The world is not simply the product of capital's requirements. Partly for that reason, and for others – technical and organisational characteristics of an industry, for instance – the range of spatial structures of production is wide. Together, they produce a particular form of spatial patterning of society – an overall spatial division of labour. But new spatial divisions of labour are also more than just new patterns, a kind of geographical re-shuffling of the same old pack of cards. They represent whole new sets of relations between activities in different places, new spatial patterns of social organisation, new dimensions of inequality and new relations of dominance and dependence. Each new spatial division of labour represents a real, and thorough, spatial restructuring. There is more than one kind of 'regional problem'.

> *   *   *

The first part of the book (Chapters 2 and 3) develops the theoretical framework. Chapter 2 deals with the most fundamental stumbling-block of all – conceptualisation. If we really are to understand spatial change as integral to social change it is necessary to go back to some of the basics, to reconstruct some of the building blocks. One obvious example: this book is about industry, but how do we relate those easy labels used in industrial studies – 'the car industry', 'coal-mining', 'the clothing sector' – to concepts of capital as a class, and more specifically to particular national capitals as a class? More generally the chapter explores some of the connections between production and social structure before turning to a consideration of the relation between these two and spatial form. This latter is largely done in Chapter 3, which examines the range of variation of spatial structures of capitalist production. Here too the argument is for better conceptualisation – this time of the geography of industry itself. A method of conceptualisation is suggested which allows a complete reformulation of most of the recent debate on intra-national uneven development, the regional problem, and spatial policy generally. Towards the end, the chapter turns from the analysis of the geographical organisation of industry to the impact on particular places. Here the problem of conceptualisation is that of recognising both that particular places are embedded in wider spatial structures, are part of broader spatial divisions of labour – a fact which they share with other places – and that each locality brings to that situation its own specific history and its own character. Once again the challenge is to hold on to both the general movement and the particularity of circumstance, and the final section of the chapter elaborates elements of an approach by which this can be done.

The purpose of all this reconceptualisation is to enable better analysis, understanding and action. One of the themes of the book is that neither theorising nor elaboration of general frameworks can in themselves answer questions about what is happening at any particular time or in any particular place. The second part of the book takes this injunction seriously and uses the approach outlined in Chapters 2 and 3 to get to grips with the upheavals which have been going on in the industrial geography of Britain since the sixties.

It has, as we have said, been a momentous period. Throughout, the British economy has been on the slide, and its international position has slumped. The post-war consensus has been rejuvenated, refurbished and then thrown out. Class relations have been remodelled and the social structure of the country has undergone a major shift. The argument here is that the changing geography of the country has been an integral element in all this.

Chapter 4 begins by setting the broad scene, sketching in the longer-term context of economic structure and class relations, looking at Britain both as a capitalist society and as a *particular* capitalist society.

From then on the analysis takes a number of different slices through the problem. The rest of Chapter 4 uses the concepts of spatial structure to analyse the quite dramatic transformations which have been under way in a number of major sections of the British economy. In the end our primary interest is in employment, and occupational and social structures – in spatial divisions of *labour*. For that reason, the focus here is on labour, on changes in the spatial structure of the labour force, changes in the use of labour in production, and labour as a determinant, both as a 'location factor' and as an active agent, of industry's choice of location. Intensified economic pressures, in various forms throughout the period, have brought with them changes in production process, shifts in the use of labour, attempts to search out cheaper and less combative workers, and enormous reorganisations of geographical form.

All this has had dramatic effects on particular places. In some the previous economic base has been removed; in others it has been substantially transformed. And just as the causes and shape of industrial change do not lie wholly within 'the economic', so the impact of industrial change has far wider repercussions than simply the percentages employed in different industries, or not employed at all. Chapter 5 takes up this regional focus and looks at the kind of industrial change analysed in Chapter 4, but from the point of view of some of the places most affected by it. In particular the chapter explores the major implications that recent changes in industrial geography have had for social structure and gender relations in particular parts of the country. Quite deliberately the chapter examines these issues in the context of two very different types of area, but areas which in the sixties and seventies were on the receiving end of the same general national change – the decentralisation of jobs 'for women' to smaller towns and peripheral regions. What the analysis shows is how different the impact of this process has been in the different regions. In spite of their being embedded in similar places in the new spatial structures of production, the areas retain their differences, their characters change under the impact of the same national process and yet remain quite distinct. As in each of the chapters on Britain, then, the analysis is not only concerned to produce a new perspective on changes under way; it is also the vehicle for a deeper theoretical argument.

In Chapter 6 the political level is examined more closely. From Wilson to Thatcher a number of very different political and economic strategies have been adopted in the UK. Chapter 6 argues that each of these strategies has had very different geographical repercussions, each pushing forward differentially particular elements of the decline of the old spatial division of labour and the emerging dominance of the new. The second half of the chapter assesses the state of play – what looks like being the new geography of class in the UK.

*   *   *

Finally, by way of introduction, one or two definitions the significance of which may already have become apparent. By *industry* is meant all economic activity, all forms of paid employment. The term is *not* used only to refer to manufacturing; indeed a large element of Chapter 5 revolves around a primary sector industry (coal-mining) and a long section in Chapter 4 is specifically concerned with the under-studied but increasingly important service industries. Second, the term *region* does not necessarily refer to standard regions, the major administrative divisions of the country, but to any sub-national area of any size. One of the arguments of the book is that the size, shape and detail of spatial variation and inequality in the UK is at present undergoing a thorough refashioning. What is more, this spatial change is not just an outcome of economic restructuring and social recomposition; it is integral to both. The phases of development of specific societies have particular geographical forms. Periods of major economic and social change are often also periods of major spatial change. It is one of the contentions of this book that we are in such a period now. And it is one of the central arguments of the book that the importance of a country's geography to its social and economic reproduction, and change, has been for too long underestimated.

2
Social Relations and Spatial Organisation

2.1 The debate

Keeble's assessment in the mid-1970s of the state, and particularly of the empirical usefulness of industrial location theory was entirely correct. Empirical enquiry into the geography of industry continued but in large part unencumbered by serious theoretical reflection or attention to problems of conceptualisation. One of the commonest empirical methods was (and unfortunately still is) the simple confrontation of two maps, one representing cause, the other effect. The effect, the phenomenon to be explained, might be a geographically-differentiated pattern of employment change. The method of establishing cause was to draw up the same map-outline but this time showing the geographical pattern of area characteristics (location factors) which were hypothesised to be influential in producing the distribution of employment growth or decline. The data on the two maps were then correlated and the production of a set of significant coefficients was assumed effectively (after all the usual caveats) to imply cause. The location factors in one map (the characteristics of areas) were deemed to explain the pattern of employment change in the other. More generally, and leaving aside the obvious 'correlation-does-not-imply-cause' objections, geographical characteristics were taken to be a significant explanation of geographical distributions.

This approach came under attack in the 1970s from a number of directions. Most obviously, it was pointed out that spatial patterns are not necessarily the result of spatial causes. Even a highly systematic spatial pattern, a clear geographical regularity, cannot be assumed to have a geographical cause. Such questions were argued out over real issues. One of them concerned regional policy. The second half of the 1960s had witnessed a not inconsiderable relative decentralisation of production activities in Britain away from the 'central' regions of the south-east and midlands and towards the peripheral regions of the north and west. The decentralisation coincided in time with a significant increase in the strength of regional policy. Regional policy at that period consisted of a set of 'carrots and sticks' distributed about the country. It was designed to change the geography which an industrialist faced when making a location decision. It was, in other words, a spatial factor, and it was soon claimed as the primary explanation for the changing spatial distribution of industry; a geographical change in one thing producing a geographical change in another. It was, however, pointed out that there might be more to it than this. Perhaps the locational requirements of industry had altered, as a result of changes in the process of production. Without necessarily saying regional policy was *ir*relevant, perhaps industry was beginning to want to decentralise anyway. Perhaps not all the cause of geographical change lay within geography itself.[1]

Another such issue concerned the inner cities. There was certainly a clear geographical pattern here; some of the highest rates of decline of manufacturing employment in these years were in these inner urban areas. So many geographers (and by no means only geographers) looked to the inner cities, to their 'locational characteristics', for the cause of decline. It was a spatial variant on the general theme of blaming the victim (the inner cities were declining, so there must be something wrong with them). There were two aspects to the rejection of this view. First, to the extent that the geographical characteristics of the inner cities themselves *were* important it was still necessary to go behind the notion of location factors and explain why those factors were important *at that time*. Locational requirements themselves are an outcome of the characteristics and ever-changing demands of industry. Second, it was pointed out that decline in the inner city might just have something to do with the more general state of economic malaise, that inner cities were getting the worst of what was in any case a bad deal. To the extent that manufacturing activity was shutting up shop in the face of international recession and national decline the cities might be suffering disproportionately, not as a result of their characteristics as locations, but because it was in these areas that was to be found the oldest and generally least profitable production capacity. The implication of both these criticisms was that, instead of passing straight from one spatial pattern to another, it was necessary to consider why particular location factors were important at particular periods (maybe the inner cities were suffering because the demands of industry had changed) and to look at how an industry was organised over space (rather than just seeing a two-dimensional surface of employment). What both implied, in other words, was that it was important to step back a bit from the immediacy of the geographical question and answer. In brief, it was necessary to look at production.

Of course, there was still the question of what 'looking at production' was to mean. In the sense of opening up the black box of the firm even behaviourism could be said in some way to be taking more account of the causes lying behind locational choices. But the more convincing answer was that the kinds of locational characteristics which will influence a company's choice of where to build a new factory, expand, run down or close will depend on the nature and demands of the process of production. In turn, changes in production, and consequently in location factors, were argued to be the result, not of some autonomous choice by management, but of wider economic and political forces, shop-floor relations within the firm, and of the company's reaction to both. So, in the debate over regional policy, the argument was not just that changes in production were an important reason, often in conjunction with regional policy, behind the geographical decentralisation but, further, that those changes were themselves often a reflection of attempts to cope with a fast-changing wider economic situation.

One of the main criticisms voiced of this approach was that it was 'deterministic'. There was deep resistance to the idea that wider forces could be part of what influenced the actions of individual companies, management teams, etc. It was a resistance born not only of a concern, if ill-conceptualised, for 'individual freedom',[2] but also from a fear that this would lead one out of the terrain of what had normally been considered 'geographical'. We would have to learn economics, maybe even sociology.

In fact, the accusation was in general anyway misplaced. There was a clear insistence from the beginning that 'macroeconomic forces' did not automatically 'produce' a response on the part of capital (see Massey and Meegan, 1979). But there was undoubtedly an early tendency for analysis to lean in that direction with capital undifferentiatedly and mechanistically, and also often without any apparent trouble, responding to a set of forces variously called 'the demands of accumulation' and 'the requirements of the law of value', whether these were conceived in terms of abstract immanent tendencies of the mode of production or in terms of historically specified economic pressures. This was not only mechanistic, it was also economistic. In fact, the way in which a firm copes with the pressures upon it depends on the kind of capital involved, on the kind of labour which it faces, and on the battle between them. It also depends on how those pressures are defined and on how they are translated through the wider political and social context. The 'requirements' of neither the macroeconomy nor the law of value are sufficient to determine the outcome.

Production really is a social process and it is in that sense that its development, including its geographical development, is not a mechanistic outcome of external forces. But that is to change the terms of debate. It is not only the personal idiosyncrasies of managers which are at issue in the debate about 'determinism', but the fact that historical change comes about through social processes and social conflict. The central question is not whether managerial strategy, personality or skill is important: 'Can MacGregor/Villiers/Edwardes/Weinstock make a difference?' They certainly can, though only within the broader context in which they are operating. But industrial location is not an issue to be addressed solely in terms of managerial decision-making. It is also part and parcel of the much broader and continuing conflict between capital and labour. In that sense this approach entails a far deeper rejection of 'determinism'. And anyway, to think back to those empirical analyses based on correlation, what could be more deterministic than the search for a high R^2?

The analysis of production, and thence of location, must be set in the context of broader social processes, both inside and outside the firm itself. In order to understand the causes and the significance of location decisions – or of the geographical distribution of an industry, the fortunes of a particular region, or the pattern of geographical differentiation within a country as a whole – it is necessary to embed that problem within the broader context of what is going on in society in general. That means actually conceptualising the firm, sector or whatever is being analysed in such a way that it can be related to the broader structures of society. What is at issue is the reproduction over space of social relations.

The fact that the United Kingdom is a capitalist society means that the broad forms of its social organisation are built around the class relations of capitalist production, between capital on the one hand and labour on the other. While it is capital which essentially controls the production process, both in its day-to-day functioning and in the broader processes of allocation of investment, the dynamic of the system revolves around the contradiction between these two classes. This is essential to all that follows. It governs the structure of society, the organisation of production and many of the unquestioned assumptions of daily life. 'It is taken for granted, "in the way things work", that profit should be the normal yardstick of investment in most areas of activity: that the living standards of the propertyless majority should be set primarily by the terms on which they sell or once sold their labour ... power is to be found more in uneventful routine than in conscious and active exercise of will' (Westergaard and Resler, 1975, p. 144). But France, the United States and the United Kingdom are all dominated by capitalist relations of production and yet there are enormous variations between them. In France there is the inheritance of a long-surviving peasantry; in the United States a recent history which has included production under slave ownership. Neither of these elements is present, or has played the same role in the social history or the social structure of the United Kingdom. Nor is it a question merely of 'additional' classes; the character of each class may vary too. 'Capital' in the United Kingdom is not the same as in the United States. In each country too the historical relations within capital, such as between banking and industry, have been different. In each case, in other words, the fundamental relations of capitalism developed historically under very different conditions and in each case, therefore, they took on different forms. While an abstract model of capitalism, by providing the necessary concepts, is an aid to analysis, it cannot substitute for the analysis itself. Each country is different, and these differences have geographical implications.

It follows also that within each country things are more complex than a simple confrontation between capital and labour. There are, for one thing, considerable variations within each of the two major classes. Intra-class, and non-class division and conflict is important. It influences the formation of government policy, it is reflected in social and cultural differences between different parts of the country and it has effects on location decisions and geographical patterns. To take seriously 'production as a social process' means to investigate the relation between these underlying structures and their particular empirical form, to investigate the actual characteristics of capital and the particular form of the social relations of the society it structures.

It is from here, then, that we shall start: looking first at some of the characteristics of 'industry' and second at the wider social relations of which industry is a part. On the way, the argument will broaden, reflecting both some more recent debates and also my own theoretical position. There is a stress on the interconnections between 'the economic' and other areas of life, a concern about how to use 'laws of the capitalist mode of production' in empirical analysis, and an emphasis on the fact that a capitalist society is far more than the capitalist mode of production. The section which follows those on industry and on capitalist social relations picks up again the debate about the relation between the social and the spatial and concludes that maybe the arguments of the seventies were not quite correct after all. Finally, an extended example, a study illustrating and linking together some of the recurring themes, concludes the chapter.

2.2 Characterising capital

The problem

'Industry', then, is more than a collection of firms. It is in general terms the embodiment of the central capitalist social relation – the exploitation of labour in production. But industry is also highly differentiated, and these differences can be important. They can affect political stance, investment strategy and locational decisions. One question, therefore, is: how can the structure of capital ownership be defined so that links can be made between these different realms? How can the study of location, and of regional economic change, be made integral to a study of UK capitalist society in general? Much depends on conceptualisation.

Although reservations are often expressed, most industrial

location and regional employment studies have for long relied on dividing the economy up by distinguishing between 'industries'. This approach has, of course, the supreme advantage of being the form in which the data is available – the sectors of the Standard Industrial Classification (SIC). On other criteria, however, it suffers from many problems.

SIC Order VI, Metal Manufacture, provides a good example. Within this Order are included both of the finer categories (mlhs) 311 and 312 (General Iron and Steel, and Steel Tubes) and mlh 313 (Iron Castings). What they have in common is the fact that their product is simple metal formed into basic shapes. Beyond that, however, it is the differences between them which are striking. In much of the iron-castings industry production is organised on the basis of short runs and one-off jobs. Much of it, too, is owned by 'small capital'. This is especially true of the craft foundries, which tend to be single-plant firms, many employing less than a hundred workers, and quite a few of them less than ten. In complete contrast, the bulk of production in mlhs 311 and 312 is on a large scale, with massive capital requirements, and under State ownership. This is the British Steel Corporation. In terms both of the technology of production and of the kind of capital involved, the two are, therefore, very different.

SIC Order VII, Mechanical Engineering, includes both mlh 338 (Office Machinery) and mlh 332 (Metal Working Machine Tools). Once again these industries are very different from each other in terms both of labour process and of capital ownership. The production of office machinery is relatively automated and routinised, and is controlled by big capital, much of it multinational. In contrast, on these criteria, the machine tool industry has more in common with iron castings.

SIC Order IX, Electrical Engineering, includes a vast range of industries, among them mlhs 361 (Electrical Machinery), 366 (Electronic Computers) and 368 (Electric Appliances Primarily For Domestic Use). All are predominantly owned by big capital (indeed much of it in the same companies), but the difference in the labour process, for instance between 361 and 366, is enormous. Further, mlhs 361 and 366 differ from 368 in terms of their place within the overall structure of the economy. While the first two industries both produce commodities which are themselves means of production, the third produces consumer goods.

These differences matter. Characteristics of scale and ownership can influence a company's response to changing macroeconomic conditions, its relation to policy formulation and its ability to respond to policy initiatives, its degree of locational flexibility and its locational requirements. Nor is this a problem which can be resolved simply by further disaggregation along the lines of the SIC. It is not the level of disaggregation which is in question but the criteria themselves. Significant lines of differentiation exist within mlhs as well. Included in mlh 450 (Footwear) are both a handful of large multinationals, often with control over their own retail outlets, and a host of extremely tiny firms run on an individual-proprietorship basis.

Such difficulties of classification and characterisation are of course well known, and the changing structure of the economy has both made the difficulties more evident and elicited a range of responses. Within industrial location studies, these responses have taken two main forms. On the one hand a wealth of detail has been produced, mainly by those working in a behavioural framework, on the great variety of company type which exists. On the other hand, there have been attempts to construct divisions of the economy based on different, non-SIC, criteria. Both these approaches have advantages and disadvantages. While it is important to recognise variety, recognition is not enough. With its essentially micro-level and voluntarist approach, the behavioural school has failed to get beyond hopeful attempts at aggregation on the basis of empirically observed similarities. Some form of systematisation and explanation is necessary if the exercise is to go beyond documentation. It is this which is provided by the new dimensions of disaggregation which have been suggested. Dimensions such as differences in labour process, or between 'monopoly and non-monopoly capital' represent attempts to tie in these recognised empirical variations to the long-term development of capitalist economies. But, at least in the way they have been used so far, these approaches also have problems.

A number of different lines of division, criteria of definition, have been suggested.

Place in economic structure

One of the most frequently advocated of these is that based on 'place in economic structure'. This means more than simply a description of the inputs and outputs of a particular economic activity. It means a specification of the way in which that economic activity relates, not just to its immediate market and suppliers, but to the broader overall structure of the economy. The most obvious such division, and one which is particularly important in the United Kingdom, is that between banking capital and industrial capital. Within industrial capital there is a similar major structural division between those parts which produce means of production (often called Department I) and those which produce consumption goods (Department II). The relation of a particular economic activity to this kind of division has a number of effects. It determines how the activity fits into the reproduction of the economy as a whole and it may therefore influence, for instance, the impact of changing macroeconomic conditions. It is a commonplace to see the banking sector booming while industry slumps, or for capital and consumer-goods production to be growing at different rates. State policies towards the economy can often also reflect these divisions. Much of the State interest in and encouragement of electronic capital goods in the late 1960s was a result of the fact that such production was vital to increasing productivity in other parts of the economy. Conversely, place in economic structure may influence the kind of economic policy a company wants to see from the State.

In general terms, then, 'place in economic structure' may be an important determinant of the kind of wider pressures with which any activity is faced. In their work on the inter-war and post-war period, Carney, Lewis and Hudson (1977) provide a good example of how division along such lines can be used to analyse the relationship between macroeconomic developments and spatial structure. They point to the broad division at that period between expanding 'Department II' production and a stagnating 'Department I' and relate that to the locational changes going on at the same time, with the bulk of Department II being located in the south-east of England, while the declining Department I was concentrated in the north. The causes of the shift in balance between these two parts of the economy were to be found in changes in the international economy and in particular in the decline of Britain as an imperial economic power. Its effects were contradictory. On the one hand the Department II industries in the south of the country needed expanding markets, but because of the decline in the north the market there was depressed. In this sense the fortunes of Department I were a constraint on the growth-potential of Department II, and decline in the north on the expansion of the south. On the other hand, the booming industries of the south benefited from the collapse to their north, for it was that which guaranteed a continuing supply of labour. The unemployed in the north, and their migration south, kept wages down and profits up in the growing Department II industries. This situation in turn influenced the political stances taken by different groups of industrialists, including their attitude to State regional policies. Carney, Lewis and Hudson argue that, for the industries of the south, the potential of the north as a market was more important than the impact of its decline in providing a reserve of cheap labour. This meant that, even though they would not gain directly in terms of their own production locations, the capitalists of Department II in the south were nevertheless in favour of attempts to revitalise the depressed areas of the north. On the other hand, this same concern for their markets on occasion led the industrialists of Department II into direct conflict with those in Department I – the coal-owners were sometimes attacked, for instance, as being too brutal in their wage-cutting (Carney, Lewis and Hudson, 1977, p. 60).

A division of the economy into Departments is therefore both important and useful. One thing it immediately brings home is the relation between economic structure, spatial form, and national and international economic change. But on its own this way of characterising industry is insufficient for our purposes. First, as a specification even of place in the economic structure, it will usually be too broad to be meaningful. In the study mentioned above, for instance, references to 'Departments I and II' did not actually mean the whole of those Departments. Strictly speaking, therefore, the terms were inadequate definitions of the industries to which they did refer. As the authors themselves point out, there were Department I industries also enjoying very fast rates of growth at this period. Moreover, and conversely, not all Department II production, by any means, fell into the category of new growth industries. Not all consumer goods came out of modern factories sheltering the new techniques of production and located on the major roads out of London, or in the west midlands. Equally part of Department II but otherwise in complete contrast were the traditional wage-good industries – industries such as footwear and hosiery manufacture. Although many, even of these, did considerably increase both output and productivity over this period (Pollard, 1969, pp. 107–10), there was no major revolution in production technique to parallel the new labour processes in motor-car production, for instance. And instead of brash and rising multinationals, these industries were still dominated by old-fashioned family firms. Instead of greenfield sites in the outer metropolitan area of the south-east, they had seen a century or more of location in the small towns of the east midlands. Completely different present characteristics, in other words, derived from completely different histories.

Reference to Departments alone, then, is often too broad to allow meaningful analysis (see also Courlet, 1977) and insensitive to such kinds of social-historical differentiation.

While the criterion of 'place in economic structure' is important in determining the kind of pressures and stimuli from the external economic environment which are faced by any particular plant, it is less significant in the determination of location strategy. The fact that the capital and consumer-goods industries in the inter-war years were located in different regions was not due simply to the fact that they were different Departments of the economy. Clearly there may be a greater degree of orientation to the final consumer in Department ii, but this is only one factor among many. And there is no such direct locational determinant attaching to Department i. 'Place in economic structure' does not of itself have much necessary relation to location. One way in which the link to location can be made is through consideration of the labour process.

Contrasts in labour process

The historical shift in capitalist societies from one major type of labour process to another has a number of potential geographical implications. A shift in labour process may involve changes in the nature and degree of the division of labour, in the number of workers required for any given level of output, and in the kinds of skills and other characteristics required of those workers. There are various ways of characterising and periodising the development of the labour process in capitalist societies. In industrial location studies, which frequently follow the work of Aglietta (1979), four phases are usually identified. The first, manufacture, consists mainly of the gathering together of previously independent workers into a factory system. In the second, machinofacture, mechanisation is introduced and the division of labour within production developed. With scientific management and Fordism job-fragmentation is further increased, particularly along the lines of separation of conception from execution, and the 'flow-line' principle, aiding these changes, is introduced. In the latest phase, with the introduction of neo-Fordism, fragmentation and de-skilling of the direct workforce (particularly through the removal of control) can be pushed further with the use of electronic information systems. Each phase represents a different way of combining capital and labour in the production process, a different way of organising the labour force, and a different kind of stratification and differentiation within that labour force.

For all these reasons, the nature of the labour process can have an important influence on location. Perrons' (1981) study of Ireland provides an example. She argues that each of the phases in the development of the labour process has different implications both for the organisation of plants in particular industries and for their geographical distribution. In broad terms, she argues that each phase represents an increasing division of labour both functionally and spatially. These locational implications are not simply logical derivations. The actual geographical pattern adopted for a particular labour process in a particular country will depend on the interaction between the requirements of the labour process and the geographical surface inherited from the previous history of the country. For Britain, Perrons argues that the earliest stage – manufacturing – tended to be widely dispersed throughout the countryside, the bulk of it organised into factories, but with homeworking still continuing to be important. The reason for this geographical distribution is stated as being 'to avoid guild restrictions and higher cost labour in the towns and also to obtain access to water power' (p. 90). This pattern of dispersion was reversed with the advent of machinofacture. Here the use of mechanical principles and power means that the constraints imposed by craft traditions are largely overcome and industry thereby freed from rural locations. This, Perrons argues, together with the need for highly developed infrastructure meant that production came increasingly to be concentrated in towns. In the next phase the growth of industries dominated by scientific management and Fordism saw the beginnings of the spatial separation of control and production, and the growth of marketing activities, the latter resulting from the expansion of consumer-goods production. Together, these led to the growth of office-based activities and, it is argued, these replaced industry in central-city locations, the restructured industry moving out to the suburbs, and subsequently, in the search for cheaper and less organised workers, beyond suburbia to the peripheral regions both of the home country and of the world. Finally, the advent of neo-Fordism in many ways reinforces this geographical pattern by increasing the spatial separability of different parts of the production process, and by extending the possibility of decentralisation of production to small-batch processes as well as large assembly runs.

It may be, then, that the different stages in the development of the capitalist labour process do have distinct geographical implications. Certainly, there is some relation between the organisation of production and locational requirements and degrees of locational flexibility. This does not mean, of course, that there is a complete reshaping of all locational patterns immediately a new type of labour process appears on the scene. At any given point in history a number of different labour processes will coexist; it is this coexistence which enables 'labour process' to be a basis for disaggregating the economy, for characterising different parts of capital. It is the major criterion operated by Perrons, who groups together sectors of the Irish economy on the basis of their being dominated by distinct major phases of the development of the labour process.

Understanding the nature of the labour process can help to make the link between changes in the broad pattern of accumulation and changes in location. At the most general level, the emergence of new types of labour process reflects major phases of capitalist development, and in turn may be reflected in spatial change. The advantage of this approach is that it enables the host of different technologies, and their associated labour requirements, to be seen in a broader context. It relates them, and the changes which take place within them, to longer-term developments intrinsic to the relation within the production process between capital and labour.

Once again, however, it is inadequate on its own. The growth of office-based activities, which is seen as a major cause of industrial decentralisation, was due in part to the completely different fact that the new industries were consumer-based. Place in the economy, in other words, was equally important. This being so there seems no reason to elevate the labour process alone to pre-eminent theoretical priority. It is, anyway, not 'labour process' which determines location, but the search after profit and the fluctuating conflict between capital and labour. All kinds of factors may influence the relation between labour process and location. Similar processes may be operated by very different groups of workers. Similar assembly processes, for example, are in some industries done by men, in others by women, in yet others by particular racial groups. The labour demand for a labour process is determined not by the process itself but by a whole host of wider social and ideological traditions. Again, scientific management and Fordism only make spatial separation of control and production possible. They do not, outside of particular circumstances, determine that it will happen. Separation within production does not in itself give rise to geographical separation. Simply to classify by labour processes is not to take account of the historical conditions in which they emerge. For that reason the actual way in which the criterion of labour process is used in the definition of major divisions within the economy must be an empirical question. It must be a part of, rather than the single input to, any analysis. But the real problem in using labour process as the main line of divide within the economy, the main way of characterising parts of industry, lies elsewhere. If the object of the exercise is to establish the relationship between wider economic and political changes and geographical change, then the conceptualisation of the economy must be relevant to that whole spectrum of concerns. While 'labour process' does have some, very broad relation to location, it is not clear that in itself it has much connection with a company's relation to the wider socio-economic and political structure.

As with 'place in economic structure' it is unlikely that the criterion of labour process will be meaningful on its own. Indeed, it will frequently be the case that divisions established on the basis of labour process will be closely related to divisions on other criteria. Courlet (1977), for instance, relates difference in labour process to place in economic structure. There is also, even more obviously, a connection to the organisational structure of capital.

The adoption of particular labour processes is often governed by size of company (making multi-plant organisation possible, for instance), financial resources (making possible the necessary investment) and management type, as well as the state of play between management and labour.

The organisational structure of capital

It is, indeed, organisational structure which has probably been the focus of most recent enquiry in geography. The debate over external control, the problems of 'branch-plant economies', the desire to stimulate indigenous growth within particular areas, the political significance of 'small firms', have all ensured that the organisational structure of companies has been a focus of attention. What exactly has been meant by the term has varied from study to study. Sometimes it has been considerations such as intersectoral spread, method of finance, degree and type of internationalisation. Such characteristics are important determinants of a firm's political and economic, as well as specifically locational, range of options. 'Size', and its associated characteristics, is probably the differentiating variable on which most attention has focused, whether the distinction has been between reflections of size such as single-plant versus multi-plant firms or between 'small capital' and 'monopoly capital'.

Once again, none of these characteristics evolve out of the blue. They are related to long-term developments within capitalist economies. The processes of concentration and centralisation are too well known to need elaboration. What is important from the point of view of the argument here is that they represent an accretion into larger units of two aspects of production, two sets of functions which stem from the fact of ownership. On the one hand there is the power to allocate investment capital. This aspect of ownership is often called 'economic ownership'. On the other hand, there are the functions of control over the production process as it exists – both the physical means of production and, through the supervisory structure, control over labour. To distinguish it from economic ownership, this aspect of ownership is often called 'possession'. The organisation of the economy into larger units of capital, both through merger and takeover (centralisation) and through internal expansion (concentration), represents an increase of the control by individual capitals over these functions. Centralisation represents a gathering-in of these powers under the direction of an individual company, replacing their operation through the unplanned relations of the market by planned co-ordination. This increasing co-ordination of production under the ownership of large companies is what is at issue in debates over 'the power of the top hundred companies', and it has important spatial consequences. It is the extension of control by individual companies over larger and larger parts of the overall relations of production.

But 'size', however it is measured, is not an adequate differentiator. One of the subthemes of this book is that what is often referred to as 'monopoly capital' is actually, from the point of view of the locational issues examined here, highly differentiated. Apart from the obvious broad divisions – such as that in Britain between the City and industry – there are also substantial differences between industrial companies. There is perhaps a tendency in the geographical and locational literature to refer to the spatial proclivities of 'monopoly capital' as though it was an undifferentiated entity. Either the petrochemicals complex, or electronics, or some ambiguous combination of the two, is taken as paradigmatic of the whole of monopoly capital. In fact, as is shown in Chapters 3, 4 and 6, different parts of big capital can have very different ways of making use of spatial variation. These contrasts, moreover, can result in very different forms of geographical inequality.

The other inadequacy of size as a differentiator is what might be called the social nature of forms of ownership. This is seen most clearly in relation to small firms. There is a world of difference, in almost every aspect of their operation, between the pushy and dynamic entrepreneurial capital to be found in some relatively new sectors of the economy and the quiet ticking-over of a family firm in, say, one of the older consumer-goods industries mentioned earlier. In the first case growth, expansion, and risk-taking are the name of the game.[3] In the second, the concern is with survival and maybe with succession. Indeed, the concern may be explicitly with the survival of a particular social form, of the 'family nature' of the firm, for instance. Accumulation in the classic sense is not the central preoccupation. Growth may even be avoided or feared because of the risk that it will change the nature of the company, by leading perhaps to the introduction of a managerial structure in place of individual owner/manager control, or to the possibility of takeover. Categories such as 'small firm', in other words, may not have much analytical meaning. If production is a social process, then the social nature of capital is of fundamental importance when it comes to characterising a particular company. Descriptions based on apparently objective (because quantitative or formal) measures may completely miss all the important differences.

Similar kinds of contrasts may exist between much larger firms, too. The difference between a wide-ranging multisectoral conglomerate and a single-industry company is not always just one of intersectoral spread. The whole orientation to production and to investment opportunities may be different. Many conglomerates are involved essentially in a financial mode of operation, commitment to particular sectors of production is minimal, and investment may be shifted rapidly and frequently between industries. Production *in general* is here subordinated to making a financial profit. Clearly, in a capitalist economy, production is always basically for profit in the sense that it could not ultimately survive without profits. That is the criterion by which production is judged to be, or not to be, worth while. But there are many different social forms by which this process can get played out. What this in turn means, of course, is that in discussing a particular economy, sector or firm, it is not sufficient to refer to 'the requirements of accumulation' to explain managerial behaviour.[4] In contrast with the financially orientated conglomerate, there is a sense in which long-established, single-industry companies may well see themselves as being 'in electrical engineering', 'in shirt-production', or what have you, as much as in profits production (although of course in fact they are in both, and in the end the latter controls the former). The nature of the calculation in these companies is different. The question is not: 'where (in what industry) are profits highest?', 'what shall we move into?', but: 'what is the market for generators?', say, or 'how many shirts can we produce and sell at a profit?' The sector of production is given. It is not just that in the latter case the company has no intersectoral spread, but that with that attitude, that kind of calculation, it is not going to develop one. Antony Pilkington, chair of the major British glass manufacturers with his surname, was recently quoted as saying that he and his board 'have never even thought half seriously of moving into anything other than glass and allied products' (Lorenz, 1982). Such a company will not, therefore, evaluate a given rate of profit in 'its' sector in the same way as might a financially orientated, multi-industry conglomerate.

'Organisational structure', therefore, includes both a whole range of potentially measurable variables (none of them on their own will do) *and* more 'qualitative' social characteristics. What is often thought of as the 'economic' level of society is itself formed and shaped through social processes, and economic behaviour is influenced by wider social characteristics.

Neither does this mean, however, that it is enough to fall back into the behavioural-school trap of endless description. The aim should be to grasp these kinds of characteristics and differentiations at a social level, and with an eye to longer-term historical developments.

Some conclusions

All of the approaches just discussed are attempts to do just that. Each tries to link the characteristics of individual firms, or parts of the economy, to the stage of development and the general characteristics of the economy as a whole. Each also tries to link short-term changes to long. Changes both in the labour process and in the degree of concentration of industry actually happen as a result of the day-to-day competition between companies. But these incremental and often hesitating processes result in identifiable long-term shifts. Recognition of this dual nature is important. It is what enables the detail of specific empirical studies to be understood in terms of the broader sweep of history. But none of these criteria on its own is adequate. All are useful, all capture something, but all seem to strain in order to gather everything under their one rubric. Organisational structure, even elaborated, will give little direct guidance as to locational strategy – labour process may be more useful here. But labour process does not in itself provide a basis for establishing a relation to the workings of the national economy and political structure. Some sensitive combination of all three criteria seems most likely to form the basis for a rethought sectionalisation of the economy. As we have seen, the three are closely linked. But which criterion is most important and *how* they are linked are empirical questions. The answers will vary between countries and over time. This is the heart of the matter. Above all, the three criteria discussed above have often failed to provide much enlightenment in practice because they have been used as externally-provided, *a priori* divisions. Each is a serious attempt to link day-to-day events in industrial location to the longer-term historical developments of capitalism, but what has often been crucially missed out in application is real history. They have been used in a static and general way, as simple, logical derivations from a mode of production, rather than as the product of an analysis of the particular capitalist society being examined. As far as industrial studies in the United Kingdom are concerned, what we need is a division of British capital which relates not only to the longer-term historical development of 'capitalism-the-mode-of-production', but to the long and specific history of *British* capitalism. Within that context, the aim is to make links between politics, macro-economy and location, and the initial conceptualisation of the economy must be part of the means by which those links are established. The basic units of analysis must be meaningful in terms of the causal structure. Most of what we have to draw on in the United Kingdom covers one side but not the other. There are investigations of British capital as a class, which study its internal divisions at a national and political level (for instance Gamble, 1981) but which do not concern themselves much with changing regional balance or with location. And there are, of course, numerous locational studies, but which fail to relate to British capital as a real historical class and its operation in the political sphere. The link between the two has not been established in studies of the United Kingdom. One of the things industrial location studies clearly need is a better conceptualisation of 'industry' itself.

2.3 Social structures and capitalist relations of production

A framework

But what of the internal social structure of capitalist production? Figure 2.1 presents a framework, borrowed from Wright (1978),

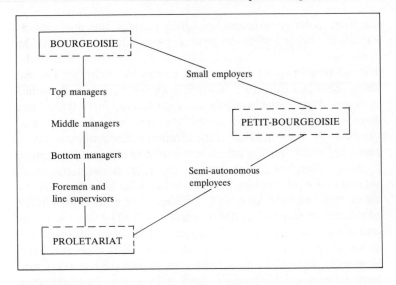

FIGURE 2.1   *A basic framework*

Source: adapted from Wright (1976, chart 8).

which allows these relations to be examined and through which connections can be made between the social relations of capitalist production and the broader structure of society. It is also a framework which enables links to be made from specific functions within a capitalist society at any point in time, and the social groups who perform those functions, to long-term processes of capitalist development. The basic building blocks of a capitalist society, the bourgeoisie and the working class, form the main axis. Each of these two classes is defined in relation to the other and by its degree of control over the process of production, its place in the relations of production. The bourgeoisie is defined by having both economic ownership and possession of the means of production – in other words, 'capitalists' control the accumulation process through decisions about investment, decide how the physical means of production are to be used and control the authority-structure within the labour process. The working class is charac-terised by the absence of these kinds of control, by its exclusion from both economic ownership and possession. These are the two fundamental, and defining, classes of a capitalist society. It is their mutually defining relationship which enables the one class to exploit the other and to do so in a specifically capitalist fashion.

*   *   *

But no actual capitalist society, of course, is so simple. For one thing, neither of the two major classes will be internally homogeneous. Within the working class there are, for instance, the lines of division between skilled and unskilled which figure so prominently as a condition of the location patterns of industry. At times industries may be effectively rooted to a particular location by long, often generations-long, experience amongst the area's working class of working in that sector. Changes in production which 'free' an industry from this tie may free it not only in terms of the labour market but also geographically. The way the skilled and unskilled operate as 'location factors' may also be very different. In some circumstances, skilled workers may exert a pull simply on account of availability, while unskilled workers may have to compete by bidding down their wages. One important factor behind the recent peripheralisation of production in many industrialised capitalist countries (as well as internationally) is often argued to be the release of industry from ties to traditional labour, and its acquisition thereby of a new geographical flexibility.

Differences such as these within the labour force (and therefore in the 'spatial surface' which capital faces) are in part derived from developments in the division of labour and the relations of production. The general role of technical change in engendering the emergence of new elements in the workforce is well recognised even if its precise form is disputed. Changes in labour process and technology are both the outcome of social relations and the basis for the creation of new forms of such relations. At the most immediate level, technical change in the production of particular goods is part of the process of capitalist competition, and it has at least two main kinds of impetus, on the one hand to lower costs of production and on the other to increase the degree of control by management over the work process itself. The two aspects are closely intertwined. Both, too, are long-term and gradually-evolving processes, and have taken place in different ways at different periods of history. In the earliest days of capitalism the individual direct producers, especially those working in cottage industries, retained a high degree of control over how fast, and for

how long, they worked. One of the reasons behind the organisation of production into factories was the need on the part of the
owners of capital to gain more control over the production process
(Marglin, 1974).

One of the ways by which both productivity and managerial
control has been increased is through the further elaboration of
the division of labour: the development of the technical division
of labour within production. Perhaps the most celebrated aspect
of this has been the dual process of separating the functions of
conceptualisation from those of execution, and of the increasing
fragmentation of the tasks of execution. It is this kind of process
which is referred to in the term 'deskilling', and the classic form
can be schematised as the breakdown of a task, which previously
involved thinking the job through, organising it and actually
carrying it out, into two separate jobs: in one the task is set up and
in the other actually performed. This development therefore
involves the creation of a whole hierarchy of jobs differentiated
from each other on a number of different dimensions. There is the
dimension from conceptualisation to execution – from, for instance, design engineering and parts programming to machine
coding and machine operating in the setting up and working of
numerically controlled machine tools. There is the hierarchy of
degrees of individual job control. In some jobs, especially where
the overall work process is based around automatic machinery,
there is very little flexibility for the individual worker in the way
the job is timed, performed or generally organised. On the other
hand there is also a whole range of jobs including research work,
various types of technical employment and skilled engineering
jobs, which involve a relatively high degree of autonomy in
relation to the work process on the part of the individual employee.[5] Nor are skills and autonomy equatable. Some relatively
skilled jobs leave very little room for the individual worker to
organise the work process; some very unskilled jobs are pretty
much outside the detailed minute-by-minute control of both
management and machinery. These are by no means the only ways
in which the capitalist labour process changes over time. Nor are
such processes as dichotomisation and deskilling as linear and
monotonic as is sometimes made out.[6] For one thing they may be
resisted, for another technological change can be accompanied by
all kinds of different implications for the constitution of tasks

within production. New skilled jobs may be created. And no task is entirely devoid of non-routine operations (even if only because things go wrong, machines break down) or mental activity. But these are processes which at various times (and places) have been important.

What is significant about them in this argument, as examples of changes in the process of production, is that the separating out of different parts of the overall work process can come to be mirrored in a parallel set of social groups, each performing different functions. This is not, it should be pointed out, in any sense technically necessary. After all, one skilled machinist used to do the job now performed by the combination of parts programmer, machine coder and machine operator.

> The unity of this process in the hands of the skilled machinist is perfectly feasible, and indeed has much to recommend it, since the knowledge of metal-cutting practices which is required for programming is already mastered by the machinist. Thus there is no question that from a practical standpoint there is nothing to prevent the machining process under numerical control from remaining the province of the total craftsman [*sic*]. That this almost never happens is due, of course, to the opportunities the process offers for the destruction of craft and the cheapening of the resulting pieces of labor into which it is broken (Braverman, 1974, p. 199).

The different tasks are allocated to different types of workers. In the United States, Braverman reports, the parts programmer is increasingly a junior technical college graduate, the machine coder a 'girl', and the operator a semi-skilled male. This hierarchy replaces the one co-ordinated function of skilled machinist. It also reflects a lot more than simple 'technical requirements'. The new array of jobs not only draws on existing differences within the workforce, but also helps to create and reinforce them. Changes in the organisation of the social relations of production reflect and are reflected in changes in the structure of society as a whole.

Some divisions within the working class, then, stem from differences within production. But there are other divisions which are constructed as much outside as within the workplace. Race and gender are the most obvious examples. In recent decades the 'economically active' workforce in Britain has been greatly extended to include large numbers of blacks and married women. The incorporation of such new groups into the paid workforce is often enabled by the kinds of technological changes mentioned above – not necessarily because less-demanding jobs are created which the new workers can perform (as is often asserted), but often simply because the very decomposition and reorganisation of the work process enables the recruitment of a social group previously excluded, perhaps on ideological grounds. The incorporation of such new groups is often bound up with continuing antagonisms and demarcations within the division of labour – sexism and racism are powerful divides within the working class.

*   *   *

In most capitalist societies there are also classes other than capital and labour. Land ownership may be the basis for a distinct class, for instance; as can self-employment. It is the latter, because of its direct relation to production, which immediately concerns us here. Because self-employment does not involve the exploitation of wage labour it is not strictly a capitalist form; it is involved in no relations, in the immediate production process, with labour. This is the petit-bourgeoisie of Figure 2.1, defined as having economic ownership and possession of the physical means of production, but as having no control over the labour of others (since no labour is employed). There are many people in industrialised capitalist societies who are self-employed simply in the sense that that happens to be the way their wages are paid. It may simply be a way of avoiding employer obligations or taxes. The 'lump' in the construction industry is the most obvious example in the United Kingdom; sub-contracted homeworking is another. By self-employment we mean here to refer to real control over a production process. It is real social relations rather than legal forms which give meaning to the groups characterised by particular labels. In this stricter sense, self-employment, as a *form* of production, is a pre-capitalist inheritance, but its continued reproduction, the fact that new areas of self-employment continue to grow and flourish, means that in this category, too, there is significant differentiation. It is a kind of differentiation which, in the United Kingdom, closely parallels that within small firms. One element is what might be called the classic traditional petit-bourgeoisie. It is typified by the shopkeeper, an element of the social structure which is genuinely pre-capitalist in the sense that it retains a foothold in those parts of the economy where capitalist firms have not yet fully taken over. For precisely this reason it is, in industrialised capitalist societies, a group typically (though by no means always) on the decline – the corner shop under threat from the supermarket, self-employment pushed out by competition from capital employing wage-labour. In contrast, there are parts of the economy in which self-employment is expanding, and where it is not, therefore, as a type, under threat. The new professional and business-service sectors are an example. Decline and expansion are not the only differences between these elements within the category of self-employment. Their social characteristics are also markedly different. The self-employed in the professions and similar areas tend to see their jobs as high-status ones. They are usually graduates, and in social terms may have little in common with the shopkeepers whose company, in formal class terms, they are sometimes said to keep.

Moreover, within any actual capitalist society there are also groups, often quite substantial, which do not fit neatly and clearly into any of these unambiguous class definitions. The criteria of definition of each of these three classes are neither all-or-nothing characteristics nor static descriptions. Classes are a product of history and of social conflict as well as being constituent of them. Their definitions are based on functions whose social organisation changes over time. Between classes, therefore, are dimensions of tension representing real processes of change within capitalist society. Take the division between bourgeoisie and working class. The former is defined as having both economic ownership and possession of the means of production (i.e. control both over what is produced and over how it is produced), the latter as having neither. Yet capitalist development has been characterised both by a separation of economic ownership from possession (mirrored, along with the disjunction of legal ownership and real economic ownership, in the debate on 'the separation of ownership from control') and by the development of complex hierarchies within each. Relations of possession concern the organisation of the capitalist production process. They involve control both over the physical means of production and over labour. On the former, there have developed hierarchies of management from top managers controlling the productive apparatus of a whole company, to functionaries at the bottom of the pile. On the latter there have developed hierarchies of supervision, from upper management to the foreperson on the shop floor. With economic ownership a similar hierarchy may stretch from the top executives who have full control of the overall investment and accumulation process (often as well as considerable legal ownership), through managers who have control over investment only in individual plants or particular functional divisions, to those lowest levels of management which mainly administer the decisions of others. Putting all this together, there is a spectrum within these 'contradictory locations', as Wright calls them,[7] from top management with some, but not full, economic ownership alongside full participation in relations of possession through to, say, someone supervising just one production line, and having, therefore, no economic ownership, little if any control over the physical apparatus of production, and limited control over other employees. There is in that sense a spectrum from the bourgeoisie (the personnel of capital) to the working class.

The dimension between proletariat and petit-bourgeoisie reflects the long process of removal of immediate job control from direct producers. It relates to such processes as deskilling. There are a number of elements here. There are skilled manual and craft jobs where the individual worker retains more flexibility in terms of how the job is done and even over exactly what is produced. There are also those new groups of employees – scientists, high-level technicians and the like – whose jobs are created in counterposition to the deskilling of others, in the larger process of the separation of conception from execution. These jobs, too, contain elements of individual job control or autonomy. Wright (1978) gives the examples of researchers in laboratories, and university academics. Neither of these jobs often involves much control over other people's labour, yet each involves a reasonable degree of control over the conditions and organisation of work. Like self-employment, this is not simply a historically-residual category on a one-way path to elimination; it is constantly being added to by new and rather different elements.

Finally, the dimension between bourgeoisie and petit-bourgeoisie. Both groups, at either end of the spectrum, have full economic ownership, and control over the relations of possession. What distinguishes them is their relation to the exploitation of labour and thereby to accumulation. The petit-bourgeois owner will be both more involved in direct production and less involved in the employment of others and in real accumulation, than is the fully capitalist employer. But once again, there is a spectrum, reflecting both the dying-out of self-employment in industries where fully capitalist relations of production are established and the continual regrowth of self-employment in other parts of the economy.

The framework, therefore, represents not a static typology, ready to be fitted on to a piece of the real world, but a set of social processes within which there is constant tension and behind which lie the conflicts of a capitalist society. These dimensions of contradictory class locations relate not just to the 'aspatial' development of the social relations of a capitalist society, but also to new forms of spatial organisation within such a society.

At a very immediate level, each of these dimensions is reflected in debates already going on, although in very different terms, about the geographical organisation of production. On the dimension of relations between bourgeoisie and proletariat lies the whole spectrum of managerial strata which has been the focus of so much of the attention of the behavioural school of industrial location. Different kinds of spatial organisation of management have been voluminously described. Study after study has examined the implications for longer-term local growth of branch-plant domination of regional economies. What both issues are really concerned with is the geographical organisation of the developing social relations of production. What is at issue, and what is the key to formulating such questions systematically, is the spatial organisation of economic ownership and the relations of possession. The empirical information gained in behavioural studies of management structure about activities and personnel can be reconceptualised in terms of the function of the activities within the social relations of production and the place of the personnel within the wider social-class structure. Likewise, the dimension from petit-bourgeoisie to proletariat relates to aspects of deskilling and the dichotomisation of the labour force. The much-studied R and D workers with their highly-concentrated geographical distribution are also to be found along this dimension. Note, too, a point which will become important later: that there are different sources of the 'white-collar middle class', some having a managerial role, others a job, such as research, with a high degree of autonomy, and that these different functions imply also rather different class locations. Finally, along the dimension between petit-bourgeoisie and bourgeoisie lie all the different kinds of small firms, differentiated by number of employees, by attitude to expansion and by social character.

*   *   *

The argument here, then, is that Wright's framework can be extended. Both the broad relations between classes and the very considerable differences within them are fundamental in under-standing locational change, both its causes and its wider effects. Both what are called 'interregional relations' and geographical differences in type of employment are in large part the spatial expression of the relations of production and the divisions of labour within society. Not only is there a relation between developments within the social relations of production on the one hand and social structure on the other, but that relation occurs over space. The changing spatial organisation of the relations of production and the division of labour is a basis for understanding changing spatial patterns of employment and the geography of social class. And the changing organisation of functions within those evolving relations of production is a basis for understanding changes in 'interregional relations'. All this will be taken up in Chapter 3.

But – once again – the framework in Figure 2.1 *is* only a framework. It is a way into the analysis of real historical diversity. Quite what the characteristics and composition of classes will be in any particular country, and how that will be related to geographic-al patterns and structures is an empirical question. What matters is not to superimpose a formal framework on the 'real world' and expect the latter to conform, or to be simply understandable when read through an abstract and pre-given taxonomy. The point of a framework is to provide an approach to analysis of the real world, not to substitute for it. The remainder of this chapter, and the next, develop the framework further, and in the second part of the book the approach is used to investigate recent changes in the relation between social and spatial structure in Britain.

Elaborations

And matters, anyway, are not so simple. It is not possible to understand the wider characteristics of social structure simply by examining developments within production. For one thing, there are many groups in society which cannot be 'placed' socially in terms of their own immediate roles in the relations of production. More significantly from the point of view of the argument here, there is no determinate, one-way relation between a function within the relations of production and the social group which performs it. What we have looked at so far is really places and functions. But 'who' does a particular job is not determined by the relations of production themselves, nor by 'technology', but by particular conjunctions of the economics of labour markets and of social tradition. There is evidence that the status and trendiness of some of the newly-emerging jobs 'in computers' is a result more of the fact that, in the present state of the labour market, graduates are usually employed to fill them, than of any real requirements of the tasks themselves. Ideologies of race and gender criss-cross the labour market, defining which groups can do which jobs. How can one square the constant, and usually unexamined, 'argument' that 'the work got lighter so enabling women to be employed' with the fact that in the Third World it is women who do most of the heavy labour? Closed shops and demarcation rules have similar effects – conveyancing in house purchase can hardly be said to require skilled workers, but it is solicitors, at high fees, who do it.

The converse is also true. The social status of a group of employees is not simply determined by the real content of the job they are hired to do. Allen (1977) writes of 'ideologically determined labour markets' and argues that 'There is no task in the whole process of production, exchange and distribution which is not ranked according to its usefulness to the system in spite of and often contrary to its own objective skill qualities' (p. 67). And differences in ideological status spill over into all aspects of the job, and therefore beyond 'Workers in high status jobs tend to have higher earnings, shorter and more congenially-distributed working hours, better working conditions, longer holidays and more social amenities in general than those in jobs ranked below them' (p. 67).

Nor does the social definition of a job as 'skilled' necessarily have much to do with the real content of the labour process. There certainly are real differences between different jobs in terms of the level of skill required. But an analysis, for instance, of trade union agreements or the Census of Production skill categories would not necessarily relate to these attributes. Whether or not a particular job is classified as skilled can be as much a result of organisational strength, bargaining power and ideology as of the nature of the task itself. The Coventry car industry in the 1920s provides a good example. The ratio of skilled to semi-skilled workers was far higher there than in the car industry in the rest of England. This was not due to a difference in the production process, but to the fact that many semi-skilled workers (defined in terms of the amount of training needed for the job they were doing) managed to gain skilled status in Coventry. 'To be classified as skilled in Coventry's car industry came simply to distinguish those workers who were being paid the district skilled rate. Increasingly workers achieved this rate on account of their individual bargaining power rather than their skills' (Friedman, 1977, p. 204). The most famous example of this kind of basis for skill-categorisation was the battle over 'dilution' in the engineering industries in Britain in wartime. It was a battle caused by the ease with which supposedly unskilled workers, particularly women, were able to take over the jobs of supposedly skilled male workers. The designation as skilled, and indeed the ability to hang on to that designation in spite of dilution, was clearly in large measure a result of historical organi-sational and institutional factors. Rubery (1978) concludes that 'workers are thus "skilled" and "unskilled" according to whether or not entry to their organisation is deliberately restricted, and not in the first place according to the nature of the occupation itself' (p. 31). The very fact that a job is done by women, whatever its content, is likely to lower its status. Subordinate ethnic groups often face the same phenomenon. Here, then, the different lines of argument come together. Technology, the physical nature of the production process and the real content of tasks are important influences on the nature of labour-demand, on who does what job and on the social status accorded to it, but they are not the whole explanation.

This kind of consideration can be important in locational analysis. As was said earlier, changes in the labour process may be introduced by management for a variety of reasons, among them being attempts to increase control over the production process and to reduce its cost in money terms. The two are not the same. 'Real deskilling' is likely to lead to both, to a potential increase in control (in so far as this is a product of the labour process itself) and to a reduction in wage costs. The fact that it may not reduce costs immediately will be due to the ability of established groups of workers to hang on to their status. And one way capital has of retaliating to that kind of defence of living standards on the part of workers is simply to shift locationally, beyond the geographical bounds of the workers with whom they are negotiating. Conversely, a sufficient degree of alteration in the labour process, even when it involves no 'real' deskilling at all, may enable the downgrading of a job in formal, and therefore cost terms. A crucial element in the ability to do this may well be a change in the workforce, from an established one which had won the accreditation 'skilled', to a new one with no negotiating basis in relation to this employment. It is simply a move from a stronger (because established) to a weaker part of the labour market. And in turn an important element in making this shift may be locational change. This does not mean that there are no differences in skill, no processes of deskilling. It does mean, however, that the formal, official categories may refer less to such attributes than to strength, status and wages, and that to detect real changes in job content the labour process must be examined directly. Much has been made in recent years, for instance, of the deskilling which seems to have enabled peripheralisation (both intra- and internationally) of units of production. Certainly in many cases these locational shifts *were* possible because of a change in the production process which meant that a less skilled labour force could be employed. In other cases, though, the change in production process freed capital from dependence on a group of workers who did the job as a result of tradition rather than specific skill, thereby enabling a change of workforce and location, even though no actual deskilling was involved. The two lines of distinction, between skill in relation to job content and the social labelling of skill, do not coincide. But both are real. They both mark important dimensions of differentiation within the workforce. Similarly, to say that an industry is looking for cheap, unskilled, female labour is an immensely loaded statement. That 'demand' cannot be taken to be simply a reflection of technology. Nor, therefore, can 'location factors' be seen as simply the reflection of the requirements of the labour process. Labour process is not in that sense determinant of location. In these and many other ways, the link between production relations, social structure and location is the product of wider social factors as well as of the characteristics of the job itself. It is not just a one-way influence; the relative weaknesses and strengths of different groups in the workforce can affect the way the production process is evolved, to take advantage of the one and to avoid the other. To say, then, that industrial location is part of wider social relations does not just mean that it is set in a larger context. The wider social relations of society also influence the internal structure of production itself. Once again, the ideological and the economic are integral to the construction of each other.

This is still to talk in terms of relations of production, of the functions within them, and of the groups which perform those functions. Because a main theme of this book argues that one of the keys to understanding the geography of employment is the geography of the relations of production, this level will be an important focus of attention. But that level of analysis is not sufficient to define 'classes' in any more full-blooded sense. As Hall (1977) puts it, production relations indicate the sites of class relations in the economic structure, but those sites do not designate whole classes as integral, empirical groups of men and women. The fact that people occupy similar places in the relations of production does not in itself imply any other empirical level of coherence, still less any kind of necessary political unity about pre-given common interests. Wright talks of class capacities, the social relations *within* a class which determine how internally coherent it is. He distinguishes between structural capacities (those internal links generated by the developments of a capitalist society) and organisational capacities (those links which are a product of conscious organisation). Skilled and unskilled workers, blacks and whites, whatever their apparent common fundamental interests, are frequently pitted against each other in the immediacy of day-to-day life, and it is in actual struggle that political subjects are constituted.

All of which means, first, that 'whole classes' are rarely actual political subjects and, second, that it is most frequently non-class subjects – blacks, women, ratepayers – who occupy the front of the political stage.

We have, therefore, come a long way from the classic conception of industrial location theory, in which an entrepreneur or a manager stares out at a 'spatial surface' and makes a 'location decision' in a context divorced from history and social relations. The 'industrial location decision' is just one moment in a much wider economic, ideological and political field. But we have also come a long way from that conception of the world which envisages a simple opposition between capital and labour in a context where the categories and the immanent tendencies of the capitalist mode of production substitute for analysis of real history.

Reflections

Three elements of this journey are of particular importance for the analysis here.

The first concerns the relationship between politics and ideology, and that realm very generally and vaguely referred to as 'the social', on the one hand, and 'the economic' on the other. We have seen that politics and ideology are not to be interpreted as simple reflections of the economic; that was clear in the discussion of class, for instance. But perhaps more important here, because the focus of this book is, in the end, on the economic, is the obverse implication – that politics and ideology are themselves important in the construction of the economic. Questions of who does which jobs, the problem of the definition of skill, the identification of different kinds of capital, all exemplify the fact that the economic aspects of society are themselves social constructions, thoroughly imbued with politics and ideological tradition. Exactly parallel points are reflected at a wider level. State policies cannot simply be interpreted in terms of 'the demands of the economy'. It is no argument to say that 'accumulation required the implementation of regional policy', for instance. For one thing, as we have seen, the process is more complex than that anyway. There are frequently highly significant divisions and conflicts within 'capital' and therefore in the requirements of accumulation. It has therefore to be analysed as to how the ruling requirement is established as general. More importantly, the economic development of society is itself subject to political determination. The stimuli and pressures of international capitalism do not arrive raw at the factory gate.

The organisation of the national economy is itself an object of political struggle; different sections of the ruling class seek to impose their own, very different, political rationalities upon it. These rationalities are truly political; they cannot simply be analysed as the product of the requirements of the economy. 'This means that the economy, like all other spheres of society, is the terrain of a political struggle, and that its "laws of motion" are not governed by a simple logic, but by the hegemonic articulation existing in a given society' (Laclau and Mouffe, 1981, p. 22). In Britain, for example, there is a world of difference between the economic and social logic of different parts of the State and between different political elements. Gamble (1981) has analysed some of these contrasting positions and their effects, pointing for instance to that important, and long dominant, strand within the British Conservative Party for which the maintenance of social power and relatively stable class relations has been of far greater importance than any particular 'bourgeois' economic ideology, such as that of the free play of market forces. There have been many times when the maintenance of the historical terms of class rule have not been simply consistent with 'the interests of the British economy'. But if that is the case then, as Laclau and Mouffe argue, the political must be a primary defining characteristic of any particular conjuncture. If that also is the case then it must be as a function of that politics, set – obviously – within the wider constraints of economic conditions but not simply relaying them unmodified, and as a function of the construction of that particular political hegemony, that the role and rationale of, for instance, regional policy, must be interpreted. This does not mean, either, that the analysis is simply reversed – that 'the political' level rules, untrammelled by other considerations. For political rationalities and interpretations are rationalities about and interpretations of the objective circumstances of the time, chief among them the requirements of capitalist production.

*   *   *

The second element of importance is that empirical analysis does not consist of references to the 'laws' of capitalist development, nor is explanation adequately established by a gesture in the direction of some 'immanent tendency'. For this reason too, it is not possible to explain the actions of an individual company or management simply by referring to the requirements of accumulation. The response of capital to such requirements will depend on its own social characteristics, the kinds of calculation which it makes, the kind of workforce with which it is faced and its actions, and on the terms of the battle between them. If the management of GEC, British Steel or British Leyland engage in long struggles with the workforce over changes in the labour process and location, and if those changes broadly coincide with the longer run of developments under capitalism, then it is important to understand that. But it is none the less insufficient to refer to those tendencies in explanation. What, then, of those cases where the long-run tendencies do not 'show up in the real world'? The same points apply to the analysis of the spatial development of capitalist societies as a whole. Again there are no inexorable trends which can be brought down off the shelf in explanation when the results of empirical analysis appear to conform with the theory.

The most obvious example within geographical analysis has been the assertion of a necessary tendency to increasing spatial concentration. Such a position has an apparent radicalism, and is clearly often stimulated by a desire to counter the conclusions of equilibration at equality which emerge from neo-classical theory. Marx himself is sometimes claimed to have identified an inevitable tendency under capitalism towards spatial concentration, and certainly there are quotations which can be read to this effect. The most obvious source of such evidence is probably the discussion of the turnover of capital, and particularly of the time of circulation, this having evident relevance to the geographical dimension. But it would be unfair to deduce from such quotations that Marx had a developed position that the dominant tendency within the geographical development of the capitalist mode of production was that towards centralisation and inequality. What he did was to point to a number of different – and contradictory – forces to which the development of capitalism might give rise.

Some attempts have been made more recently, however, to produce a more systematic analysis. While numerous writers refer to 'increasing spatial concentration under capitalism', few argue the case in detail. The most thorough attempt is in the work of Läpple and van Hoogstraten (Läpple, 1978; Läpple and van Hoogstraten, 1979; and van Hoogstraten, 1979). In their various papers, Läpple and van Hoogstraten argue the case for the existence within the capitalist mode of production of a dominant tendency towards increasing geographical concentration. Their argument has a number of strands. They postulate that increases in the social productivity of labour require, under capitalism, a corresponding expansion in the scale of production. It is argued that any locational decision in any unit of production within any particular sector will be subject to two sets of influences – 'natural' conditions (such as the availability of raw materials, the existence of 'natural' transport routes) and 'social' conditions (such as the nature of the labour force, accessibility to other sectors). It is then suggested that the direct influence of 'natural' conditions must diminish over time in relation to that of social conditions, and further that that shift in balance implies an increasing degree of geographical concentration. But must this change of emphasis between different types of 'location factors' produce an increasing degree of spatial concentration? The authors argue that two things, the increasing emancipation from a direct dependence on 'natural' location factors, and the development of the division of labour both work towards such concentration; that the reduced importance of natural factors entails a corresponding reduction in the tendency of units of production to disperse in response to their differing dependencies on such factors; and that the increasing division of labour entails also its opposite, the need for every individual plant to be in spatial contact with the rest of the social collective labourer. 'Along with the increasing socialisation of production the productivity of social labour becomes even more strongly dependent on the possibilities of the systematic combination in space of the different stages of production' (Läpple and van Hoogstraten, 1979, p. 10). The mechanisms being pointed to here are certainly real. The increasing division of labour is at variance with the (corresponding) increase in the need for contact between the different parts of total labour. But does this mean that production will be increasingly spatially concentrated? The conflict is between anarchy and the need for socialisation, which is not necessarily the same as between dispersion and concentration. Certainly the need for contact will provide a pull in that direction, but other factors will also be operative. The growth in the productivity of labour will also increase the ease of crossing space (the annihilation of space by time); some social factors, such as costs of labour, may work in the opposite direction, increasing precisely as a result of concentration. Clearly, the growing division of labour will reinforce the need for systematic combination and organisation of spatial contacts, but this does not necessarily imply spatial concentration. What has been unearthed is one influence. It has not been established that it will necessarily be dominant. Exactly the same reservations apply to the next stage of the argument, which concerns the tertiary sector. Once again an important tendency has been highlighted, but what does not seem to have been satisfactorily established is that this is in any sense the dominant tendency.

Läpple and van Hoogstraten do indeed consider the possibility of counter-influences, that is, tendencies towards the spatial dispersion of production. They identify two. The first is that the increasing size of individual capitals, in the context of the increasing division of labour, enables the splitting up of different functions within the production process, and their separate, and differentiated, locational responses. The second is, as already mentioned, that the fact of spatial concentration may itself produce negative effects and consequently a tendency to decentralisation, especially on the part of relatively weak firms and sectors of production. But, they argue, these are not the dominant tendencies because of the increasing necessity for State provision of the general conditions of production and of reproduction. At this point the explanation amounts not so much to an argument as to an empirical observation. Indeed, for many writers the elucidation of necessary spatial tendencies under capitalism has consisted of observation of actual empirical tendencies followed by attempts to re-read them as logically necessary outcomes of a pure capitalist mode of production. Quite apart from all the epistemological disadvantages referred to earlier, such a procedure opens itself up to simple refutation by reference to empirical examples of the opposite tendency. At the time of writing, for instance, the phenomenon of '*usines isolées*' is probably the most discussed aspect of the changing geography of production in western Europe.

Finally, what is meant, after all, by spatial centralisation? Clearly most authors on the subject are referring not only to the centralisation of control over production, but also to the centralisation of production itself. But what is meant *exactly*? How would one go about evaluating it – by proportions of wage-earners, by wages of wage-earners, by amount of capital investment or some measure of production? The responses have been varied, and often ambiguous. The implication we draw here is that centralisation – and indeed geographical inequality in general – is not to be measured on some simple linear dimension of inequality but must refer more to a structure of dominant relations between elements of the economies of different 'regions'. But how does one compare such structures of dominance to decide whether or not centralisation is increasing? Indeed, might not such structures vary not just in degree but also in kind?

The issue is yet more complicated than this. Apart from the problem of the variables on which it is to be measured, what does 'increasing centralisation' mean in *geographical* terms? Does it mean that those regions which gain the initial advantage become increasingly dominant, and the peripheral regions increasingly poor? This pattern is what is implied by most versions of the 'cumulative causation' model. Yet how, in that case, can clear cases of reversal to dealt with? What of Belgium, where once the industrial might of the south was dominant but where the main centres of accumulation are now in Flanders, with the old industrial areas lying neglected and depressed?

One of the main characteristics of the developing geography of capitalist societies so far has been precisely the development of new areas and the abandonment of old. Even if we accept that the existence of production in a region does not in itself make that region a centre of accumulation, the whole history of capitalism indicates that what we need is not some single concept, such as 'centralisation', but a whole range of concepts which will allow the analysis of complicated, and changing, *structures* of geographical inequality. To return to our original theme, even had some general logical spatial tendencies of 'a capitalist mode of production' been established, they would not in themselves be an explanation of the enormously complex geographical history of actual capitalist societies. What is needed is an approach which can deal with this ever-changing complexity.

*   *   *

The third element, and putting all this together, is that what we are concerned with in empirical analysis is geographical and historical specificity. Indeed, what lies behind the whole notion of uneven development is the fact of highly differentiated and unique outcomes. That form of analysis which combines economism with a simple application of deduced laws has created a divorce within certain strands of Marxism between 'theory' and the analysis of particular situations. It is a divorce which parallels that between the patently inapplicable mathematical industrial location theory and the collapse into simple description by much of the behavioural school in geography, and by many concerned with real empirical analysis. Further, when attempts are made to use such theory in empirical analysis then, just as with models of firms and their imperfect realisation in the world, so with laws and actual historical developments: behaviour is split into two and the world is divided between the inexorable *a priori* and the purely descriptive deviation. The models of firms developed both in classical industrial location theory and subsequently in the behavioural school, both interpreted the fact of specificity as one of mismatch between theory and reality. It was a problem; and both coped with it by dividing analysis, and by implication company behaviour, into two completely different parts – that which accorded with the *a priori* model and that which was attributed to 'additional factors' derived simply from observing and describing this particular individual case (Massey, 1976). Certain forms of Marxism stand in danger of reproducing the same mismatch and the same untenable dichotomy. Moreover, 'precisely because no "fact" can represent a challenge to the inexorable course of history, we can afford to be negligent with facts. This attitude, paradoxically, creates two orders of reality. The first, that of the necessary laws of evolution, which is theorised in a rigorous fashion, represents the latent meaning of history. The second, the order of facts, in the absence of any perspective which would allow a theoretical analysis of the conjuncture, amounts to no more than a sum of empirical circumstances' (Laclau and Mouffe, 1981, p. 18). The implications of such an approach are deleterious not only to analysis but also to political intervention. On the one hand there is little that can be done about the inexorable. On the other hand, mechanistic analyses are followed by a politics with which they have little connection (see, for example, Dunford, Geddes and Perrons, 1981). 'An ever-greater chasm is thus established between the expedients of day-to-day political practice and the aprioristic knowledge of the laws of history' (Laclau and Mouffe, 1981, p. 18). The point of theoretical concepts, and of frameworks such as those elaborated here, is to provide tools for the analysis of specific situations, analyses on which action can be based.

2.4 The social and the spatial: an impossible dichotomy

Geography matters

Just as most locational studies have failed to relate geographical changes to wider social relations, so have most studies of social relations ignored geography. Conceptual work in economics and sociology frequently proceeds as though the world existed on the head of a pin – as though it were distanceless and spatially undifferentiated. The academic disciplinary division of labour between 'substance' and 'space' has done harm to both. The 'substance laws' of economics and sociology have been spatially blind, while geography has been periodically thrown into paroxysms of self-doubt about whether it had a real object of study, and if so, what it was.

Geography's answers to this conundrum have varied over time. For much of its history, a central focus of human geography has been 'the region', defined as a distinct area of the earth's surface, and the concern of geographers was to understand the interrelationship between different aspects of the natural and social world, 'from geology to politics', which went to make up the distinctiveness of different places. The emphasis, then, was on the unique. All this was overthrown in the 1960s. As in other disciplines, that decade brought with it a new dominance of a variety of forms of positivism. There was a search after empirically-generalisable laws and an obsession with the quantitative. Uniqueness was now something to be normalised-away, reduced to conformity. In method, geography thus became indistinguishable from other disciplines. Its *raison d'être*, therefore, had to be defined in terms of its object of study, and geography set itself up as 'the science of the spatial'. The approach to the analysis of spatial pattern by correlation between maps with which we began this chapter is a lingering and low-key empirical inheritance from geography's theoretical self-definition of the sixties. A realm of 'the spatial' was demarcated. Spatial distributions were analysed as the result of spatial processes (processes operating over space but defined without any substance referents), there were attempts to identify purely spatial mechanisms (gravity models were much in vogue), there was a search after 'spatial laws'.

Along with much else, this came under fire in the seventies. It was pointed out that there were no such things as 'purely spatial processes'. There were only particular social processes operating over space. Spatial form and spatial distributions, it was argued, are the result not of spatial processes (for there are no such things) but of social processes. It was at this point that many geographers went off to learn sociology or economics, or whatever discipline related to the substance laws of their bit of the subject. The introduction of production into industrial geography was thus a particular instance of the more general move to introduce social processes into the explanation of geographical form.

But this reaction of the seventies itself had problems – the relative importance of the social and the spatial was simply reversed; the two continued to be conceptualised as separate realms. Geographical patterns were now understood as simply the result of the distribution of social processes over space. Geography was reduced to mapping the output of other disciplines; 'space' was reduced to a passive surface over which social processes were distributed. The equally dispiriting corollary, of course, was that the social processes themselves could continue to be conceptualised in aspatial terms. At this point, both spatial and substance disciplines were underestimating the importance of geography.

For geography matters. The fact that processes take place over space, the facts of distance or closeness, of geographical variation between areas, of the individual character and meaning of specific places and regions – all these are essential to the operation of social processes themselves. Just as there are no purely spatial processes, neither are there any non-spatial social processes. Nothing much happens, bar angels dancing, on the head of a pin. The title of this section refers to the frequent separation of the inseparable. Nor do any of these processes operate in an environmentally characterless, neutral and undifferentiated world. Geography in the fuller sense implies not only spatial distance but also physical differentiation, of terrain, of vegetation, of climate. Such physical features and variations are important. Their impact, use and meaning will, of course, be socially constructed, but that construction is *of* something. Timpanaro has written of biology: 'To maintain that since the "biological" is always presented to us as mediated by the "social", the "biological" is nothing and the "social" is everything, would ... be idealist sophistry' (1974, p. 16). The same applies to the physical differentiation of the earth's surface. There are real environmental influences and constraints. But even to conceptualise space and natural physical features in this way (as influence on, or constraint) is to presuppose a separation, parallel to that supposed between the social and the spatial more generally, and which is equally untenable – first the social processes, then the influences on them (Williams, 1978). 'People and Nature are not separate: we are part of Nature and to start in the conventional manner with such a separation followed by a listing of interactions would be to prejudice every other aspect of the exposition' (A. Sayer, 1979, p. 22). Geography in both its senses, of distance/nearness/betweenness and of the physical variation of the earth's surface (the two being closely related) is not a constraint on a pre-existing non-geographical social and economic world. It is constitutive of that world.

What does it mean, then, to say that geography, or space, has an effect; that geography matters? Clearly it is not to say that space alters the processes themselves. That would be to re-posit the separation. The statement concerns our analysis of those processes. Substance laws and analyses of social processes might be different were they to make integral the fact of their necessarily spatial character. It is certainly invalid for geographers to seek to define abstractly spatial processes without reference to substantive content. But it is equally invalid for those in substance disciplines to ignore the fact that the relations they study take place over space and in a geographically-differentiated world.[8]

*   *   *

When we take seriously the fact that the social processes involved in the development of capitalist relations of production take place 'in a geographical world', our analysis of them changes. Take a few examples.

Production change (the development of the forces of production, changes in the labour process, etc.) and locational change may often be alternative ways in which capital can achieve the same ends. The fact of spatial variation in the labour force may give management greater flexibility in decisions about production. If a production process is potentially mobile it may be easier to move to an area of low wages than to introduce, through investment in technical change, a shift in the nature of the labour process. Either strategy, production change or location change, can be used to achieve the same result – a lowering of labour costs. This is a relation (in this case a choice) between production change and geographical change which presents itself at a particular moment. It is more likely to change the speed rather than the overall direction of major tendencies. But it is not just a localised or minor effect. What would have happened to the development of the labour process in clothing, in textiles, in electronics assembly, over the last twenty years had multinational capital not found the desperately cheap labour reserves of the Third World? Nor is it just a case of the availability of cheap labour slowing down the necessity for automation or other forms of technological change. The ability to keep processes manual, as opposed to automated, can speed up technological innovation in the product. Froebel, Heinrichs and Kreye (1980) found examples of this in their study of the new international division of labour. They quote the United States Tariff Commission: 'Manufacturers state that such rapid changes in the market discourage economical automation of product lines; automation would tend (1) to prevent product innovation because of the investment required, and (2) slow the advance of technology vital to maintaining their competitive position with regard to imports' (quoted on p. 335). It is not just that production shapes geography; the historically-evolved spatial configuration (both the fact of spatial differentiation and its particular nature) has its influence on the course taken by accumulation itself.

So the pace, certainly, of changes in the labour process will be influenced by the kind of labour available, and the variation in it. And much of this variability will be spatially organised. Indeed, spatial separation may be a condition of the variation itself. To take one obvious, simple example: the fact of spatial separation is often an important element in the preservation of particular, local, conditions of production – low wages, loyalty to the company and a concomitant lack of militancy may be easier for a company to ensure in an isolated area where there is a degree of local spatial monopoly over the labour force. And more generally distance, as we shall see, has been a great divider of the working class, an important condition for the perpetuation of differences.

Further, whether or not the adoption of a particular production technique and its constituent labour processes is accompanied by spatial separation of different stages of production will depend on whether or not there are spatially-differentiated labour markets, or spatial differentiation of some sort. And, in turn, that spatial response itself may influence the internal organisation of the firm.

Particular forms of organisation of technology may be adopted to enable advantage to be taken of particular geographical patterns. The fact that companies become multilocational (still more, multinational) may be the impetus for the development of particular forms of management hierarchies, particular subdivisions of the relations of economic ownership and possession. Different ways of breaking down the production process, to take advantage of specific forms of spatial variation, may in turn stimulate different ways of disaggregating the relations of ownership and possession, and therefore give rise to different kinds of managerial social groups. It is not just that the growth of the multilocational company means the distribution of the management hierarchy and the associated relations of production over space but that the fact and form of spatial distribution may itself influence how those hierarchies and relations develop. In an early and important work, Stephen Hymer (1972) pointed out how in multilocational companies different functions of management (i.e. within the overall relations of production) were distributed in hierarchical fashion between different geographical places. It is interesting to reflect on this, not just for its implications for uneven development over space, but also for whether the need to devise some form of spatial structure itself influenced the development of the division of labour within managerial functions.

Historically, of course, the whole process is a circular one. Distributions of class relations and different social groups over space are in part a product of these processes and operate as location factors in subsequent periods of investment. Reserves of labour, for instance, are the product of social relations; they don't just happen. And such local variations in class and social structure can in turn have significant effects on location.

This is to concentrate on what happens to the analysis of specified processes when we recognise their necessarily geographical character. There may also be categories and processes the operation of which cannot be understood without recognising their internal spatial structuring. The national rate of growth of wages may be set by the region where labour is strongest (something which happened in Britain in the fifties) – what economists, when they look spatially below the national level, might explain by geographical rigidities. An assessment of the supply of and demand for labour at the national level, or of its national-level strength, would not be able to isolate the process at work. Not, it should be repeated, that space, or geographical variation, has any necessary consequences in and of itself – workers in the region with the highest level of economic activity could have been constantly undermined by an influx of unemployed labour from elsewhere (which did happen, as we have seen, some decades earlier). It is not that a particular form of spatial variation will have a particular outcome, itself produce a necessary effect. But the fact of spatial variation will demand some social response. It is not 'space' itself which accounts for the impact on the national economy but social and economic processes operating spatially. The fact of regional inequality and differentiation can either help or hinder the national rate of accumulation, and can be a profound influence on State policy towards the economy.

It is not, then, just a question of mapping social relations (economic, sociological or whatever) *on to* space. The fact that those relations *occur over* space matters. It is not just that 'space is socially constructed' – a fact with which geographers have for a while been coming to terms – but that social processes are constructed over space.

Thinking back to earlier arguments, part of the necessity for the specificity of empirical analyses results from geographical variation in the operation of economic and social processes and from the particular local combinations and local developments of those processes which go to make up the uniqueness of place.

So far, we have given just a few examples to illustrate the fact and the variety of the influences of 'the geographical'. But the subject can be approached more systematically. Quite centrally, location and geographical mobility are key factors in the conflict between labour and capital within production. The simple fact of distance, of spatial separation, can be important. Dual-sourcing, by avoiding complete dependence on a single workforce or a single site, is an obvious example. Another is that mentioned earlier where a simple shift of location may make it easier for management to introduce a new production technique, or even simply new work practices Geographical mobility is often involved in attempts to bring new social groups into the workforce. The detailed choice of a local site might have a kind of symbolic significance and effect. In Greenock, Scotland, the detailed location of IBM is significant and apparently highly effective. The company employs male workers in an area traditionally associated with shipbuilding and heavy engineering. Into this context IBM brought a demand for relatively unskilled labour and a determination to establish a non-union plant (Steuer *et al.*, 1973). Workers were chosen carefully, not on the basis of skill but on being 'the right sort of person' for the IBM project, people who would fit in with the task required, 'a reliable and responsible type of person'. Unionisation was to be avoided at all costs, and conditions and starting pay were good relative to the area. The resulting social set-up at the factory cut across many of the established work mores of the district (Steuer *et al.*, 1973). And the whole effect was reinforced by the site of the plant. As the Steuer report put it: the company stands apart, both socially and geographically. The location far from the town, in a pleasant valley, away from all other places of employment, contributes to the separateness and symbolises the philosophy.

One of capital's crucial advantages over labour is its great, and increasing, geographical mobility. Time and again through the historical development of industry whole sectors have shifted location to escape a well-organised workforce, thereby both lowering labour costs and re-establishing the controlling power of capital over labour – the movement of the hosiery industry in the United Kingdom from London to the midlands from the eighteenth century (Wells, 1972) and of the textile industry in the United States from New England to the south are just two of the better known examples. In these cases, and in some of those given earlier, it is not simple geographical mobility which is at issue but mobility beyond the spatial boundaries of organisational coherence of the employees. Again, 'space itself' (in the sense here of separateness, or distance) guarantees no particular outcome. The spatial mobility of capital is pitted against the geographical solidarity of labour. Finally, and implicit in all of these, capital can make positive use, in a way labour cannot, of distance and differentiation. The approach to the analysis of spatial structures which is introduced in Chapter 3 is designed precisely to enable this to be examined.

The 'order of analysis', then, in social sciences should not be first the aspatial, or the 'aggregate' (often conceived as the aspatial) and then the distribution over space; first production and only then location. 'Geography' should be part of the specification from the beginning. The reproduction of social and economic relations and of the social structure takes place over space, and that conditions its nature.

Places and politics

Social relations and social structure, and the character of both labour and capital, can vary quite dramatically within an individual country. One element of this is simply that the relations of production are unevenly distributed over space and so, therefore, are the constituent social classes and social groups. That is a large part of the subject matter of this book. But it is also that the constitution of social groups actually occurs 'spatially', i.e. in places. We have already argued that economic function within the relations of production is not an adequate basis for 'whole empirical classes' and that other social relations and ties and commonalities can form the basis for intraclass, and cross-class, variation and antagonism. Geographical separation and distance can operate in precisely that way. One element of this is that the wider social relations (wider, that is, than the world of work) in which social groups are constituted and reproduced are in many ways spatially bounded. The place-based relations between work and community, for instance, form part of what Wright would call structural class capacities. And they are an important influence on local class character, and thus on geographical variation in that character. The nature of the economic base itself can give rise to long-lingering local characteristics. Compare the individualistic stroppiness of Merseyside workers, with a long history behind them of casual labour on the docks, with the organised discipline of miners from South Wales (see Beynon, 1973, pp. 70–1). The enormously varied geographical patchwork which forms the industrial base even within one advanced capitalist country is still of fundamental importance as a basis of social and cultural variations, local loyalties, and therefore potential misunderstandings and antagonisms within, in particular, the national working class. It is never just a question merely of industrial history, of course. The contrast between catholicism and nonconformism has clearly also been important in the difference between Liverpool and the Welsh valleys. Local cultures and traditions of organisation can develop a life of their own – the bargaining strength of Coventry car workers is an example.

There have at times in recent years been flurries of debate over whether one can identify in Britain today 'regional classes', and what such a term might mean. A 'regional class' would seem to refer not to a national class or stratum which is geographically concentrated (there are examples of these) but to such a degree of geographical differentiation within a class that the elements demand separate definition. For a while the debate was bound up with that about the use of dependency theory in intranational analysis. The understanding which informs this book is that what we are dealing with in the United Kingdom are geographical variations within national classes. The importance of the debate, though, was to emphasise the considerable, and geographically-structured, variety which lies behind a term such as 'the British working class'. Nor is it just the working class which is thus differentiated. Clearly, the very different nature of 'capital' and the high degree of its spatial mobility, in money form and as a social relation, means that as it develops it can, more quickly than labour, free itself from particular geographical bases. But long histories in particular parts of the country can still be important, even in moulding the character of capital. Local histories and local distinctiveness are integral to the social nature of production relations which we have already argued should be central to any attempt at 'characterising capital'.

For both capital and labour two parallel and related processes are in operation. On the one hand the business of overcoming distance, of the flexibility of relations over space and the movement towards the formation of supraregional and supranational links and allegiances. On the other hand, and in parallel, the gradual destruction of local distinctiveness. For capital, both changes are proceeding apace, and on the whole both add strength to its arm. For the working class the process is more one-sided and ambiguous. The formation of any kind of interregional and international consciousness is slow and halting. Yet even while wider links are difficult to establish, local distinctiveness is often being undermined. And for the working class, local distinctiveness can be both a disadvantage – in producing divisions at a higher level – and the source of local coherence and strength. The balance between gain and disadvantage is the object of struggle and open to question. But whatever the future holds, it is clear that geography, and class relations to geography, will remain of fundamental importance.

All this is still to talk in class terms, of differentiation within classes. But political subjects, as we have seen, are not always defined in class terms, and one possibility is that non-class political subjects are defined in spatial terms – in terms of locality.

Some intraclass (or cross-class) spatial differences can develop to such an extent that geography itself may become a politically self-consciously chosen and defining characteristic. People in different parts of the country experience different economic fortunes at any one time; 'the crisis' hits different regions in different ways. People demand jobs – for their region, their locality, their inner city. Variations in levels of prosperity, in the kinds of class dynamics, in kinds of conflict, mean that local subgroups may face highly contrasting immediate problems, and have very different immediate interests, even antagonistic ones, at any one time. Such differences and antagonisms are often exacerbated through tacit encouragement. The open hostility of people in London and Birmingham to the regional policy of the 1960s, designed to divert jobs to the peripheral regions, is a case in point. At such junctures, the primary aspect of group definition and allegiance may become geographical.

More obviously, the constitution of some political subjects is from the beginning and by definition spatial. Community groups are a clear example at the very local end of the geographical spectrum, while at the other is the whole host of 'regional' issues which, at least in Europe, from Catalonia to Lapland and from Croatia to Scotland, have figured increasingly prominently in national political debate. A number of analysts, such as Urry (1981a) and Nairn (1981), in rather different ways suggest that this kind of impact of geography may be increasing in importance at the moment within the United Kingdom. Either way, the general point is that, whatever the political subjects, they are formed in the context of social processes and conflicts, and these take place in places.

A particularly clear example today of the importance of geographical variation can be seen in Belgium. There, the very process of forming a national government has been made extremely hazardous by interregional differences and antagonisms which result from a combination of contrasting economic fortunes and cultural and linguistic backgrounds, and which at times have erupted into street violence. In an early article, Mandel (1963) pointed to the very different class histories of Flanders and Wallonia as the conditioning force behind the long-running antagonisms. The competitive strength of Belgian industry, he argued, was based on a combination of advanced technology and depressed wages. And one of the causes of the very low wage levels was regional differentiation. 'Belgium was only half industrialised, for Flanders remained essentially agricultural. The cost of living, therefore, remained low and there was always an abundant reserve army of labour to keep wage levels to a minimum' (p. 8). It is an old story, and one which can be told, in different ways, for many European countries at different stages of their development: from Britain in the early nineteenth century, and again to some extent between the wars, to Italy for virtually all of the last hundred years.

Those regional wage differentials in Belgium were not simply a product of different industrial structures. Nor indeed was it only wage-differences that were in question. The 'rural areas' of Flanders were dominated not only by a particular branch of the economy (agriculture), but also by a specific set of social relations. (Once again, sic Orders were not an adequate characterisation!) Mandel outlines the broader structure of causes behind the nature and price of labour in Flanders. He points out that the endemic unemployment in that rural area made any kind of industrial work a boon. In this context an alliance was established between 'a still omnipotent clergy', which controlled its own system of education, and a class of employers which sought every means possible to ensure that it was Catholic trade-unionism which was promoted. This alliance proved to be an almost insurmountable obstacle to the widespread influence of Socialist trade unions. It was an obstacle made even more effective by the internal spatial structuring of the region.

Catholic governments . . . sought to *prevent the concentration of the proletariat* and *to stimulate the petit-bourgeois inclinations* that were latent in a working class which had only just emerged from the peasantry. A system of extremely cheap railway season-tickets ensured great mobility of labour for the economy, while at the same time allowing workers to remain permanently in their native villages. A legislative encouragement of the purchase of land helped to make these workers into owners of minute cottages dotted about the country or along the roads. Consequently, apart from the ancient centres of Ghent and Antwerp, there have been no real concentrations of the Flemish proletariat comparable to those which marked the birth of major industry in Wallonia in the nineteenth century. The mass of Flemish workers – and there are more of them today than Walloon workers – continue to live in the country or in small provincial towns (Mandel, 1963, pp. 13–14, emphasis as in original).

Mandel argues that this dispersion has reinforced the ideological hold of the clergy, and also that it has put straightforward physical difficulties in the way of organisation: 'Many Flemish workers have to travel to work five to six hours every day on top of an eight-hour working-day. All this has combined to prevent the awakening of socialist consciousness' (p. 14).

Here, then, we have it all. Intraregional spatial structure operating as an important conditioning force on the local development of social relations and working-class organisation. Differences between regions being a significant factor, for a period, in determining the rate of national economic growth. And, at the present, those same regional differences (though reversed in economic fortunes) by providing an organisational focus, being a serious barrier to the smooth operation of State economic policy and the formation of a national government. Geography matters.

2.5 An example

Aspects of this approach have been illustrated in some recent analyses of Italy, in particular those by Secchi (1974 and 1977). Secchi's thesis is that an important link between the development of the Italian economy as a whole and the development of regional disparities within it has been the changing use of labour and the related technical changes in production. He points to the fact that since the end of the nineteenth century the Italian economy has experienced contrasting phases in the use of labour and that these have coincided with changes in interregional disparities. He argues further that these different stages of development have reflected different economic and locational strategies in the major divisions of the Italian economy and the economic and political hegemony of different social groups, themselves related to these major divisions. Secchi's characterisation of different parts of the economy enables him to establish a relationship between, first, various characteristics of production (production technology and the organisation of labour, labour demand, size and social structure of capital), second, locational strategy, and third, the connections to the various arms of State policy, including regional policy, and consequently to the main systems of political alliance and conflict within capital as a whole.

The divisions identified by Secchi in his characterisation of Italian capital reflect the particular importance in that country of differentiation between large and small companies and of the role of the State in production. The 'organisational structure of capital' emerges, in other words, as particularly important, with numerous industries (textiles, food and drink, mechanical engineering, light chemicals, etc) being dichotomised between a few large firms and numerous small ones. This division is one which is also often reflected in the organisation of the labour process. Thus the distinction between large and small firms in sectors such as textiles and food, drink and tobacco mirrors a difference not only in the kind of capital involved but also in the typical production technology and labour process. The second main, though very broad, line of partition reflects major structural divisions within the economy. Secchi's characterisation of Italian capital, in other words, is both specific to Italy (there is no chance of importing it unmodified to the United Kingdom) and bears a clear relation to his analysis of the main factors in the country's economic development. It reflects the importance, within that development, of the dual processes of high levels of technological advance, in certain periods and in certain industries, alongside the continued preservation of important 'traditional' sectors.

Moreover, this characterisation of Italian capital makes it possible to establish coherent relations between the division of the economy and a wide range of other characteristics and forms of behaviour. Apart from obviously closely related aspects such as changes in technology and the organisation of work and the movement of labour productivity, these include also such things as the flows of labour between sectors, the relation to the land market, the relation to different arms of State policy, and the main systems of alliance and conflict. This last – the main systems of alliance and conflict – refers to the positions taken by capital in each part of the economy to a whole variety of issues, both political and economic. The fact that each part tends to be affected in a particular way by national and international economic changes, and that within each the constituent elements have similar internal characteristics, leads to characteristic groupings (i.e. alliances and conflicts) on such issues as foreign trade policy, domestic policies on nationalised industries, on labour supply, training, etc., on incomes policy and, of course, on regional policy. The introduction of this aspect of the differentiation of capital within an economy is extremely important, for it allows links to be made not only between national and regional policies, and the attitude of different parts of capital to these, but also between the more purely economic and the political determinants of uneven regional development, and the influence of each upon the other. This system of political alliances is a main organising principle of the analysis. It is through that political level that the impact of economic forces is translated.

Secchi's characterisation of the development of the Italian economy as an alternation of phases of extensive and intensive development, each of which has distinct implications for the degree and nature of the disparity between north and south of that country, is not therefore a characterisation merely of 'economic' phases. The periodisation refers also to changing class relations, and in particular to changing relations between different parts of capital on the one hand and different parts of labour on the other. Secchi states that his 'thesis is that the different phases correspond to different development strategies pursued by the various leading economic sectors and social groups' (Secchi, 1977, p. 47). The analysis takes account not just of the major economic phases of development, but also of the political strategies adopted to deal with them. The effects of economic changes are understood as being translated through politics; they are not the raw requirements of accumulation. The essential unifying characterisation of a particular period is both economic and political, and it is contradictions articulated at that level which mark the shift from one phase into a new one.

Thus, the crisis of 1963/4 – the end of the Italian miracle – was not simply an economic crisis, though it certainly was that; it also marked the collapse of a political alliance between different parts of capital, an alliance which had in the preceding period held sway over the main lines of economic and regional policy in Italy. Both 'miracle' and subsequent crisis must, in other words, be defined in political and class terms. Secchi argues that the extensive development of the 1950s was a product of the dominance of an alliance between sectors of industry producing intermediate goods, largely dominated by big capital, and large and medium firms in a range of other industries on the one hand, and those in the building industry on the other. It had been characterised by a high rate of increase of employment (corresponding to the notion of an 'extensive' phase), and by a high rate of aggregate growth and of exports. Moreover, this fast rate of growth in employment occurred mainly in the north, attracting increased migration from the south. These flows of labour led in turn to faster urbanisation and, particularly, to a high rate of investment in housing (hence the participation of the building sector in the alliance). As a result of this, and also because of increased wage differentials between the advanced sectors and others, the regional effect of the alliance was an increase in the disparity between north and south. By 1958, this strategy of extensive development was beginning to come up against deep internal contradictions (Secchi, 1977, p. 43). The profligate use of labour was leading, in spite of migration, to tighter labour markets and increased money-wages. But more importantly in Secchi's analysis it was leading to 'excessive' development of the building sector, a development which was due, precisely, to the geographical concentration of the labour force and of the population and which brought in its train soaring rents and all the problems of over-rapid urbanisation. And, of course, that urban concentration was itself due in large measure to the priorities of the industrial strategy of the 1950s.

The economic crisis of 1963/4 was also a political conflict between two parts of the ruling alliance: the advanced industrial sectors, and the building industry. It was, moreover, a crisis in which spatial disparities and the results of locational change were themselves an important component. The political alliance, through its economic strategy, had major spatial effects (over-rapid urban concentration and exacerbated regional inequality), and the repercussions of those effects were, in turn, part of the reason for its collapse. Spatial structure was cause as well as effect, inextricably intertwined with the development of economic and political processes.

It was at this period that the Centre Left was formed, and the crisis in the ruling alliance was countered by proposals for 're-form'. These proposals had a strong territorial content, both urban and regional, and on both scores led to further conflict. On the urban side there were proposals for planned control of city development and for transfers of resources towards those social groups most affected by the increase in rents which had accompanied urbanisation and the boom in the building industry. The proposals to curb urban growth were resisted and sharp intracapitalist conflict ensued (Secchi, 1977, pp. 48–9). Similar battles took place over the attempt to establish a regional policy which, while having aspects of a social reform, could also have increased the total amount of labour available, thus reducing pressure on wages.

Obviously, these conflicts were not just between different parts of capital. 'Tight labour markets' and 'pressure on wages' were indications of increased potential strength among the working class. In a situation of near 'full employment' capitalist discipline became harder to keep; the threat of dismissal became less effective. Those who, migrating north, had for the first time joined the national industrial working class, understood and used their new-found strength. In this battle, too, policy on the employers' front was by no means united. In a situation of relative labour shortage there were frequent competitive wage increases and attempts by different parts of capital to monopolise types of labour which had become particularly scarce (Salvati, 1972, p. 15).

Much of the energy of the ruling alliance was thus also directed, often through the reforms themselves, against this new-found strength of the working class. The results of all this, and therefore the future of location patterns and of regional inequality, thus rested on the outcome of a political battle, in which 'geography' itself was an integral element.

3
Uneven Development and Spatial Structures

3.1 The approach

If the social is inextricably spatial and the spatial impossible to divorce from its social construction and content, it follows not only that social processes should be analysed as taking place spatially but also that what have been thought of as spatial patterns can be conceptualised in terms of social processes.

One of the problems of the 'correlation of maps' approach to industrial location is that it is inclined to interpret the geography of employment as a two-dimensional pattern – more jobs in this region than that, more white-collar jobs here than there, etc. In a very literal sense it looks at the surface phenomenon and conceptualises it in terms of its pattern as a surface. It is on the basis of this patterning that explanations, which are often embodied in similar kinds of patterns, are sought. (Hence the desire to explain geographical regularities?) But if such geographical patterns are the outcome of socio-economic processes (operating over space) then in order to understand a pattern we must go behind it and *interpret* it in terms of the structures and processes on which it is based. The geography of employment, in other words, can be conceptualised, not only as a two-dimensional pattern – as though it were a purely spatial phenomenon – but in terms of the social structures on which it rests and the social processes of which it is the outcome. The primary social process which the geography of jobs reflects is production. The spatial distribution of employment, therefore, can be interpreted as the outcome of the way in which production is organised over space. The question is, how to do it.

One key to getting behind the two-dimensional view of the geography of employment is *to begin by conceptualising that geography in terms of the social relations of production*.

The fact that one region has jobs only in direct production while another claims all the headquarters, or that areas differ in their dominant industries, or that in one area the jobs on offer are overwhelmingly manual while in another there is a sizeable slice of white-collar and well-paid employment in research, all these differences reflect different forms of geographical organisation of the relations of production. What are often called 'interregional relations'[1] reflect the same thing. Structures of dominance and subordination between economic activities in different places mirror the way in which, in any particular case, the relations of production are organised over space. 'Interregional relations' are the relations of production over space.

The aim, then, is to link two discussions – the one concerning production and social class, and the other concerning spatial organisation. In relation to much previous analysis within geography, the argument is that what has been seen simply as the spatial distribution of employment is underlain by, and can be approached through, analysis of the geographical organisation of the relations of production. In relation to the substantive social sciences the argument is that the social structure of the economy, the social relations of production, necessarily develop spatially and in a variety of forms. These forms we shall call *spatial structures of production.*

From both disciplinary vantage points this approach highlights the fact that 'space' is not a passive surface on to which the relations of production are mapped, nor yet simply a negative constraint (in the sense, for instance, of distance to be crossed). The fact of spatiality is an integral and active condition. In relation to production, spatial form and spatial strategy can be an active element of accumulation. Capital can make positive use of distance and differentiation. This chapter will begin to formulate some of the ways it can do this, and to examine their effects.

It is important to stress that there *is* a whole variety of ways in which capitalist production can be organised geographically and great variety in the way the relations of production can be structured over space. Many different ways in which, in other words, the facts of distance and of geographical variation can be actively used in the process of production and the accumulation of capital. This enormous variation is not immediately apparent from the literature, particularly that concerning large capital. There has been an unfortunate tendency to assume that the form of organisation identified in a particular study is replicated in all other parts of the economy, or if it is not, then it soon will be, for the tendency is in that direction. A whole range of different archetypes have formed the basis for this urge to universalisation. Ford's world car, General Motors' J-car (and now J-truck and S-car) with their combination of world-wide, part-process organisation and dual-sourcing. The product-cycle, or variations on the theme of it, where different plants specialise not in parts of the same commodity, but in different commodities defined by their degree of 'maturity'. The ponderous complexes of the chemical industry with their huge demands for State infrastructure and organisation. The organisation of labour in some firms and industries into primary central groups and secondary, peripheral groups, with concomitant geographical forms.

All of these exist. Each refers to an actual form of geographical organisation of production, and most of the studies either start from or are backed up by empirical investigations of firms and industries. But the evident corollary is that none of them can be the model of geographical behaviour for the whole of multi-locational capital.

The argument here is that there is no need for such a model, such an archetype. What this chapter does is to recognise from the start the existence and importance of variety. It attempts to formulate an approach to conceptualising and examining the apparently endless adaptability and flexibility of capital. Three different forms of geographical organisation of production are elaborated and analysed, but the function of these forms is *not* to be archetypes. The examples are merely examples. They are vehicles to demonstrate *dimensions of potential variation*. They do not exhaust that potential. They represent three out of many ways in which the relations of production can be organised over space. Indeed, in the chapters on the UK which follow many other forms will be identified. As in Chapter 2, what is being presented is a framework, not a blueprint.

But, as was also emphasised in that chapter, this stress on the need to confront empirical variety should in no way be seen as licence to retreat into unsituated descriptive empiricism. Much of the factual information produced by such studies, for instance of managerial structures, can indeed be given meaning by reformulation in terms of the approach suggested here. Many of the empirical characteristics of companies referred to in subsequent sections of this chapter have been described before. The aim here is reconceptualisation; the construction of a broader framework.

The challenge is to construct an approach which is neither detailed description and empiricism nor a 'mechanistic Marxist' insensitivity. It is possible both to recognise specificity and to situate it within the grander historical movements of capitalist societies.

3.2 Spatial structures of capitalist production

Conceptualising the spatial organisation of production

Each of the different archetypes mentioned in the introduction to this chapter represents a possible form of organisation of the relations of production over space. Let us begin by examining one of them further, and uncovering its underlying characteristics. One of the best-known forms of spatial organisation at present is that which draws on the characteristics of multi-locational companies in industries such as electronics. It is usually described in terms of a hierarchy in which R and D and strategic functions are performed at the headquarters location and there are a number of other plants, for simplicity say two, each in a different region, one branch plant manufacturing complex components, the other being where the final assembly is carried out. It is a spatial structure which is well recognised at both international and intranational levels.

What is interesting about this geographical form is that, when examined in terms of the organisation of the relations of production over space, it is not one hierarchy at all, but a whole complex of them. For the moment they are conveniently treated as two groups. Moreover, what these two different bundles of hierarchies represent is two distinct, though related, aspects of the development of the relations of production in capitalist societies; two distinct aspects of the dynamic of capitalist economies.

The first hierarchy is that which connects the different plants, and hence the different locations, in terms of their status as headquarters or branch plants. This is what might be called a managerial hierarchy and along it run the functions of financial and administrative control. It may be that at HQ the long-range investment decisions are taken, which then form the parameters for action for management at branch level. It is at HQ too that ultimate control over the production process, and ultimate authority over the labour force, is likely to lie. Such a hierarchy can be conceptualised in terms of the relations of production. What this aspect of inter-plant relations represents is a particular form of spatial organisation of the relations of economic ownership and the relations of possession. Figure 3.1 indicates one broad and general form which these relations might take.

Capitalist development has been characterised both by the separation of economic ownership from possession and by the development of complex hierarchies of functions within each. In this aspect of the organisation of multi-locational companies we see these complex hierarchies spread out over space. Behind the descriptive terms 'headquarters' and 'branch plant' lies a form of geographical organisation of parts of the relations of production. Indeed, the development and increasing complexity of these relations *took place* over space and in a geographically differentiated context. Multi-locationality itself, as much as the increasing size of firms (the only thing usually referred to) must have been important in producing the need for such hierarchies and in influencing the forms which they have taken and the kinds of division of labour which have developed within these functions. 'Geography' has been an essential constructive element in their development.

One bundle of relations in this 'electronics archetype', then, can be referred to broadly as a management hierarchy, and it represents the spatial hierarchisation of the relations of economic ownership and possession.

In the electronics example, however, this hierarchy is paralleled by another – that within the process of production itself. R and D is separated from the production of technically more complex components, and that in turn from the final assembly of the commodity. In this spatial structure each of these stages of production is both located separately from the others and under the control of the same company.

In other words, in this case not only is the hierarchy of relations of ownership and possession spread out in different locations but so also is the technical, or detailed, division of labour within

DEGREE OF CONTROL OVER:		
Relations of economic ownership	Relations of possession	
	control of means of production	control of labour power

HQ

FULL	FULL	FULL
i.e. control over the overall investment and accumulation process **and** PARTIAL participation in decisions concerning either sub-units of the total production process or partial aspects of the entire production process	*i.e.* control over entire apparatus of production	*i.e.* control over the entire supervisory hierarchy

BRANCH

PARTIAL	PARTIAL	PARTIAL
participation in decisions concerning a sub-unit of the total production process **or** MINIMAL participation in decisions concerning narrow aspects of sub-units of production	control over one segment of the total production process	control over one segment of the supervisory hierarchy

FIGURE 3.1 *Managerial hierarchies and relations of ownership and possession: a basic shape*

Source: adapted from Wright (1976).

production. And in the electronics example some of the 'classic' characteristics of that division of labour show up very well. The sequence of stages of production forms a hierarchy which represents different degrees of removal of job control (the individual worker's control over the physical means of production), and deskilling. In this particular case the hierarchy represents also a very clear distinction between the functions of conception on the one hand and execution on the other, with the parallel division between an emphasis on mental labour and manual. At one extreme are those who work in research, design and development, involved primarily in mental labour, and with tasks relating to overall strategic conceptualisation. Such positions, while they do not carry much control over other employees, do enable the individual workers to retain considerable immediate control over their own conditions of work (Wright, 1976, p. 36). In class terms, these are not completely 'proletarianised' forms of work. At the other extreme, the assembly workers perform repetitive tasks of execution, manual labour in which the individual worker has very little individual control over the form, or even the pace, of the job. In between on all dimensions is the skilled craftworker whose job is not completely routinised, and who retains some control over the pace and method of work (Wright, 1976, p. 36). These different aspects of the production hierarchy are schematised in Figure 3.2.

R AND D	high levels of conceptualisation and mental labour; high degree of autonomy in immediate labour process
CRAFTWORK	skilled manual work, mixing conception and execution; some control over immediate labour process
ASSEMBLY	manual work; repetitive; execution; very limited individual autonomy in immediate labour process

FIGURE 3.2 *The division of labour in production in parts of electronics*

As in the case of the managerial hierarchy, the fact of this division of labour does not in itself imply geographical separation. It could quite easily remain (as it does in many cases) a technical division of labour on one site. In this example, however, the different stages in the technical division of labour are distinguished also by locationally relevant characteristics – above all by the kind of labour which each predominantly needs. Braverman (1974), in his analysis of the development of the technical division of labour in capitalist economies, points out that not only are the operations separated from each other, but they are assigned to different workers. An exact parallel can be drawn here with locations: not only is there a technical division of labour within production, but the different stages of it are assigned to different regions. Moreover, just as the division of labour between different workers can increase productivity and thereby profit, so can its division between regions, by enabling the different stages of production each to respond more exactly to their own specific location factors. Spatial structure, in other words, is an active element in accumulation. Moreover, precisely *because* geographical form can influence the rate of accumulation, it may well be that one of the conditions for the development of particular kinds of technical division of labour within production in the first place is the existence of particular kinds of geographical differentiation, for instance in the labour market. In other words, it is not only that 'the different stages in the technical division of labour are distinguished by locationally relevant characteristics' and are therefore spread out in different locations. It is also that the very existence of such differences between locations may be a stimulus to the development of a technical division of labour which enables advantage to be taken of them.[2]

There are, then, even at the most general level of analysis, distinguishable within this classic spatial structure two hierarchies, or bundles of hierarchies, each reflecting different aspects of the division of labour within a capitalist society, and each representing a different set of functions with different internal relations of dominance and subordination.

*   *   *

Not all multi-locational companies, not even the biggest and most modern ones, have this kind of spatial structure. The way the relations of production are organised over space may vary enormously both between sectors and between individual firms. Take, for instance, the case where there is a headquarters/branch-plant structure but where the whole process of production takes place at each site. The only difference between the plants is that one is the headquarters and the others are branches.

Here there is one hierarchy only, that of 'management functions', broadly defined. Only the functions of investment, supervision and control over the production process – the relations of economic ownership and possession – are spread out over space. The production process itself remains geographically undifferentiated. It may be that there is a division of labour within production but that, for one reason or another, the various parts are kept together on one site, or it may be that there is not a very marked technical division of labour within the process of production under the ownership of a single capital. In contrast with the part-process structure of the last example, this is a case of what might be called simple 'cloning'. Examples abound. Medium-sized firms in the clothing industry often have this structure, as do many multi-plant companies manufacturing final consumer goods which need to be produced very near to the market, large numbers of plants simply being replicated in different geographical areas – Coca-Cola bottling plants come to mind. Dual-sourcing is a strategy of cloning adopted for a different reason – to guarantee continuity of production, usually by undermining the potential monopoly control of a workforce in one place over a particular production process.

*   *   *

As a third example, take what is probably the simplest spatial structure of all – the autonomous single-region firm. Here the whole process of production of a commodity is concentrated within a single geographical area.[3] Whatever managerial hierarchy exists, and whatever the division of labour within the process of production, it is all located within one area. Such a spatial structure is obviously most likely to characterise companies which are small, not just in these geographical terms, but also in employment and financial terms. Crum and Gudgin (1977), for instance, comment on the fact that most British-owned companies which are small in employment terms are confined to one region (para. 275). Such companies are likely also to have a relatively simple internal structure. There may be no well developed technical division of labour within the process of production, and little in the way of a complex division of labour within the relations of economic ownership and possession. Although there is by no means a one-to-one correspondence between the lack of a sufficiently developed technical division of labour and small companies, nonetheless the lack of a significant division of labour within production, since it frequently implies also a lack of major economies of scale, is often an enabling condition at least for the survival and continued entry of small companies, and certainly there is considerable empirical correspondence between the two.

*   *   *

These three examples of spatial structures – part-process, cloning and concentrated – are set out diagrammatically in Figure 3.3. What the three structures illustrate are three fairly simple cases. In these clear forms they are unlikely to be found very often 'in the real world' and the intention is not to set off a search for them. The examples are intended to illustrate something of what it means to say that the relations of production can be spatially organised in a variety of different ways, and indicate a means by which the complexity with which empirical analysis is faced can be approached. It is easy to think of numerous other possible structures. Conglomerate ownership, for example, in which the production of a wide range of different commodities is under the same financial control. Product-cycle structures, where the grip of both financial and scientific control is relaxed as products mature. Or combinations – part-process structures combined with dual-sourcing, for instance. And once again it is not legal forms but real relations which are crucial. Subcontracting systems can involve one company in 'real ownership' of another, for instance, or a firm may be operating in a situation where part of the functions of ownership and possession lie with a bank or financial institution. All of these potentially represent different structures of the relations of production over space. The point here is not to establish an all-embracing typology, but to use a few examples as vehicles for illustrating an approach.

Moreover, *within* these broad forms there may be great variation in the way in which each part of the relations of production is organised spatially. Within the managerial structure there are many ways in which the different functions can be organised; those of economic ownership may not form a hierarchy in parallel with those of possession, for instance. Fashions change, too. The 'matrix approach', pioneered by consultants in the days of technocratic rationality in the 1960s, is now seen, in the face of un-dreamt-of economic difficulties, as overwhelmingly complex and over-formal, and there is a return to more pragmatic, less co-ordinated structures (Hunsicker, 1982). Such shifts influence directly the geography of the relations of production.

The same applies to the production hierarchy. There are many different kinds of technical divisions of labour within individual

1. *The locationally-concentrated spatial structure*

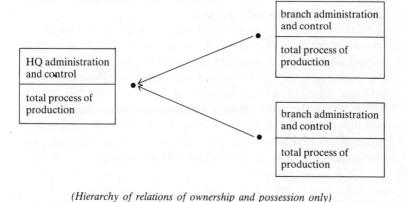

| all administration and control |
| total process of production |

| all administration and control |
| total process of production |

| all administration and control |
| total process of production |

(*No intra-firm hierarchies*)

2. *The cloning branch-plant spatial structure*

| branch administration and control |
| total process of production |

| HQ administration and control |
| total process of production |

| branch administration and control |
| total process of production |

(*Hierarchy of relations of ownership and possession only*)

3. *The part-process spatial structure*

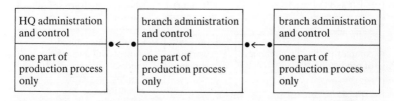

| HQ administration and control |
| one part of production process only |

| branch administration and control |
| one part of production process only |

| branch administration and control |
| one part of production process only |

(*Plants distinguished and connected by place both in relations of ownership and possession and in the technical division of labour*)

FIGURE 3.3   *Three locations showing three different spatial structures*

firms, technical divisions of labour which may be organised into geographical hierarchies. And they vary widely in their implications for the pattern of employment and thus for the structure of interregional social difference. Figure 3.4 gives some examples. The diagram is *not* meant to imply that such part-process hierarchies always typify the sectors named, still less that the different stages are always separately located. What it shows is the different kinds of technical division of labour which can exist within the ownership of single companies in a number of modern branches of industry. Again, other technical divisions of labour exist which, although hierarchically organised in terms of flows of inputs, do not have such an obviously hierarchical form in social terms. Part-process plants exist in many industries, and in some cases do not employ distinct kinds of labour.

All these aspects of social relations are integral to the organisation of production within capitalist societies. There is a clear distinction within such societies between the planned organisation of production within each firm and the unplanned market relations between them. The development of the technical division of labour within the production of a particular product increases the viability of the individual company in the overall competitive battle. Such divisions, once evolved, may provide the basis for whole new branches of production, under separate ownership.

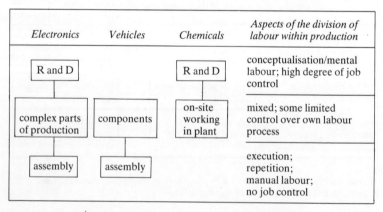

FIGURE 3.4   *Three different part-process possibilities*

The emergence of 'producer services', first as a function within the division of labour in manufacturing companies and subsequently as an independent 'sector', is a case in point. Conversely, it is as part of, and as a result of, such competitive pressures that different patterns of ownership are constructed. Strategies of vertical and horizontal integration, for instance, undertaken as responses to competitive pressures resulting from changing macroeconomic circumstances, represent the progressive transfer of parts of production, whose relation was previously that of the unplanned competition of the market, to real control and co-ordination under a single ownership. The different aspects of the division of labour within production reflect each other and develop in relation to each other. Moreover, both these facets of the social relations of production have shown clear long-term developments. Over the long term within the development of capitalist economies, the pressures of competition have led both to increases in the size of individual firms and to the incorporation within them of different processes of production, and to the finer and more complex development of the division of labour within each individual process of production.

This is, then, not a static taxonomy of spatial structures. The emergence of particular kinds of spatial structure will depend on the level of development of different aspects of the relations of production. They will only become possible at certain points in the overall development of capitalist societies. The tendencies in the development of capitalist economies for the size of individual companies to increase, and for multi-plant, multiregional and multinational companies to become more common has as its corollary that the significance of the simple-concentration form of spatial structure will recede. In contrast, the part-process structure is a relatively late arrival on the scene.

To talk, however, of 'the overall development of capitalism', does not imply that all parts of the economy are at the same stage of development. The part-process structure is not only a late arrival, it is also relatively rare and typical only of certain kinds of 'advanced' sectors of production. It by no means typifies even the whole of the electronics industry, nor indeed has it always been a possible spatial structure, even in this part of the economy. For it to become possible it was necessary for specific developments to have taken place both in the scope of individual companies and within the technology of production. It was necessary to have companies of a sufficient size and degree of integration to include within one ownership all the stages from research and design to final assembly. These conditions should not be taken for granted: there are plenty of mono-functional companies which perform only research (UK mlh 876), and there are plenty of small firms, within the manufacture of industrial instruments (UK mlh 354) for example, that perform the whole range of functions, but on one site. Neither of these situations involves the use of spatial differentiation described above. Particular characteristics are also required of the technology of production. The part-process structure in electronics has indeed only evolved with the long-term technological development of the industry, and especially with the emergence and development of commodities and components which can be produced by mass-production techniques, and with the reinforcement of these longer-term processes by the conditions of fiercer competition of the last twenty years (see, for instance, Saxenian, 1979). It has, indeed, been precisely the conjunction of technological and organisational possibilities which has enabled the establishment of this form of spatial structure. And the corollary is also true. Not all firms with a spatially concentrated, even single-plant, structure are technologically backward. Similar spatial structures can be established by very different kinds of capital. In the production of scientific instruments, mass production and economies of scale are difficult to achieve (save for certain small subsectors such as the production of numerically controlled machine tools) precisely as a result of continuous technical change, particularly in the nature of the product (Oakey, 1978) and the marketing conditions which frequently demand individual customer specification.[4] It may be, however, that there is indeed a well-developed internal division of labour, but that the associated production requirements and possibilities do not lead to a geographical separation of the different tasks. This in turn may result either from the lack of different locational requirements for the different processes or from the organisational structure of capital being of insufficient scale or complexity to allow geographical separation. Or it may be that such a division of labour within production would be technically feasible but that its development is not encouraged by the existing character of geographical differentiation. So while there is a tendency for this kind of spatial structure to become less important, it is not a unilateral tendency; as was seen in Chapter 2, small firms are not simply a dying breed. Although it may decline in overall importance, therefore, single-region production is not a spatial structure which can be uniquely associated with old-fashioned capital. And it is unlikely to disappear.

Neither are other tendencies all in one direction. While electronics has been typified by the spreading out and geographical differentiation of its stages of production, the metropolitan complexes of the chemicals industry represent a converse process of locational integration. Within petrochemicals there is a clear series of technical stages within production, the output from each stage being a different product in the chain (Laurençin *et al.*, 1977). Sometimes these products are marketed, sometimes they are retained as inputs for the next stage of production (G. Taylor, 1979). But while there is a clear series of stages, they are not located separately. This is the opposite of what has been happening in electronics, where changes in the nature and degree of competition have stimulated changes in the organisation of capital and in the process of production, all of which has both encouraged and enabled locational subdivision. In petrochemicals, in contrast, changes in production concerning in particular the relative importance of different raw materials, and the competitive need for economies of scale, have encouraged the relocation of previously separate sites in large groups, or complexes. This process has been further stimulated by two things: firstly, by the fact that the different economic and technical stages of production are neither a response to nor, once established, responsive to distinct locational considerations; secondly, because the sites, which would in any case be large, require such a vast amount of preparation, infrastructure and often State aid, that economies are attainable by minimising their number and grouping different processes together.

It is not enough to point to the stage reached in the development of capitalist relations in order to understand the complexity of spatial structures. There is a need also for specific and detailed analysis of the levels and forms of development in different parts of the economy, and of their more specific causes, which will be found in an analysis of more immediate conditions – in a particular development of managerial structure, perhaps, or a recent merger boom, or a low level of technological development. But, conversely, neither is it sufficient only to do the more immediate analysis. It is important also to see the particular developments within the broader frame of evolving social relations of which they are part. And one aspect of this, as we have been arguing, is to conceptualise these 'geographical patterns' in terms of the spatial structuring of the relations of production.

*　　　*　　　*

But why does all this matter? The argument here is that *each different kind of spatial structure implies a distinct form of geographical differentiation, of geographical inequality*. This is so in two ways – in terms of the structures of interregional relations and in terms of the patterns of social differentiation between areas. Geographical uneven development does not vary only in degree, as some of the arguments about increasing uneven development imply, it varies also in nature. And this variation reflects the plurality of ways in which the relations of production can be organised spatially. Finally, in turn, this way of conceptualising geographical inequality enables the reformulation of some 'spatial' issues at present on the political agenda.

Before pursuing this argument, it is important to look at one or two other aspects of these spatial structures.

Some issues

The concern of this book is with intranational geographical differentiation, but this concern cannot be divorced from its international context. A country's internal economic geography reflects its place in the international political economy, the international division of labour. It is well recognised that countries on the receiving end of imperialism, as it were, reflect in their internal spatial structure their subordinate and externally orientated position within the world economy. The same applies to metropolitan countries. The geography of 'Britain the dominant imperialist and trading power' was structured by booming, export-based industries on the one hand and a sinking agriculture on the other. A well-known attempt to point to possible future developments in French regional geography started by taking a number of different possible scenarios for the international role of that country as a whole (Michon-Savarit, 1975).

Intranational spatial structures are embedded in an international system. It may be that the economies of different parts of the world are 'specialised' in the production of different commodities. Increasingly today, on the other hand, many of the industries which are organised along part-process lines, for instance, are internationalised in terms of their production facilities. Different national economies will have different balances of the various stages of production and their internal geography will be affected accordingly.

The electronics industry is a case in point. The United Kingdom occupies an intermediate position in the international spatial structure of this industry. It is both a location for inward direct investment in the lower orders of the part-process hierarchy, and the source of outward direct investment. In this it is different from, say, Third World countries, which tend to have only inward direct investment, little ownership in these industries by local capital, and consequently no presence of the upper tiers of the management hierarchy, and little in the upper echelons of the part-process structure either. The inward investment in the United Kingdom, much of it from the United States but more recently including also facilities owned by German and Japanese companies, tends to be 'headless', to be lacking the top end of both management and production hierarchies. Even if development (the 'D' of R and D) is carried on in the United Kingdom, very often the basic research is not (Scott, 1974). This, then, tends to give added weight to the production – assembly locations rather than to the sites of control and innovation. The outward investment tends to be more balanced. A number of British owned companies do farm out some – though not all – of their humdrum operations to countries with lower wages than those offered in the United Kingdom. But there is also some tendency to carry out advanced research in the United States. The State-owned Inmos has opted for this strategy, and a considerable fraction of the high-technology investment in the early years of Silicon Valley was owned by British capital. The net result of this complex relation to the international sectoral division of labour is probably that the spatial structure established in the United Kingdom, while clearly representative of all stages of production (in contrast to that in a Third World country) is under-represented at the top end of the hierarchy. Thus the position of the United Kingdom in the overall world capitalist economy is reflected in the geographical structure and balance of this industry within the country.

The basic chemicals industry is also organised at an international level and once again each national spatial pattern is part and parcel of an international division of labour. The national geography cannot be understood at national level alone. In chemicals this is a fairly complicated phenomenon, but a few points are clear. The non-R and D production in Figure 3.4 is that of the huge chemical complexes typical of the metropolitan countries where, as we have seen, each of the major stages from refining and the production of basic products through to the main derivatives will usually take place. There may also be a second tier of organisation linking production and distribution across a number of different countries. Such an organisation exists within the EEC, for example, and is made possible by the vast size of the individual companies. There is thus little by way of a hierarchy – in the sense of a differentiation between sites of production which could form the basis for inequality – either within each of these metropolitan countries or between them. Things are different, however, in the division of labour which exists between these countries as a group and many of the Third World producer countries. The latter have for long often had little other than raw-material production itself. In contrast to the electronics case this international hierarchy is not a response to variations in the cost and type of labour. Above all it is a response to the location of raw materials on the one hand and to political relations between the companies and States, and between the different States, on the other. Fear of nationalisation of a set of products seen as 'strategic' and requiring high levels of capital investment in their production figures largely. There is, of course, as a result of distinct political strategies, considerable variation between countries (Laurençin *et al.*, 1977), but broadly speaking an international division of labour at present exists in which most of the physical and economic conditions for accumulation are

confined to metropolitan countries, and many Third World producer countries lack even the production of a range of basic
products.

*   *   *

This brings us back to another issue. The evolution of different
kinds of spatial structure, their establishment, maintenance and
eventual collapse and change, are not simply determined by the
characteristics of the labour process, the requirements of accumulation, the stages of the mode of production, or even the
demands of capital. None of these things in themselves 'result in'
specific spatial forms. Spatial structures are established, reinforced, combated and changed through political and economic
strategies and battles on the part of managers, workers and
political representatives. The presently dominant international
division of labour in petrochemicals is now subject to political,
backed up by economic, pressure. It is the object of political
struggle. And the outcome will be the result, not only of technological and economic requirements and constraints, but also of a
multi-sided political and economic battle between the politics of
Third World producer countries, international companies in the
sector, and metropolitan State strategies (Laurençin *et al.*, 1977).
This is clear at the international level, but it is true also within
individual countries.

Some of the best examples of this can be seen in the conflicts in
the car industry in recent decades. Many of these conflicts have
been precisely over what kind of spatial structure would be
established. One dimension of the technical division of labour in
this industry was illustrated in Figure 3.4. Car production consists
technically of the manufacture of a large number of component
parts (engines, gearboxes, suspension units, axles) which are then
assembled.[5] This is represented in Figure 3.4 but without any
spatial connotations. The question is how this structure of production relations, in terms of both ownership and technology, is to be
combined with the form of spatial differentiation which faces it.
This can be both the object and the result of conflict. Spatial
separation and variation have been, in the car industry, as much a
part of capital's strategy against labour as have changes within
production. Two contrasting examples make this clear. Fiat in
Italy, on the one hand, and the companies operating in the United

Kingdom on the other, have both attempted to establish intranational, hierarchical, spatial structures.

From the early 1970s, and indeed initially following an agreement with the unions in 1969, Fiat began to restructure its geographical pattern of production within Italy. It was a change which was itself allied to a more general realignment of Fiat's position within the system of car production. One element of that spatial reorganisation was the decentralisation of part of the company's production away from its traditional base in Turin, to the south of Italy. This geographical shift in turn entailed an explicit process of segmentation of the stages of production so that some of them could be separated off in a different region. Production change and geographical change were planned together. The parts of production which were decentralised to the south were different from those remaining in the north (Courlet, 1977; Deaglio, 1975). Above all, what went south was assembly work, along with other factories providing supplies and certain kinds of subassemblies and parts. What was established, therefore, was a part-process, hierarchical, spatial structure, with the south at the bottom of the hierarchy. Jobs there were primarily low-paid and defined as low-skilled (Courlet, 1977, p. 273; Deaglio, 1975). The interregional difference in production jobs was reinforced by the fact that none of the higher managerial, financial and service functions left Turin.

The new spatial structure was founded on inequalities already accepted within the workforce on the basis of the technical division of labour (that assembly workers were classified as less skilled, were less well paid, etc.) and upon geographical differences in the workforce which enabled even greater disparities to be enforced. The workers of Turin were relatively strong and well organised, and their increased militancy is cited by some (Courlet, p. 7) as being a factor behind the new locational strategy. In contrast, the workers of the south were new to modern industry and had little experience of union organisation. These characteristics in themselves, however, were not enough. There had been attempts by Italian industry to use southerners before. We saw in Chapter 2 that a few years earlier, in the Italy of the fifties and early sixties, southerners had been drafted into the working class through migration to jobs in the booming industrial north.

In this earlier period Italian industry wanted southern workers both because, as we have seen, this was a period of extensive growth and also because in some cases, including Fiat, new labour was being sought to work new machinery. Technical change and a change in the workforce were implemented together (Partridge, 1980). Fiat ran an advertising campaign in the south to entice workers north, workers who, largely from a poor peasant background, management hoped would put up with the job's increased monotony. For a while the strategy worked, backed up by encouragement to racism against 'the Meridionale' as a means of dividing the workforce. 'In this period there wasn't even one southern foreman – the southerners were treated as pure machine fodder with absolutely no chance of promotion' (Partridge, 1980, p. 423).

But it was not to last. We saw earlier that the newly arrived industrial workforce was often in the vanguard of the wave of militancy at the turn of the decade. In part it had a lot to do with 'place'. The southerners had come north with promises of high wages and high standards of living. They found themselves caught in the margins of a spiralling urbanisation. They lived in hostels, paid rents that ate into the higher wages and discovered that those 'higher wages didn't go far with the higher prices of the north and the added expenses of laundering and catering that young unmarried immigrants had to face' (Partridge, p. 430). (Southern males were clearly used to relying on unpaid labour for food and clean clothes!) In that combination of industrial and community conditions, of work-life and home-life, what had been a potential weakness turned to strength. 'Lack of industrial experience' can lead to indiscipline as well as to submission. 'But the southerners, especially, weren't really used to discipline like the northerners . . . they talked among themselves, sometimes they didn't give a shit . . . they didn't understand anything – but precisely because they didn't understand the rules of Fiat, it was really they who began mass discussions, who began to break discipline . . . So I think it was really the southerners at Fiat with their "bad manners" . . . who started to discuss the problems' (Parlanti, undated, quoted in Partridge).

It was in the context of this experience that Fiat's movement south began. Maybe in a different geographical setting, home-based in their own region, out of the company of the students and the other manufacturing workers of the industrial triangle, and with less strength in the labour market, southern workers would be different. The spatial strategy of dispersion within the south, moreover, seemed designed to the same end, reinforcing through isolation of labour markets the general characteristics of the region. What Fiat had managed to do was to combine particular aspects of the technical division of labour with spatial differentiation in the workforce. It managed to establish a spatial structure which was hierarchised in terms both of administration and control and of stages and statuses within production and for a while at least it was successful.

British capital in the United Kingdom car industry has not succeeded in achieving the same results. Until about 1960 the car industry in Britain was overwhelmingly concentrated in the west midlands and the south-east of England. In 1959, these areas accounted for 72 per cent of total United Kingdom employment in the industry (Keeble, 1976, p. 181). But in the early sixties this pattern changed considerably with all the major car firms setting up new factories or large plant extensions in the depressed areas of the country, primarily in Merseyside and in Scotland. In 1959 the depressed regions – the north of England, Wales, Scotland and the north-west of England – had only 11.8 per cent of workers in the car industry in the United Kingdom; by 1968 they had 22.4 per cent (Friedman, 1977, p. 243). The basic reasons for this decentralisation of production activity are fairly generally agreed, regional policy and government pressure ranking first, but combined with availability of unemployed male workers (see, for instance, Friedman, 1977, p. 221; Keeble, 1976, pp. 186–7). Whatever the precise balance of these two factors, the *fact* of decentralisation created the possibility of establishing conditions of production more favourable to capital than those which existed in the older-established locations. The car workers of the west midlands, as we have seen, were strongly organised and had won for themselves good rates of pay and favourable skill ratings (Beynon, 1973, p. 65; Friedman, 1977, pp. 221–4). This local strength was an inheritance of decades and of the long-established importance of engineering in the west midlands region. One strategy for the car companies was clearly to undermine this strength simply by changing location, by moving outside the geographical reach of this level of organisation.

The workers in the new areas faced bleak prospects as a result of job losses in the industries previously dominating those regions, and it was clearly possible that such gloomy conditions would produce a vulnerable workforce. Certainly an attempt was made to play upon these disparities, though to different degrees in the different firms. Wages in Ford's and Vauxhall's large new factories were quickly brought into line with those in their older factories in the south-east. But Rootes, BMC and Leyland continued to pay far lower rates than in their midlands factories. The difference in approach among the firms reflected wide pay differences between midlands factories (especially those in Coventry) and those of the south-east (Friedman, 1977, p. 221).[6]

The attempt to impose different conditions on workers in different regions did not confine itself to pay. Friedman points out that managers hoped the 'vulnerable' workers in the new plants might be 'more amenable to managerial initiatives' (p. 243), and he quotes Chrysler's attempt to initiate Measured Day Work at its Linwood plant in Scotland. The importance of this aspect of control over the workforce, as well as the more obvious money differentials, is also stressed by Beynon (1973) in his examination of the establishment of Ford's Halewood factory. Quoting managerial directives, he points out that expansion away from traditional areas made it possible for the car companies to organise production free of the job control that had built up in the old factories: 'when Ford came to Liverpool "restrictive practices", the activities of shop stewards and managerial prerogatives dominated the minds of management and supervision' (p. 65). Management and foremen in the new plant were recruited from Dagenham. Most of the labour, on the other hand, was 'green' and recruited locally. 'Many of the management team had been involved in conflicts with steward organisation at Dagenham and were determined to prevent a similar situation developing at Halewood' (Beynon, p. 65).

The strategy, however, did not work. Those employed in the new factories resisted the imposition of such differentials. From the mid-sixties on, disputes demanding parity between factories, both within and between companies, began to replace disputes over differentials within factories as the major source of wage grievance in the industry. A series of major parity strikes in the late sixties and early seventies began with a six week long dispute in 1966 involving 4000 workers at Leyland's Bathgate factory in

Scotland over parity with its Standard–Triumph factory in Coventry. 'Coventry's high wages, made more visible because of the Coventry Toolroom Agreement, were held up to employers as a standard for the whole industry in Britain ... the strategy of building a periphery of workers within car firms in this country, separated from Coventry and other traditional motor areas, began to crumble during the late 1960s' (Friedman, 1977, pp. 221–4).[7]

Similar battles took place over attempts to establish differentials in shop-floor organisation. At Halewood the policy failed, stimulating instead much conflict. 'By 1964 a strong shop stewards committee had been established in each of the three plants on the Halewood estate, and the company had been forced to amend its policy of restriction' (Beynon, pp. 66–7).

The establishment of a spatial structure, then, is not just a matter of a simple calculation on the part of capital. Its success or failure can be a function also of workers' own attitudes and strategies, in this case their determined resistance. 'The requirements of capital' do not always have it their own way.

There were also interesting differences between the British and Italian cases. Most importantly, perhaps, in the United Kingdom the technical division of labour was not so clearly co-ordinated with skill difference and spatial separation as it appears to have been in the case of Fiat. Both were part-process spatial structures, but in the British case there was a less systematic and clear-cut hierarchical relationship between technical division of labour and geography. Halewood and Ellesmere Port included major assembly plants, but then, as we have seen, Ford and Vauxhall did not succeed in the strategy of wage-differentials for very long. Certainly it has not been the case that only less skilled jobs have gone to peripheral-area locations. Without that basis of division, therefore, the way was open for worker resistance on the basis of direct parity claims, based on identical work, and management's strategy of paying lower wages was, therefore, dependent entirely on the workers in the new areas being more vulnerable than those in the old. It depended, in other words, on management's assessment simply of geographical differences within the labour force, of its greater strength in relation to labour in the depressed areas and on a lack of solidarity between regions. It was a division based on location rather than race, sex or skill (Friedman, 1977, p. 221). It depended entirely upon geographical differences in the strength of otherwise similar workers.

But neither were the geographical disparities in the labour force the same in the two countries. They were undoubtedly more marked in Italy, where the contrast was between the organised workers of the industrial north and people being drafted in from a rural peasant society in the Mezzogiorno. The distance from Turin to Naples is far greater than that from Coventry to Merseyside, not just in terms of kilometers or miles but also in terms of social relations.

The workers who were recruited on Merseyside and in Scotland were not green workers in the same way as those of southern Italy. They may have been vulnerable to the threat of unemployment, but they were not without experience of organisation. This was a working-class area and some of the new recruits had been union workers. Few, however, had been activists, and Ford's recruitment policy was designed to keep things that way. Given the employment conditions elsewhere in the area 'everybody wanted to go to Ford's but not everybody was allowed in. Ford's had the pick of the labour market, and the Company followed a recruitment policy ... consistent with ... obtaining a trouble-free plant on Merseyside ... Family men with commitments came first. Stable men who were tied down with debt and responsibility were given priority. Men under twenty were formally barred and there was little welcome in Halewood for men off the dock or the buildings. Seamen weren't very high up the list either. Neither were the unemployed' (Beynon, p. 89). Vauxhall at Ellesmere Port operated a 'points system' for recruitment, based on similar criteria (IWC Motors Group, 1978, p. 11). The aim, in other words, was to overcome the potential militancy of the workforce and to reinforce its 'geographical' vulnerability. Beynon reports a steward recollecting that it was 'not a typical Merseyside labour force at all' (p. 89). But it was still in, and part of, Merseyside. Much the same was true in Scotland. What began as green labour, hand-picked for docility, 'soon developed strong shop steward organisations. Remember the "new" car factory areas themselves were strong "old" centres of worker resistance' (Friedman, 1977, p. 224). By the late sixties the car workers of Scotland and of Merseyside were among the best organised and most militant in the United Kingdom.

Compared with the Italian case, then, in Britain not only was the attempt at divisiveness more dependent simply on specifically geographical differences in labour's strength, but also those differences, in spite of managerial efforts to reinforce them, were themselves less marked. Both management strategy in relation to geography, and geography itself, were different.

Such things are influential, but they are not determinant. It still took a conscious effort of organisation (Wright's organisational as opposed to structural capacities) to build strength in the car plants of the peripheral regions of Britain. And in the factories of southern Italy such effort has eventually been able to overcome the structural difficulties and to establish a reputation for organisational strength.

In the British case certainly, and increasingly in the Italian, locational separation and the hoped-for effects of differences in the situation of workers, proved to be an insufficient basis on which to establish further differences, in wages and conditions, between those workers. In the British case it was a locational strategy both within a single country and between areas all of which had a long history of unionisation, even if not in that particular sector of industry. In the years since the failure of that attempt within one country, many major car firms *have* managed to establish such differences but on an international scale, both between metropolitan and peripheral Europe and between Europe as a whole and the countries of South America and the Far East. The plants established in the British Development Areas in the sixties operated in a context where there was essentially a United Kingdom car market, with the relationship to the world production and market system operating primarily through exports and through United States ownership of groups which operated as separate entities. There was some degree of managerial subordination but little in the way of an international part-process structure. But by the seventies the multinational producers were well on their way to establishing a technical division of labour at international level. Imports to Britain rose sharply, but a sizeable proportion of the increase was due to imports by US/UK manufacturers themselves. In 1982 Ford imported more than it exported from the United Kingdom (Gooding, 1982). It was a reflection not just of increasing trade, but of the establishment at international level of a spatial structure which included the geographical separation of different stages of production. The next round of car plants in the Development Areas, such as Ford's engine plant at Bridgend, were part-process plants but not for assembly, and they were sited on the basis of an international choice of locations. In early 1983, British car workers were contesting the form of General Motors' international spatial structure with, interestingly, different unions taking different positions. Skilled workers were demanding the location of component manufacture in the UK, semi-skilled workers the location of assembly. Once again the national pattern must be analysed in an international context. And in that wider context the difficulties of organising battles over parity are far greater. Once again, geography matters.

An example

The development of the footwear industry in the United Kingdom over the last 200 years illustrates a number of these themes. Up to the beginning of the nineteenth century the industry was largely concentrated in London. But around that time rising labour costs and increasing militancy among workers stimulated a major geographical shift. Foster (1974) writes of 'the efforts of the great London contractors (for long the controlling power within the industry) to sidestep the effects of wartime wage inflation' (p. 85). In cost terms the contractors were being pressured on both sides. For markets, they relied mainly on export orders and fixed-price purchasing from the Army and Navy. They were, therefore, particularly vulnerable to rising labour costs. The way out which they chose was to divert more and more of their orders from London to the secondary, provincial centres of production in the north and, especially, the midlands. The crucial differences between London and the provinces lay in the cost of labour and the organisation of the workforces. The provincial centres 'offered not just cheaper subsistence but a labour force that was unorganised' (Foster, p. 85). The shift in the geographical centre of gravity of the industry resulted from what Foster calls 'this blacklegging diversion of work from London' (p. 86). Conversely, geographical mobility enabled accumulation to continue.

Northampton was one of the main centres chosen for this expansion. There were a number of reasons for this. There was, for instance, an easily-available supply of leather from the surrounding agricultural area. But, as Foster indicated, perhaps the most important considerations had to do with labour. The labour force here was abundant and it was cheap. For the social relations in agriculture in this area were changing, and this ensured a constant stream of landless, workless people. The east midlands was a region where the establishment of large-scale commercial farming came rather late, in comparison with the rest of England. 'In most parts of the region the open field system of agriculture persisted for a long time – as long as anywhere in England – enclosure not being completed until the early nineteenth century, and compact villages and well-knit village communities remained typical' (Dury, 1963, p. 363). This was, then, just the period when, in this part of England, labour was being thrown off the land and was therefore abundant. It was also cheap, partly because of its very abundance and partly, Foster suggests, because it was 'probably open to covert subsidy from the poor rates' (p. 85).

But the attraction of Northampton was not simply that labour was *available*, but also that labour was, in contrast to the workers in London, completely unorganised into any form of union. In part this was because most of the workers were new to the industry. But also the fact that there was a constant stream of this surplus labour coming in from the rural areas to Northampton itself and to the villages made it likely that the workforce of the newly-established footwear industry would *remain* unorganised. Northampton did not have anything approaching a labour movement. It was not for want of trying. There were a number of attempts to organise unions but on each occasion it was possible to attract only a small number of workers for any length of time and 'from the 1830s to the 1850s every single strike in the shoe-making industry seems to have ended in disaster' (Foster, p. 102). As Foster points out 'Given the nature of the local economy, this of course is just what one would expect. The whole pattern of Northampton's growth depended on the cheapness of its labour, its lack of militancy and the constant influx of new workers from the surrounding countryside' (p. 102). He quotes a union organiser, speaking in 1834, early on in this struggle to build a labour movement. 'There is no class of being in Christendom that more requires the aid of a well-conducted and properly regulated union than the operative cordwainers of the county; they having long been reduced to the lowest stage of poverty, privation and want and far sunk in the black night of ignorance.. . .' (quoted on p. 102). Sixteen years later, by the middle of the century, the situation was much the same. The continued influx of people desperate for work made union organising virtually impossible. According to a journalist of the *Morning Chronicle*: 'The society [of shoemakers] has endeavoured for some years to keep up the price of labour, but all their efforts have been ineffectual. "Two or three years since," said the secretary, "we struck in one of the shops in the town. It was no use our holding out for the scabs from the country went in and fetched the work for whatever price the masters liked to give"' (quoted in Foster, p. 103). Indeed, by this time, instead of functioning in the main to improve the pay and conditions of workers in its own area, as might be expected in a locality where the industry had now been well established for some decades, the Northampton shoemakers' society operated mainly as a tramping organisation which helped its members find work in *other* parts of the country! 'In all this the root problem was clearly a labour market that stretched far beyond the town itself and included (as a result of the rural clearances) a pauperized mass of labour willing to do almost anything to get work' (Foster, 1974, p. 103).

Now, as the industry established itself in the Northamptonshire area, it took on a particular spatial structure, and this too, like the weakness of the labour force, was a direct function of existing, wider social relations. It was during the mid-nineteenth century that one important aspect of the organisation of production in the industry was established which has remained ever since and which has affected both labour-movement organisation and locational strategy. A system developed whereby men were employed direct by capital, on a factory basis in the town or village, to make shoes. Very frequently, however, the men would in turn farm out to women the 'closing' process – stitching the uppers on to the soles. The women were subcontracted labour and worked at home, mainly based in the 'compact villages and well-knit village communities' which Dury referred to as still being so important in the area around Northampton. Within the industry a sexual division of labour thus developed which reflected social divisions in the world outside – and in particular the confinement of women to the home. New relations of production, a sexual division of labour, and a local internal spatial structure were thus established simultaneously.

Later in the nineteenth century, however, pressure from imports increased and capital in the industry was again faced with the need to cut costs. 'Once again, therefore, with no help from machinery, and with wages already down to subsistence level, some further way had to be found of maintaining profitability' (Foster, p. 86). The solution adopted this time was to change the social relations within the industry and, as part and parcel of this, once more to alter its spatial structure. The major shift was a massive expansion in the direct employment by capital of women and children in factories in the town of Northampton itself. By the middle of the century over half the wage-labour force of the industry in the area consisted of women and children. 'The larger social importance of this was not so much their employment itself (they had to some extent been employed at home before) as the fact that they were now employed together, under supervision, in the town centre workshops' (Foster, p. 86). This shift in both the social and the spatial organisation of the industry had a further geographical consequence. Along with the increasing severity of the poor laws it encouraged a mass influx of immigrants, this time from the surrounding villages to the town itself. 'Where previously shoemaking families had been able to work without difficulty in quite distant villages, they now had to be within daily reach of the town's closing shops' (Foster, p. 86). The by-now established sexual division of labour in the industry, combined with the fact that women continued to be responsible for domestic labour in the home and therefore were unable to travel far to work outside the home, meant that a change in the social relations in production (the establishment of the closing process on a factory basis) had considerable geographical implications. The changing organisation of production and the stubbornly unchanging relations between the sexes together accelerated the process of urbanisation in the nineteenth-century east midlands of England. By 1851 Northampton's population had reached 26,000 and almost one in two of its families were dependent on the shoe industry.

Inside the production process the previous division between factory and domestic (closing) organisation was formalised as two separate stages of production, performed by different groups within the workforce, but both now operated on a factory basis.

Labour costs were reduced at this stage, not by a change in the kind of labour which was used, nor by a change in production technique (for the work of closing the shoe remained exactly as it had been when performed in the women's own homes) but by a change in production relations. This enabled the more direct enforcement of discipline over the actual work process: control over the time, amount and pace of work for each individual worker. This change even though it was confined to something as apparently intangible as 'social relations' in turn had major and immediate implications for the spatial organisation of production in the industry.

But while production relations and social structure underwent major changes, the sexual division of labour, established initially because of 'the place of women in the home', became more firmly inscribed in the organisation of the industry. From now on, men did cutting (clicking), women did closing (see also Massey and Meegan, 1982). It was a social allocation of different kinds of workers to different stages in the process of production, and along lines of division accepted within and by the workforce, which was based on a sexual division of labour in the wider society, and taken up and thereby reinforced within production. It was to have further implications for the spatial structure of the industry.

First of all, it played an important role in the course of labour relations within the industry. The level of labour militancy in the footwear industry has remained low. The two main unions (NUF-LAT and the Rossendale Union) are seen by the employers themselves as moderate and accommodating. A report by the Economists Advisory Group (undated) commented that 'workers in the industry are organised into two industrial unions rather than on a craft basis. EAG believes that this is most satisfactory and is a partial explanation of the generally good industrial relations in the industry.... We consider that the present union leadership is aware that bad industrial relations could cripple the footwear industry at a time when it is already vulnerable' (p. 133). 'Evidence of the fairly moderate attitude of the unions at local level' is then detailed. The importance of this union amenability was revealed when employers readily agreed to a closed shop in the industry. The quid pro quo for this seems to have been twofold. First, it was a deterrent to the unions' being taken over by a more general union, which might be more militant: 'The introduction of the closed shop in March this year will significantly increase the two unions' membership and funds.... This strengthening of the unions is desirable to the extent that it makes them less vulnerable to take over by some other union. We doubt whether of itself it will make much change in relations within the industry' (Economists Advisory Group, undated, p. 133). Second, the sexual division of labour was retained: 'We are unaware of any restrictive practice in the industry save two which are so glaring as apparently not even to be described as such by managers in the industry; the restriction of clicking to men and of closing to women. We do not accept that there is any aspect of either operation which precludes the use of either sex. We doubt whether this custom conforms to the requirements of recent sex discrimination legislation' (p. 134). It still continues to exist in practice, however.

This sexual division of labour still has effects on the geography of the industry. Much of the footwear industry in the United Kingdom today is located in the small towns and villages of regions such as the east midlands and East Anglia. But these are regions to which, since the Second World War, other female-employing industries have begun to decentralise. This has meant competition for labour and pressure on wages. Women's wages in the industry have been pushed up. Such changes have not been taking place in the market for male labour (though in absolute terms men's wages remain higher than women's). This differential availability (at those wages) of male and female labour has led to an increasing degree of geographical separation between the two stages of production: a new spatial structure. The Economists Advisory Group reports that the shortage of closers (women) has necessitated the establishment of closing rooms away from the main factory (p. 134). In other words, a social division of jobs between workers, which has absolutely no technical basis in the present form of organisation of the industry, continues to influence its spatial structure. It is a story we shall take up again in Chapter 4.

In the footwear industry in Britain today, then, it is not just that there is a variation in the balance of employment between men and women in different areas. Divisions which have been established within the organisation of the process of production itself have been a necessary precondition for these variations in the geographical pattern of employment. But neither has it been true that the technical division of labour itself, or the nature of the labour processes within the industry, have been the determinant of the kind of labour sought by companies in the industry. The allocation of different groups of people to different jobs has had more to do with social and ideological structures established outside the factory than with any requirements of the labour process itself. And 'place' has been important in the history of the industry too. The spatial separation of home and work reinforced the initial sexual–social division of labour within production. The wider characteristics of the region and its social organisation, and in particular the nineteenth-century changes in agriculture, have left their mark on union organisation within the industry. Such were the problems posed by the continual influx of new workers that, to refer back to Wright's terminology, the organisational attempts made within the industry were powerless in the face of the lack of structural capacities, in this case largely the product of the kind of geographical area in which the industry was located. The relation between the technology of production, social conflicts and definitions within and outside the factory, and geographical form continues to be one of mutual interaction and determination.

3.3 Spatial structures of production and geographical inequality

Not two-dimensional patterns, but underlying relations

The geographical organisation of production can, then, be conceptualised in terms of the spatial structure of the relations of production. And if this is so then what are often referred to as 'interregional relations' are also a reflection of the spatial structure of the relations of production. The notion of 'spatial relations', in this sense, refers to the fact that one function in the organisation of production is operating between two different places. While other functions operate in a single location it is at this point within the division of labour that spatial separation is combined with the aspatial division of tasks. Different regions have allotted to them, in different spatial structures, particular bundles of functions within the overall relations of production. It is what is often referred to as 'the role of the region' in the country as a whole.[8] And this in turn means that the geography of dominance and subordination can take many forms. For different spatial structures – different ways of organising the relations of production over space – can then be seen to imply very different kinds of 'interregional relations'. Different ways of organising capitalist production underlie, and lead to, different kinds of 'regional problem'.

*   *   *

The spatial structure characterised by the locational concentration of ownership and production does not, in itself, necessarily produce any sort of interregional relations of dominance and subordination. The total span of functions of real ownership and possession and the full range of production activities under any individual ownership are present within each region. All 'planned' relations, those of direct control within a firm, are intraregional. And all interregional relations consist of 'unplanned' market transactions between firms or between firms and consumers. It is, moreover, at least in some logical sense possible for every region to have exactly the same mixture and spread of locally-owned production. This logical sense, however, is one which considers only the formal range of possible patterns, rather than the mechanisms of their production. Such idyllic pictures of balance and equal exchange do not, of course, have many historical referents. Historically, this form of spatial structure has been associated with specialisation and differentiation, and unequal market relations.[9]

In particular, in so far as this use of space has been associated with regional differences, it has most usually been one based on interregional relations structured around industrial spatial concentration. The role which any region plays within the larger system is thus defined by its sectoral contribution or specialisation. This was the dominant situation in interwar Britain, analysed by Carney, Lewis and Hudson (1977). There are a number of ways in which such industrial differentiation between regions can produce a structure of interregional subordination and/or inequality. Much of the history of capitalist societies so far has consisted of the opening up, domination and subsequent desertion of areas by particular industries. The kind of dependence which can exist in such cases is, of course, structural (meaning sectoral) dependence – 'over-representation' in the production of particular commodities or ranges of commodities. The employment structure of such areas may become heavily dependent on the fortunes of particular industries, and at any particular historical moment some will be leading and others lagging in the process of economic growth. In terms of this use of space, it is sectoral concentration – the kind of commodities produced – which is likely to differentiate regions one from another, and which defines their role within the overall regional system.

*   *   *

This form of interregional distinction does not characterise either the cloning or the part-process spatial structures. In both these latter cases all the regions in the system may have exactly the same industrial structure, and conversely any industry may be present in all regions. What distinguishes the regions in a case like this is their relation to a single unit of ownership. In both these cases even an equal distribution of industries will be associated with inequality, with interregional relations of domination and subordination. But there are also significant differences *between* these two spatial structures. In both, branch plants are subject to external ownership and control, but in the part-process structure, where there is both a managerial hierarchy and geographical separation of stages of production, regions 'lower down' the hierarchy will be subject to both external ownership and production-dependence, and the effects of these two forms of subordination are very different.

Take first the case of the cloning spatial structure. Here it is only the relations of economic ownership and possession which are disaggregated over space. In other words, the production activity – itself the same in all regions – is in the non-headquarters region ultimately subordinate to administrative and financial control located outside the region. It is this which has come to be referred to as 'the problem of external control', 'the problem of the branch-plant economy', and as such is reputed to have all kinds of undesirable effects. Conceptualised more precisely, however, what external control really means is that, in these regions, certain parts of the functions of economic ownership and possession are missing. And conceptualised like this, some of its effects look rather different.

One commonly-claimed effect of external ownership is the leak-age of profits from the region of production to the region of control. The complaint is that external control leads to remissions of profit to a parent plant from where it need not be reinvested in the region of origin. In its usual form this is a complaint which is overstated and misformulated.[10] What are at issue are the relations and functions of economic ownership. Full economic ownership consists of control over the overall investment and accumulation process. It is the loss of this function which leads to the likelihood of the leakage of profit and investment funds from the region. But what does 'the region' mean? There is usually an implicit comparison with times gone by, yet in fact neither 'the region' as an entity, whatever that would be, nor the direct producers within it, ever had control, under capitalist relations, over profits and investment. The usual argument puts the focus entirely on geographical location to the complete exclusion of class location. Even with geographically local ownership of production such profits could be withdrawn from 'the region' and invested elsewhere. Regionally-based capital is not necessarily regionally 'loyal'; indeed, given that it is reasonably enterprising, it would be foolish to be so. Here the social nature and organisational structure of capital is important. Certainly ownership by larger and already multi-regional companies will go along with increasing geographical flexibility and mobility. There are likely to be *higher* leakages of profit, therefore, but it is not by any means a new phenomenon introduced by external ownership. Nor does the solution to the problem lie in spatial redistribution – in a fairer distribution of capitalists between the regions of a country – but in a change in, not just the geographical, but also the social location of full economic ownership.

This reformulation of what the question of external ownership is about, in other words, changes also the political question – what does it mean politically to complain of external control? One of the recent policy responses in the United Kingdom, partly to this issue and, conveniently, to the fact that big, multi-regional firms are no longer a source of so much new employment, has been an emphasis on a small-firm strategy; 'backing local business', 'encouraging local entrepreneurship'. As a response to the simple complaint of external control this strategy is perfectly adequate, but it thereby precisely shows up the dangers of such a complaint. For it fails completely to attack the deeper issue, the combination of geographical *and* social control over investment. Even in the (unlikely), event of such strategies succeeding, in terms of the growth of local control, that control would simply mean the emergence or re-emergence of a local capitalist class. For anything which could meaningfully be called local control, reorganisation is needed not just of the spatial but also of the social form of the relations of production. It is a function, not a class, which should be reclaimed.

But that raises a further issue about what 'control' means in this context. It is often argued that one of the major effects of external ownership is that it leaves the plant or locality 'at the mercy of external forces'. Again, however, is this really new? It was external forces – the external forces of the market and of changing international relations – which laid waste the coalfields of Britain in the early part of the twentieth century. What is different is that 'blame' can now be laid at an identifiable door – in Detroit, in New York or in London. The locus of responsibility is now personified. Instead of suffering directly from the unplanned relations of the market, people working in a branch plant experience them through the mediation of planned relations within a company. But to see that as somehow 'worse' than the previous situation is to blame individuals while accepting as inevitable the operation of market forces. It is to give credence to the market as 'natural', to accept in other words one of the fundamental underlying ideological tenets of capitalist social relations.

Where, anyway, does 'control' lie? It does not lie in individual personnel (in spite of the very real and considerable degree of autonomy exercised by large corporations, and the degree of control over the market conferred by monopoly power) but in the wider relations of which they are part. To return to an earlier discussion, the personal qualities of a Henry Ford, a Michael Edwardes or an Ian MacGregor, are not negligible in their effect on company behaviour but they have their effects within their historical times. Neither Edwardes nor MacGregor is likely to revive, single-handed, the production of cars or of steel. The logic of economic forces does not determine the precise response of individual managers or of different types of companies, but neither is action simply taken in a vacuum. It *is* a response *to something*, to wider conditions of which those companies and managements are a part.

And that, too, has its implications for policy. If real control, in that ultimate sense which would be restricted by circumstances not being of one's own choosing, lies outside the relations of production in an individual firm, it follows that it is not only insufficient to change the geographical location of control, it is also insufficient to change its class location if all that means is that different people take over. A profit-oriented co-operative in a sea of market forces may have all kinds of other social and political advantages, but it is no less subject to the 'external forces' of the market than is the straightforward capitalist firm. To get real local control over employment it is necessary also to remove production from the play of market forces. It is not just that the claim should be for functions of control rather than for a new breed of local business people, but that the functions too must be redesigned. They cannot, if local control is to be real, remain simply as defined by the wider structure of capitalist relations.

Some effects of that broad, descriptive thing 'external control' have, then, perhaps been overestimated or misread. They are real, but in forms, and with political implications, rather different from those commonly adduced.

There are other effects too, also more easily interpreted when external control is conceptualised – and therefore disaggregated – in terms of geographically absent functions within the overall relations of economic ownership and possession.

First, branch plants may have lower local multipliers than would be the case if the whole enterprise were located in one place. This results from the loss to the headquarters region of the more strategic functions of possession, in other words from the centralisation of major purchasing functions dealing both with capital investment and with services, particularly the whole range of business services. It has been found in a number of studies that such functions may be missing from branch plants and that that in turn may mean a lower proportion of purchases being made locally – hence the lower local multiplier effects. The importance of such effects is open to empirical investigation and will certainly vary, for instance depending on whether the market areas for such goods and services would in any case be constrained to regional or local level. To the extent that such an effect does result, however, it has a number of implications. It reduces the potential propulsive effect of State regional policies designed to attract into declining regions investment by multiregional and multinational capital. And it impoverishes the level of integration of a local economy, reducing it to a collection of isolated production units with little connection in economic terms to each other. Both of these may make it more difficult to provide the momentum for 'self-sustaining growth' in a region.

Branch-plant economies can be a problem in other ways, too, for those who work in them. Branch-plant status may greatly increase the difficulties facing trade union negotiators – and here the problems are exacerbated if the headquarters is abroad and not merely in another region of the same country. The difficulties are twofold. Above all, local management, low down the management hierarchy but still required to sit across the negotiating table, may simply not have the functions and levels of control and responsibility which are being bargained over. Those functions are located elsewhere. Further, where the branch plant is part of a cloning structure, or where there is any degree of dual-sourcing, it is all too easy for management to threaten to play off one plant against its duplicate elsewhere.

These, then, are some of the characteristics and problems of the absence from a locality with only branch-plant status of some of the higher-level functions of economic ownership and possession. They are attributes, therefore, which will characterise, to one degree or another and in some form or other, all branch-plant forms of organisation. They will characterise both the cloning and the part-process spatial structures.

*   *   *

While in the cloning structure it is 'only' these functions of ownership and possession which are removed from the branch-plant location, in the part-process structure branch plants are doubly penalised. Not only are managerial functions removed but so also are whole sections of the wider technical division of labour into which the plant is embedded. Not only is the plant subordinated to an externalised hierarchy of ownership and possession, it is also subject to what might be called 'production dependence'. And the effects of this kind of dependence are quite different, and have different political implications, from those of external ownership alone.

First, the part-process structure is also likely to result in low local multipliers in the branch-plant regions, but the reasons for this, and the implications, are very different from those which result from external ownership alone. To begin with, the cause is different. In this case the lack of economic relations with the local economy results not from the centralisation of ordering proce-

dures and decisions at head office but from the fact that the actual
material flows of inputs and outputs to the plant will come from
and go to other plants within the same corporate structure. A
factory or office is just one stage in the company's production of
the commodity. This means that while external ownership may
affect service links more than material ones (because of its relation
to the functions of control), part-process dependence overwhelmingly affects material linkages (precisely because of the nature of
the plant's insertion into the spatial structure). Because external
control does not require production dependence but production
dependence does entail external control, one would expect that,
when 'branch plants' are considered as an undifferentiated category, service links will be more affected than material ones. Thus
Marquand's survey (1979) finds that the effect is more marked,
when branch plants as a whole are considered, in service than in
manufacturing linkages. On the other hand, studies of individual
sectors whose forms of spatial organisation include production
dependence (e.g. some parts of electronics, and cars) often have
almost no local material linkages. This difference also means that
the economic isolation of plants – their lack of connection to the
local region – is likely to be much stronger in the case of
part-process dependence than in that of external ownership alone.
Plants which are embedded in both managerial and part-process
hierarchies really are 'cathedrals in the desert'. Again, as with
external control, a part-process structure will make life difficult for
trade unions and worker organisations, but again the reasons are
different from and additional to those which result from external
ownership alone. One obvious reason is that in a part-process
structure local sympathetic action by workers in nearby related
plants and industries may be more difficult to organise. The very
isolation, the linkage into corporation rather than region, will
mean that there are few, if any, nearby plants and industries which
are related.

Finally, a part-process structure will make more difficult any
attempts at local takeover and the establishment of autonomous
production. Now it may be asked what is the difference between a
whole series of plants owned by different companies but providing
each other with inputs, and the production hierarchies of a
part-process structure? Are they not just all part of the general
division of labour within society? In fact not; for plants in a

part-process hierarchy are subject to an additional kind of dependence. Where all the stages of production in different regions are under one ownership, a particular region's economic activity is embedded within a specific larger structure of production on which it is dependent and from which it cannot easily be made autonomous. It is subject to planning and co-ordination with other plants through control by an individual company. Thus in the case of part-process dependence the unit of production is established not as part of the more general social division of labour but as a stage in the technical division within the production of one commodity or group of commodities.[11] It is both monofunctional and almost inextricably linked to other *particular plants* (as opposed to another sector), and those external links are subject to the control of a single company rather than being a function entirely of market forces. As such the plant cannot so easily be established as a separate point of production of profit; it is less easy to take over and run as a locally-autonomous entity.

Obviously much, too, will depend on the technical nature of the production process, on the degree to which the capital equipment is particular to the individual product, but in general terms exactly the same contrasts apply in comparison with a simple cloning structure. The high degree of specification of production itself to a particular broader structure entailed in a part-process spatial form substantially increases the difficulty of any moves towards local control, whether in the form of nationalisation, where the interregional dependence is also international, or in the form of workers' control. With production dependence, it is not only full economic ownership which is missing – a situation rectifiable by takeover – but the broader productive structure as a part of which the particular factory has been planned.

* * *

Each of the three spatial structures, then, can be the basis for a different set of interregional relations and form of interregional dependence. In each of the three cases just looked at the individual regions play different kinds of 'roles' within the overall system. So it matters in what kind of spatial structure a plant is embedded. It matters in terms of the kind of relations of dominance and subordination which exist between plants in different localities, it matters for the people who work in the plants, and it matters politically.

It also matters methodologically and conceptually. One of the underlying themes implicit in all this is that it is important to get away from discussions of apparently simple 'objects', and to conceptualise processes and relations. Objects are not simply given to analysis, but are themselves products, and must be conceptualised in such a way as to incorporate, not just their descriptive characteristics, but also the process of their production, the larger dynamic of which they are part. The notion of 'branch plant' is a good example. It is probably fair to say that the phenomenon of 'branch plants' is too often treated either as an unproblematical and undifferentiated category, or as differentiated only according to managerial preference, current fashions in corporate organisation or descriptive dimensions such as size.[12] There clearly are interfirm differences in branch-plant autonomy, etc., which do depend on such factors, and which do have effects. What is important is also to conceptualise the different roles branch plants can play in terms of the different spatial structures in which they are embedded and the different larger processes and relations which they reflect. The contrast between branch plants in a part-process hierarchy and those in a simple cloning structure is an excellent case in point. The possible differences in levels of service and material linkages have already been referred to, and there may be other distinctions. For while the first kind of branch plant represents one stage of production, the second represents additional capacity for all stages of production. This characteristic might lead the two types of branch plant to have very different relative propensities to closure during downturns in economic activity. Closures or reductions in capacity in branch plants in the part-process structure could not really take place without other production locations experiencing similar cutbacks (this does not, of course, apply to R and D facilities). Such branch plants do not in any way perform the function of flexible extra margins to capacity. It is, however, precisely this function which is played by branch plants in the cloning spatial structure and it is this kind of branch plant which one would expect to be more vulnerable to closure in business downturns. There has been considerable debate over the years over whether or not 'branch-plant economies' are more liable to employment cutbacks and fluctuations because of a higher propensity to closure. It would certainly be worth investigating whether an analysis of their

distinct roles within different spatial structures affects the implications for recipient regions of new employment with a high branch-
plant component. A more analytical distinction along these lines
might help to throw light on the apparently conflicting empirical
evidence, and perhaps even point to a variation over time as
different kinds of 'branch plant' became more common.

These examples of the connection between spatial structures
and spatial relations could be multiplied. A conglomerate form of
enterprise structure, for instance, is different again, and has
different implications. In this case the specifically intersectoral
nature of ownership may, as a result of the kind of characteristics
discussed in Chapter 2 (Section 2.2, Characterising capital) add a
further degree of vulnerability because of greater flexibility of
investment. In the case of subcontracting, the technical division of
labour, and the overall production process, is under the control of
one firm which sends out certain stages, or parts of certain stages,
to other companies. Thus the legal independence of the producing
company is nullified by the actual control of many aspects of
ownership and possession by the larger enterprise, while the form
of the product may be influenced by its *de facto* subordination into
a part-process hierarchy. The effects of this in terms of dependence and potential instability of employment are well known.
Subcontracting may also take on a systematic spatial form.
Pedersen (1978) analyses such a situation in Denmark, and its
relation to regional inequality. The three examples being used
here are to illustrate an approach, and within each there are
numerous possible variations. And many other different kinds of
spatial structure exist.

Spatial structures and social structures

Apart from leading to distinct kinds of interregional relations,
each of the different spatial structures can also be associated with a
different pattern of social differentiation between localities. This
can be shown by linking up the distinct geographical patterns of
relations of production which define each spatial structure with the
social characteristics of the groups performing the different functions. It is not just the relations of production which have a spatial
shape: so does the division of labour between the social groups

performing the different functions within those relations. It is possible, therefore, to link up the discussion of social class in Chapter 2 with that of spatial structures earlier in this chapter. Figure 3.5 summarises the argument so far. It takes a number of occupational groups, defines them in terms of functions in the relations of production, and thereby schematises their typical class location. If these connections are now related to the specifically geographical organisation of functions in each spatial structure, the different social–geographical implications of each structure are immediately apparent.

First, and most obviously, while a spatially-concentrated structure may leave each region with a locally-based capitalist class, this class will be lacking in those regions subject to external ownership under the other two spatial structures. Even in the region of ownership, moreover, the nature of the capitalist class may well be different from that typical of spatially-concentrated production. While in the latter case it may consist of individual owners and traditional capitalists, in larger multi-regional corporations capital is more likely to be personified in the shape of top corporate executives and top managers. In non-headquarters regions the hierarchy of ownership and possession is most likely to be carried by middle management, a stratum occupying, according to Wright, a contradictory location between working class and bourgeoisie. In other words, the class characteristics of management are likely to vary between regions of the hierarchy of relations of economic ownership and possession.

One of the questions much exercising regional geographers, planners and policy-makers since the late sixties is what is seen to be the lack of white-collar, high-status jobs in management, in particular in the United Kingdom in the peripheral areas of the north and the west. Certainly, regions dominated by spatially-concentrated production will include the full range of administrative jobs within their industries. It may well be, however, that those companies, precisely because they are small and confined to a single region, are the ones with the more compressed managerial hierarchies. This is indeed to be expected because the development of such service functions, through the extension of the division of labour in control and supervision, is part and parcel of the emergence of the other spatial structures. Such contrasts may significantly reduce (or reverse) the difference, *within* the

Occupational group	Functions in relations of production				Typical class location
	Economic ownership	Possession		Sale of own labour power	
		Means of production	Labour power		
Traditional capitalist	Full	Full	Full	–	⎱ Bourgeoisie
Top corporate executive	Full	Full	Full	–	⎰
Top management	Partial/minimal	Full	Full	–	⎱ Between
Middle management	Minimal	Partial	Partial	✓	⎰ Bourgeoisie and Proletariat
Lower management/supervisors	–	–	Minimal	✓	
R and D workers	–	Minimal	–	✓	⎱ Between Petit-Bourgeoisie and Proletariat ⎰
Manual workers	–	Minimal or none	–	✓	Proletariat

FIGURE 3.5 *Occupations, relations and social classes*

(This diagram does not contain all the criteria used in this kind of determination of class location. Juridical ownership of the means of production, for instance, is omitted. The figure is restricted to the criteria on which attention is mainly focused in the chapter.)

Source: derived from Wright (1976).

peripheral regions, between plants in this spatial structure and those in the other two. This is a matter for empirical investigation. But the main point is that the comparison at issue is between regions, and between interregional variation in different spatial structures. It is not, as is sometimes supposed, between externally-owned plants and locally-owned ones within the same region. The argument is not primarily – as it is sometimes seen to be – that spatial structures with interregional hierarchies of control are 'worse' in this way *in absolute terms* for peripheral regions than the locationally-concentrated spatial structure, but that they exacerbate the *difference* on this score between peripheral and central regions. Indeed, in the United Kingdom, many of the local areas which are now suffering the highest levels of external control are those in which white-collar administrative jobs have anyway for long formed a relatively small proportion of the employment structure. The low *number* of such jobs is not a new phenomenon. It is as a result of a comparative, not an absolute, worsening of their representation in administrative and managerial jobs that the issue is now coming to the fore as an aspect of the regional policy debate.

Once again, moreover, conceptualising things in terms of capitalist relations of production brings home the real issues. What has actually been lost to these regions is not a type of job and associated personnel (since such jobs and elements of the social structure hardly existed in these regions before) but a function within the overall social relations of production. The spatial inequality consists not so much in the uneven distribution of jobs of different social types (and thus in some way of geographical 'equality of opportunity') but in the removal from some regions, and the concentration in others, of the more powerful, conceptual and strategic levels of control over production. Moreover, it is precisely the development of the division of labour and the social separation of such functions to be performed by a separate social group within an extended hierarchy, which enables their geographical removal. Once again the organisation of production and the organisation of space go hand in hand. Particular forms of geographical inequality have as a necessary condition particular forms of organisation of production. And in turn, the desire to take advantage of spatial distance and difference can be what stimulates those developments within production.

The three uses of space will also differ in their implications for the range of jobs available to production – as opposed to administrative – workers. Obviously, the implications for this part of the employment structure will depend on the actual nature of the technical division of labour, the nature of the associated labour processes, the kinds of wages and status attached to jobs, and so on. What *can* be said, however, is that in the case of locational concentration, the whole range of workers involved in production in that sector will be present in one region. This range may be narrow, but such narrowness is not a function of the spatial structure itself. Much the same is likely to be true of the simple cloning structure – this use of space does not involve a part-process division and the existence of a managerial hierarchy does not in itself imply any differentiation in production jobs. Where there *is* a part-process structure, however, the monofunctionality of the different plants may well lead to an accentuated separation of particular types of production workers into different regions. And these different types of production worker may belong to different parts of the overall class structure. Once again, therefore, the pushing forward of the division of labour, this time within production, when this also takes the form of a geographical hierarchy, is mirrored in interregional social difference. In the case of the 'electronics hierarchy' this social differentiation is particularly acute. If the description of jobs in Figure 3.2 is put together with the definitions of social class in Figure 3.5 it is clear that the spatial hierarchy of production coincides with a social hierarchy. This time the social hierarchy is, following Wright's characterisation, that between petit-bourgeoisie and working class, along a dimension related to the level of individual job control. This contrasts with the social class spectrum associated with the hierarchy of ownership and control which, being primarily a function of control over production *as a whole*, and with supervision, follows the gradations between working class and bourgeois. This element of 'the middle class', the R and D workers, thus has a different origin from that of the management hierarchy. Here the control is over their own labour process, rather than the labour of others. Once again, this aspect of spatial structures of production has been raised as a political issue. This time the problem is interpreted as being a lack of R and D jobs in peripheral regions.

But once again the claim for a 'fair share' of the high-status technocrats, as for a fair share of upper-management or capitalists, seems a curious one for the labour movement to make. In local State policy terms the issue is mirrored in the establishment of science parks for the private sector, in advertising the area's universities and its environmental attractions (usually of the 'rural idyll' variety). Everywhere wants to be Silicon Valley.

But it is clear that not everywhere *can* become Silicon Valley. Both the impossibility of such plans and hopes and the fundamental ambiguity of demands for more high-status jobs are clarified by seeing, behind the kind of employment itself, the social function it performs in the overall structure of capitalist relations of production – and the fact that it is precisely the result of the division of labour into such unequal specialisms. The very fact that there *is* Silicon Valley means that there must be production-only outposts in peripheral regions, both inter- and intranationally. For what is distributed about the world is not just 'kinds of jobs', but functions within the overall structure of capitalist production. It is the fact of a particular form of technological development, and of a corresponding technical division of labour within production which enables this form of spatial inequality to develop. The absence of R and D workers from the Third World and from national peripheries, and their congregation in such areas as Silicon Valley, has as a necessary prerequisite the development of a division of labour in production where some people have a monopoly of that kind of strategic brain-work, and where such work is attached to high status and high reward, while others are relegated to the tedium of assembly. Once again, it is not so much types of jobs which people in peripheral regions should reclaim, but functions, integral parts of the overall structure and relations of production.

These are very simplified examples. The position in any real case will be more complex. There will, for instance, be accountants and other professionals within the managerial hierarchy. Such employees are really part of what might be called the production process of management. They are outside the direct supervisory structure of authority and have a considerable degree of autonomy in organising their own work. They will be more likely to fall in the spectrum between proletarian and petit-bourgeois. Conversely the division of labour within production generates its own specific supervisory structure. Alongside the assembly workers at the bottom end of the hierarchy will be technical 'testers' of various sorts whose social position – as formally derived from their position in the job structure – might take them out of the straightforwardly proletarian and on to (though only just on to) the spectrum with the bourgeoisie. The actual form of differentiation in any instance is an empirical question.

This, then, lays out a formal means for investigating the links between spatial structures of production and the geography of social structure. In later chapters it will be developed in relation to geographical patterns in Great Britain. But, to pick up again the argument of Chapter 2, relations of production are not all that matters. Figure 3.4 includes two industries in which assembly work often forms one stage of production: electronics and cars, yet the social implications of assembly work in the two industries are very different. In electronics, the job is usually done by women, sometimes working part-time and always receiving low wages. In the car industry the equivalent workers (if they are not replaced by robots) are male and form part of the core of trade union economic militancy. This difference is not obvious from the nature of the job itself. Such aspects of social structure are not derivable from simple examination of the job structure involved in a particular organisation of production. Neither, therefore, is the geography of social differentiation simply derivable from spatial structures of production. It is at this point that the processes of social allocation of different parts of the population to different kinds of jobs becomes important. Existing social conditions outside the firm/sector, in other words, help determine the social organisation of production within it. And geography is important here too.

*   *   *

It has been argued in this section that different uses of space by industry (different spatial structures) may produce distinct effects on particular regions, as well as alternative structures of differentiation and possibly inequality between regions. But equally, if not more, important is that underneath this has gone a parallel argument which emphasises still further the need for theoretical clarity. For what may look like a very similar regional phenomenon can have very different implications in terms of the interregional structure of which it is part. Take an example: three different regions may each have the same employment structure, all in branch plants, but in different industries and, crucially, in different spatial structures. In one it is the closing process in the footwear industry which is dominant, in the second electronics assembly, in the third, light engineering. In terms of employment in each of the regions the effect is broadly the same – a job structure dominated by low-paid and distinctly uninspiring jobs for women, and only middle-level administrative jobs. But, apart from the common fact of external ownership, the structures of differentiation in which the regions are embedded are different in each case.

In footwear, the region will be playing a role in a technical division of labour within the industry. The other stages are not research and skilled production, as in electronics, but the cutting process. As we have seen, this is performed by men and the two stages may be separately located when the cost-surfaces of the two kinds of labour are different. To the extent that this is a hierarchy at all, it is one based on differences within manual workers and on sexual discrimination. Simply, in one region the men have jobs, in the other the women, and in the first region wages are, in consequence, higher than in the second. The income and status differences in the electronics case, and consequently the degree of overall regional inequality, are far greater. They involve a span between semi-skilled, skilled manual and high-status technical jobs. In the case of light engineering, no technical division of labour may be involved at all, in which case the region will have the same production employment structure as others in which production exists.

There is more to a 'distribution of employment' than meets the eye. Such a distribution is not just a pattern; it is the result of an underlying structure. What is at issue is the way in which different localities can be incorporated into the developing relations of capitalist production. In this example, similar employment effects in a particular region actually result from very different structures and consequently have different implications for 'interregional relations'. And what this means in turn is that they have also very different implications for action if those relations of dominance and subordination are to be combated.

3.4 The uniqueness of place

No two places are alike. People who only stop over at airports (to and from conferences, perhaps) might get the impression of a pervading similarity, but any deeper exploration will soon dispel that illusion. Geographical variation is profound and persistent, and this is true even within a country as apparently homogeneously developed as the United Kingdom. We talk of 'the peripheral regions', but they are all very different. The term 'inner cities' includes Merseyside, Glasgow and London, as different as can be in culture, political history and the character of the labour movement. Any train journey across country provides ample evidence: different kinds of people get on and off at Lancaster, Grange-over-Sands and Barrow-in-Furness.

As we have already argued, these differences matter. Most people still live their lives locally, their consciousness is formed in a distinct geographical place. At any one time different areas may be changing in contrasting ways; different battles are being fought out, different problems faced.

So how can this variety be analysed? Spatially-differentiated patterns of production are one of the bases of geographical variation in social structure and class relations. They are not the only cause, but they are significant. The analysis of regional contrasts and conflicts in Belgium in Chapter 2 showed clearly how the organisation of production can be an important condition for the development of social and political culture. Gramsci's analyses of Turin bring out many of the same points: 'Turin ... is the industrial city, the proletarian city, *par excellence* ... like one great factory ... powerfully united by industrial production. The Turin proletariat was able to advance so far along the road of Soviet-type mass organisation precisely because of this powerfully united character of the city's industry' (1920, p. 151).

It is not, of course, as simple as that. For one thing, local areas rarely bear the marks of only one form of economic structure. They are products of long and varied histories. Different economic activities and forms of social organisation have come and gone, established their dominance, lingered on, and later died away. Viewed more analytically, and concentrating for the moment on the economic, the structure of local economies can be seen as a product of the combination of 'layers', of the successive imposition over the years of new rounds of investment, new forms of activity.

These new forms of local activity are each related to a wider setting. Spatial structures of different kinds can be viewed historically (and very schematically) as emerging in a succession in which each is superimposed upon, and combined with, the effects of the spatial structures which came before. In each of these spatial structures economic activity in an individual local area plays a specific role and exists in certain relations of dominance and subordination with economic activity in other areas. Each spatial structure is a system of interdependence into which the industrial activity of any local area is inserted. So if a local economy can be analysed as the historical product of the combination of layers of activity, those layers also represent in turn the succession of roles the local economy has played within wider national and international spatial structures.

Each new layer, each new round of investment, brings with it potentially new economic bases of social organisation, new 'structural capacities' and a new overall position within the broader geographical division of labour. In the preceding section we drew out some of the internally necessary implications of a range of different spatial structures. But the effects of spatial structures in a particular situation cannot be predicted from such a logic alone. The actual implications will depend, not just on the nature of the new round of investment, but also on the existing character of the areas affected. The combination of layers is a form of mutual determination, of the existing characteristics of the area or regional system with those of the geographical pattern and effects of previous uses. Thus, for example, while a spatially-concentrated structure implies a local capitalist class and other spatial structures do not, if those uses of an area succeed each other, one question will be how the class related to the earlier spatial structure reorientates its position within the region. Clearly, the kinds of changes which do occur will depend both on the characteristics of the incoming industry, the way its activity in the area is incorporated into its overall spatial structure, and on the existing structure of industry in the area (e.g. Lojkine, 1977). Lipietz (1977, pp. 85, 89 *et seq.*) points to the kinds of battles between different parts of capital, and the consequent changes in the local balance between them which can ensue from the entry of national and international firms into an area hitherto dominated by smaller and more regionally-based companies. The incorporation of a local area into a new division of labour is likely to cause change and disruption, economically and socially. This, too, is a social and historical process. So Foster's (1974) analysis of the footwear industry in Northampton does indicate how the nature of the labour market there, and the particular use made of it, was one condition for the weakness of the labour movement. But 'if this was the problem, it only proved insurmountable because it was not possible to use the same tactics as in Oldham' (p. 103). And this in turn was due to an inheritance of history: 'Unlike Oldham, Northampton had experienced little wartime radicalism and certainly no breakdown in law and order. A food riot in spring 1795 had quickly been smashed up by the Horse Guards and by the second quarter of the century there was an efficient police force and a permanent garrison. Consequently without any tradition of anti-state labour solidarity and with strong-arm tactics ruled out, there was almost no way of imposing union discipline on the constant stream of immigrant workers'. It was not just labour-market conditions but the lack of a history of organisation which made unionisation so difficult. And this in turn was the result of conflict. 'In terms of industrial coercion the boot was very much on the other foot. Savage punishments – flogging, imprisonment – were inflicted for work offences, jailings were successfully used to break the trades movement of 1834' (p. 103). And the effects of this were to colour local politics for a long time ahead. 'So, instead of a labour movement, all that existed were small islands of organised workers . . . Northampton politics reflect this situation closely . . . Indeed it is this . . . that holds the key to Northampton politics right up till the ascendancy of Bradlaugh' (pp. 103–4).

The outcome of the disruption, and the form and direction of the change, that results from the insertion of a local area into a new division of labour, will depend on the existing character of the area, itself the result of an already long and complex history. Local changes and characteristics are not just some simple 'reflection' of broader processes; local areas are not just in passive receipt of changes handed down from some higher national or international level. The vast variety of conditions already existing at local level also affects how those processes themselves operate.

It is also more than this. We are talking primarily of the economy and 'the economic', yet the sequence of wider contexts within which localities are set is also ideological and political; social in a much broader sense. The social changes in an area, the shifts in prevailing ideology and temperament, are not bound up only with economic changes within that locality. They reflect also broader shifts and in other aspects of society. The layers of history which are sedimented over time are not just economic; there are also cultural, political and ideological strata, layers which also have their local specificities. And this aspect of the construction of 'locality' further reinforces the impossibility of reading off from a 'layer of investment' any automatic reverberations on the character of a particular area.

Conceptualising things in this way makes it possible to combine an understanding of general trends with a recognition, alongside and within that, of very great diversity. The uniqueness of place and the constantly evolving and shifting systems of interdependence are two sides of the same coin.

*   *   *

When, in the middle decades of the twentieth century, geographers switched their main concern from understanding the complexity and uniqueness of regions towards the vigorous pursuit of empirically-generalisable laws, the debate was often posed in terms of the specific and consequently descriptive versus the generalisable and supposedly scientific. There was, it was argued, little one could do with the unique save contemplate it; the aim should be to identify empirically-observable relations which had a sufficient degree of regularity to be graced with the status of 'law'. The argument here is that the opposition presupposed in that debate is itself a false one. 'General laws' are about causation, not empirical correlation. They are as well if not better established in causal studies of the particular, the much-maligned 'case study'. And by the same token, the unique, the product of many determinations, is certainly amenable to analysis. It is indeed time that regional and local particularities were reinstated as a central focus of geographical thinking. This is not to argue for a return to 'good old-fashioned regional studies' but to suggest that the same subject matter can now be approached within a rigorous analytical framework, with some understanding of the relation between the general and the particular, and with an appreciation of how each local area fits into the wider scheme of capitalist production and social relations. There is a basis for a new regional geography.

The implications of this impinge on other debates, for if the actual empirical implications of any given spatial structure cannot be logically deduced, but must be analysed as the result of its combination with the existing character of an area, it follows that the effects of any given productive activity may vary from region to region. Merseyside and the Mezzogiorno, São Paulo and Bridgend have all been drawn into the world-wide production of cars, but the implications for each have been very different. The effects of the installation of major coastal steel and petrochemical complexes have not been replicated in each case. The investments at Dunkirk (Castells and Godard, 1974), Fos-sur-Mer (Bleitrach and Chenu, 1975) and Taranto (Courlet, 1977) were not exactly the same in their impact. They varied according to the particular characteristics, the history and present conditions, of each local area. And the fact that these effects of particular spatial structures will vary according to the conditions in which they operate means that it is fruitless to examine the real world for an empirically-generalised outcome in order to substantiate some inherent logic. The internal necessity of a spatial structure does not get 'acted out' in the real world in pure form. What takes places is the interrelation of the new spatial structure with the accumulated results of the old. The 'combination' of layers, in other words, really does mean combination, with each side of the process affecting the other. So this way of looking at the world is in no sense deterministic. 'Structural analysis' as it has sometimes been called, does not necessarily mean 'top–down' analysis; far from obliterating the possibility of variety, it provides an approach to its explanation.

Moreover, not only may a given production facility have different effects in different regions, but areas with different histories may also provide advantageous locations for the same kind of production. Brittany, Alabama and the mining towns of Northumberland all have reserves of cheap, unorganised labour. All have attracted decentralised, labour-intensive production. But those labour reserves came out of very different social histories. Location theory has tended to see labour availability as a 'location factor'. It is, of course; but such 'location factors' are also the product of social relations, of a region's previous succession of roles in the wider national and international spatial structures. This brings us full circle: it is precisely because areas have different histories that the arrival of a new form of economic activity has in each case distinct social and economic results.

So far in this section it has been implied that the economic structure of a region is the product of a series of simple and discrete rounds of investment, in each of which one new spatial structure will be articulated with a given spatial surface. But the historical process is more complex than this. At any given time, more than one new spatial structure may be in the process of establishment, be undergoing changes, or be disappearing with decline. It is the effect of the combination of all these changes with the existing geographical pattern (itself the result of previous uses of space) which contributes to the distinctive economic character-istics of local areas. The very fact that a region may, through the variety of its economic activities, be embedded in a multitude of spatial structures, each entailing different organisations of domi-nance and subordination, serves to emphasise that it is not regions which interrelate, but the social relations of production which take place over space. The results of all this in terms of the geographical distribution of social classes and groups is *a geographical, or spatial, division of labour* in the country as a whole. And it is this which forms the basis – the new locational surface – for subsequent patterns of investment.

The incorporation of an area into a new, dominant, spatial structure may have one of a number of different effects on the social and economic status of that region. It may well be that its new role simply reinforces the social and economic advantage or disadvantage of the area. It may, however, be that the fortunes of a region are reversed, that in terms of a given range of indicators its 'performance' becomes closer to that of the national average. Yet again, it may be that the relative advantage or disadvantage of the region is maintained in some general sense but that it is changed in its nature in terms of the indices on which it can be measured. In other words, both the economic structure which underlies interregional inequality, and the way in which that inequality is expressed socially, are transformed. Geographical differentiation has been reproduced, but in a changed form. Each of these situations is entirely different, but any approach to regional analysis must be able to handle them all. The cumulative causation model of Myrdal (1957), and adopted by Holland (1976), can only handle the first case. The equilibrating mechanisms of neo-classical economics are happy only with the second. Neither of them can deal with the third. But they all happen. Unfortunately, some of the alternative approaches to analysis developed recently (see Chapter 2) also tend to be restricted to expecting only one outcome – in this case usually increasing inequality. Any adequate framework must be able to deal with any of these cases. It is not enough to resort to a separate, and therefore deterministic, 'model' for each different empirical outcome.

Up to now we have been dealing with the effects of the combination of new forms of economic activity with the existing characteristics of a particular area. It was implicit that this 'area' had already been defined. In fact, however, shifts in the dominant spatial division of labour may produce a complete change in the very geographical pattern of spatial differentiation. This has important implications for what is meant by 'a region' or 'a locality'. It is very possible for the pattern of geographical inequality to change. Regions themselves are products of these processes, so the geographical framework for studies of spatial structures must allow for the possibility of its own transformation.

$$*\qquad*\qquad*$$

This historical process can also be schematised at national level. Here, successive layers of spatial structures of production lay the basis for a sequence of spatial divisions of labour. At any point in time the geographical pattern of economic activity which is associated with the new spatial structures is overlaid on and combined with the pattern produced in previous periods. And each new combination of successive layers produces, or may produce, a new form and a new distribution of inequality, which in turn is the geographical basis for the next round of investment. 'The regional problem', or spatial inequality more generally, is thus a very complex thing. It will change over time in both form and pattern. It may alter in terms of the nature of the underlying interregional relations, in terms of the social differences and inequalities on which it is measured, and in the terms of its geographical shape. And this shifting intranational inequality is itself locked into a wider international set of spatial structures and division of labour.

The fact that there is such geographical differentiation within a country, that there is regional inequality or an 'inner city problem', has an impact on the operation of what are often thought of as 'national' processes. It may help or hinder national rates of accumulation. It is not possible to make any *a priori* assumptions about whether the effects of the pattern of spatial difference will be problematical or positively useful for capital, but there will be effects. Indeed, it is entirely possible that the implications will be different for different parts of capital. This was clearly the case in Italy over the past few decades (see Chapter 2). Spatial inequality and geographical differentiation may also be influential in the formation of national political alliances and the formulation of apparently national, as well as clearly spatial, policies. There will be effects, too, on national class relations and class structure. Seen in one way, the sum total of all the changes going on in the different parts of a country may add up to an 'aggregate' national effect. But it may also be that geographical separation and geographical differentiation are important to the production of that national effect. Once again, 'geography' is not just a product of social relations; it is an integral part of their development. Lipietz (1977) writes: 'La structuration de l'espace est la dimension spatiale des rapports sociaux, et, ceux-ci étant luttes de classes, *la structuration de l'espace est luttes de classes*, non seulement en ce sens qu'elle en est le produit, mais en ce qu'elle en est un enjeu et même un moyen' (p. 90).

One of the arguments of the rest of this book is that changes of this sort, where geography is an important component of class and political relations, are going on now in the United Kingdom.

4
Some Changing Spatial Structures in the United Kingdom

4.1 Setting the scene

The inheritance: social and spatial

Much of what is peculiarly characteristic of 'British capitalism', of British economy and society, stems from the long inheritance of its international position and role. From merchant capitalism, through the heyday of Empire and the dominance of international trade through its role as workshop of the world, to the long twentieth-century process of decline, this international orientation, though changing in its form and in its implications, has been fundamental (Gamble, 1981). And this inheritance has not been one which registered only in economic terms. The economic role within the nineteenth-century international division of labour left its mark in the form of a particular set of class relations and particular contours of class structure. It is through these class relations and their consequences for national politics that 'the British economy', accumulation within the geographical boundaries of the nation state, continues to be affected, constrained, and often undermined, by its inheritance from the past.

The structure of the capitalist class still shows these marks very clearly. Probably the most celebrated effect is the unusual degree of separation which has historically existed in Britain between banking capital and industrial capital (see Brett *et al.*, 1975; Gough, 1975; Groves *et al.*, 1975; National Economic Development Office (NEDO), 1976; Hu, 1975). The fact that for years British banking capital had the whole world to choose from when selecting profitable investments enabled the growth of a powerful financial centre and encouraged in it an international and speculative character rather than any propensity to invest in home-based British industry. The growth of Empire and of a wider world role, which went hand in hand with the development of the power base of 'the City', afforded too many other opportunities. The corollary, of course, is that the health of the financial sector has a high degree of independence from the health of the home-based economy. The money which British banking capital lends to British industry tends to be in the form of short-term (and more recently medium-term) loans rather than of long-term commitments. The effect is not so much a shortage of cash for investment in industry (the claim sometimes made) but a certain separation of interests between 'the City' and 'industry' and a relative lack of institutional connection between the two.

But that division within British capital is not the only one, nor even always the most important. The character of industrial, and particularly manufacturing, capital has also been moulded by the legacy of Empire and the international domination of a century and a half ago. Again for reasons of opportunity historically available to British capital more than any other, British manufacturing industry has had a particularly high tendency to direct investment overseas. One effect of this has been the development within British industry of a veritable chasm between on the one side highly internationalised sections with a major, often *the* major, orientation overseas and on the other sections where production is confined to the national or even regional levels. The importance of the internationalised sections in turn lies behind the relatively low levels of investment 'at home', the increasingly outdated capital stock and the tendency to fall behind competitors in levels of productivity. Much of the investment which goes overseas is in the newest technologies and the newest products. British industry provides at the international level a telling example of the point made in Chapter 3 that having your capital owned locally, 'your own capitalist class', is no guarantee at all of local reinvestment.

These lines of divide, between financial and industrial capital and between international and national elements within industry, cross-cut each other, each having its effect on political formation and on policy. Their combination has meant that financial and international perspectives and interests have been more powerful politically than has nationally-based industrial capital. This has been reflected in the organisation of the State. The nature and dominance of the Treasury is frequently acknowledged, but the impact goes deeper than that – as Gamble (1981) points out 'there has never ... been a permanent government department to speak for and represent the interests of the national economy and national industry' (p. 180). Not surprisingly, this internal structure of British capital has also found its reflection in policy, and in particular in the concern for the strength of sterling. The two strongest and most dynamic parts of British-owned capital – the banking sector and big, internationalised industry – have interests which coincide neither with the requirements of a strong internal economy nor on all occasions with each other's. British capital and the British economy are by no means the same thing. And both the political strength of the City and of internationalised industry and the conflicts between those interests and those of the British national economy continue to this day.

The early and wide extension of capitalist relations of production, and the legacy of Empire and international dominance, had effects also on the working class. The British labour movement is strong in economic and industrial terms. It is a strength which in part derives from both its sheer numerical importance and the ability of British capital in the nineteenth century to appease its 'own' working class with a share of the imperial spoils. But it is an economic strength rather than a political one. The relation between party and trade unions is the reverse of that in, for instance, Italy and France. In the United Kingdom the unions gave birth to the Labour Party, and thus was established a separation between the political and the economic wings of the labour movement. The trade union movement's considerable strength, its comparative independence from the State and the importance of its shop-floor level of organisation have, with notable exceptions, tended to be associated with a sphere of activity more or less confined to economic defence and a resistance to changes in production which has occasionally been characterised as Luddite. In fact, over the period dealt with here, the union movement has countenanced huge losses of jobs in the name of technological progress. But in many sectors of the economy capital's attempts at modernisation did not come until too late, until decline had already set in. Under such circumstances, programmes of investment, modernisation and technical change inevitably produced consequences more at odds with the immediate interests of labour than they would have if pursued in a period of expansion.

The conflicts, then, were complex. Within capital there was a straightforward conflict between the dominant elements with their political commitment to the maintenance of the traditional world role, and the requirement to modernise the society and the economy. The dominant political interests have been reflected in the liberal bias of a State which has been consistently unwilling either to tackle the archaic institutions of British society, which served to preserve Empire and class rule rather than the interests of accumulation in the home economy ('interests' for which there was no powerful political voice), or to intervene directly in industry to promote rationalisation or greater productivity. This went together with the indisputable fact that such a process would in any case be problematic, given the economic and defensive strength of the organised working class.

*   *   *

Geography was integral to all of this. The internal geography of the country reflected its international position. The dominance of City, Empire and trade contributed to the importance of State, financial and commercial activities, and of the employment associated with them, in London. The dominant form of regional problem in the United Kingdom throughout the earlier part of the twentieth century was also in part an inheritance of Empire. It resulted from the decline of major sectors of the economy with particular forms of spatial structure. It was those spatial structures which moulded the national geography of employment from the nineteenth century up to the 1930s, and which were characteristic of a small group of industries – coal-mining and exporting, iron and steel manufacture, shipbuilding – which owed their dominance in the geography of employment to the role of the United Kingdom over that period in the international division of labour. It was the United Kingdom's position as an imperial power, its early lead in the growth of modern industry, and its consequent commitment to free trade and to its own specialisation in manufacturing *within* this international division of labour, which enabled the rapid growth, up to the First World War, of these major exporting industries. The spatial structures which were established by those industries were those where all stages of production of the commodity are concentrated within single geographical areas. The comparatively low level of separation of functions within the process of production, and the relatively small variation in locational requirements between such potentially separable functions, were not sufficient to make geographical differentiation a major attraction. In establishing this spatial pattern of production within the United Kingdom these industries sought access to ports for import of raw material and for exporting goods, a plentiful supply of labour, and, to some extent still, access to coal. Since these were characteristics not evenly distributed over the country, the geographical pattern which evolved was simply that each of these major industries concentrated its production on one, or a small number of, regions. Ships in Clydeside and the north-east of England, coal in south Wales, and so on. Conversely, given the simple quantitative importance of these industries, a number of major regions of the country became heavily specialised in one or two of these industries.

This geographical structure was based on the dominant role of Britain in the world economy and on the characteristics of the consequently dominant industries. It was the former which ensured the importance of the latter. In the early twentieth century, half of British iron and steel production and a third of coal output was exported directly (Deane and Cole, 1967), while both were further used in other industries which in turn were also based on Britain's international role. On the other hand it was the stage of development of the industries themselves which influenced the kind of spatial structure which was adopted.

The spatial division of labour within the country as a whole was thus based primarily on different sectoral specialisations. It was only when the United Kingdom's relation to the international economy changed, with its decline as a world trading power, that production in these industries fell drastically and these previously-dominant spatial structures produced a regional problem. Much of this old basis of Empire and international dominance has over the years been nationalised and the capital which once owned them, often itself regionally based, has moved off into other sectors and other geographical areas. The new industries of the twentieth century grew up in the south-east and midlands of England. At first, too, there was some acquiescence on the part of the upper echelons of the trade union movement (itself for the same reasons undergoing a change in its internal balance of power) to this sectoral and geographical refocusing of the economy. 'The demise of the basic industries was accepted as a "second industrial revolution" particularly by Citrine (The General Secretary) and Bevin (TGWU General Secretary)' (Cooke, 1981b, p. 25). Such union leaders, as representatives of the new industries and in the context of their new co-operation with the State, thereby eased the way for the establishment of the newly-emerging spatial division of labour. 'The interests of the right-wing general unions (TGWU and NUGMW) in the new semi-skilled industries, and their subsequent involvement in government, most obviously in the shape of Bevin, reflected the regional as well as the sectoral shift that had taken place in the power-relations of industrial Britain' (Cooke, pp. 26–7). But the decline of the old basic sectors produced appalling poverty and a persistent 'regional problem'. For, because of the spatial structure of these industries, and their dominance of particular regions, the effect of this change in economic and political relations was simply that sectoral decline brought with it regional decline. The indices on which this kind of regional inequality was registered (in other words, the kind of regional problem which was produced) were the ones which became the classic measures of 'the regional problem' in Britain. The most important of these measures was unemployment, with the level of outmigration, per capita earnings, and the level of manufacturing employment playing subsidiary roles.

There were, of course, other groups of industries which were important, both in the national economy and in the geographical structure, which derived much of their pre-eminence from Britain's international position and which have subsequently declined. Textiles, primarily cotton textiles, are the most obvious example. But there are interesting differences between textiles on the one hand and coal, iron and steel and shipbuilding on the other. First, they are from different parts of the economy and have developed very different forms of capital organisation. These two factors are linked. The vital economic and political place of coal, steel and even shipbuilding was an important consideration in their subsequent nationalisation. The change in capital organisation as a result of decline was very different in textiles and although there was considerable government intervention to organise the process of decline the industries have remained entirely within private ownership. A further contrast arose from the sectors' different labour processes and labour requirements. The higher proportion of female workers in textiles, together with women's lower pro-

pensity to register when unemployed and the lower political significance attached to employment for women, was undoubtedly a
major reason why declining textile areas never gained Development Area status.

It was, then, the decline of the major basic, and male-employing
sectors which produced the form of regional inequality which came
to be recognised as a regional problem. The decline of these
industries has continued, in employment terms, since the First
World War, though its pace has varied considerably. Spatially, the
decline has been accompanied by interregional consolidation into
larger units of production, but the main change in spatial structure
has concerned ownership, with nationalisation and centralised
control replacing private and, often, regional ownership.

The fifties: a wasted decade

These characteristics of the United Kingdom's economy, society
and geography were reinforced during the fifties. The long post-
war boom of the international capitalist economy allowed British
industry to coast along without thought of serious reorganisation.
At the beginning of the period, British manufactures still
accounted for 25 per cent of world exports. But this decade was to
see the beginning of the end of that position. The traditional
orientation of the State and of important sections of capital
continued. Politically there was more concern with Suez and with
organising a reasonably dignified withdrawal from Empire, than
with the domestic economy. And British capital invested massively
abroad. 'The opportunities that Britain's imperial trading and
financial connections provided led to the development after 1950
of some vast and very successful international businesses' (Gamble, 1981, p. 113). The world vision of sections of manufacturing
capital was thus reinforced, and the conflict between the interests
of internationalised industry and finance, and the requirements of
the domestic economy was exacerbated. Little was done to update
production within the United Kingdom itself. Moreover, extensive
expansion drew heavily on domestic supplies of labour. Immigration provided extra workers, but that source too began to be cut
back with the increasing restrictions from the early sixties on. The
fifties were a decade when the complacent claim that we had never

had it so good temporarily concealed the fact of yawning structural weaknesses.

Much the same complacent inactivity applied also to questions of geography. In the fifties regional inequality did not figure prominently on the political agenda. Throughout that decade the main concern expressed about geographical differences was that the differential tightness of regional labour markets might cause 'overheating' in the economy as a whole. It was reasoned that the strength of labour in the relatively full-employment regions of the south-east and midlands of England, combined with national bargaining structures, would push up wages to a level above what could have been won had unemployment been more evenly distributed about the country. The argument seems never to have carried sufficient political weight to get an active regional policy off the ground. This omission was akin to British capital's tardiness in updating its production techniques, and it too was to have serious consequences. It should be noted, to begin with, that the lack of regional policy was in no way a reflection of what was happening to regional inequality. Differences in unemployment levels were in fact quite high during the fifties. Absolute levels of unemployment, however, except for those in Northern Ireland, were low, with the old basic industries enjoying for much of the decade a relative boom. The low absolute levels seem to have had more political effect than the relatively high levels of disparity, and 'the regional question' was not a major political issue. This relative quiescence, combined with a Conservative government committed to decontrol, resulted in almost a decade of virtual inaction, a passivity broken only by the occasional *ad hoc*, and sometimes ill-judged, intervention in direct response to social pressure (see Board of Trade, 1955–6). The decision to split investment in a steel strip mill project between Llanwern in south Wales and Ravenscraig in Scotland was such a political response. In this way, the rest of the long boom, the period which provided the most propitious conditions for a successful regional policy, was wasted. Indeed as Hudson (1982) amply demonstrates, there were clear decisions *not* to attract jobs for men to the north-east, for fear of losing labour from the mines. The subsequent period of active regional policy has been conducted under conditions of manufacturing employment decline. For the end of the long boom brought with it also the return of the regional problem.

The cracks begin to show

By the early sixties the long-term weakness of the British economy was clear. The set-back of the late fifties had given the first intimations, the recession of 1957 revealed the vulnerability of basic sectors, and by the early sixties it was irrefutable – every indicator of growth and competitiveness was on the slide. The international capitalist economy was heaving itself into a new position, a new international division of labour was asserting itself, and the British economy was both changing its role and losing out.

In employment terms, 1966 was the turning point. It was in that year that manufacturing employment began to decline, not just relatively, as a proportion of total employment in the economy, but in terms of the total number of jobs it provided. And since 1966 the decline has continued, with only occasional and very brief periods of growth. It was around the mid-sixties, too, that unemployment began to shift upwards to a level markedly higher than that about which it had oscillated for most of the period since the Second World War. Even before 1966, of course, many major sectors of the economy were declining in employment terms. Agriculture, mining, metal manufacture, shipbuilding, textiles, clothing, transport ... all had been losing jobs since well before the mid-sixties. Indeed, production industries as a whole were showing employment decline. But in 1966 many of the industries associated with post-war growth began to employ fewer people – the SIC Orders of food, drink and tobacco, mechanical engineering, electrical engineering, construction, gas, electricity and water, and the distributive trades. The group symbolises the building and consumer boom of the fifties. Between 1966 and 1979 other industries followed, equally symbolically – instrument engineering and public administration. By the end of the 1970s insurance, banking and finance, professional services and miscellaneous services, were the only SIC Orders still registering a net increase in employment.

It has, of course, been a decline which has varied in intensity between different parts of the economy. The old basic sectors, and mechanical and electrical engineering-based means-of-production industries, declined the fastest, while some consumer and producer services continued to expand employment for much of the period. The decline has also varied in nature, being more combined with investment and technical change in the early part of the period, more dominated by simple cut-back at the end (Massey and Meegan, 1982). But, in one way or another, employment decline has been important throughout the period.

The decline in production industries is not, of course, peculiar to Britain. It is taking place in most industrialised capitalist countries, and the diminishing proportion of employment in manufacturing is a reflection of long-term and generalised changes in the labour process and the division of labour. The absolute decline in the number of people employed in manufacturing is also common to a large number of countries. The fact that this generalised downturn took place rather earlier in Britain than elsewhere, and that it has been more severe, is a reflection of the long-term structural weaknesses in British economy and society. In the context of a shifting international division of labour and, later, a slowdown in the world capitalist economy as a whole, these structural weaknesses came home to roost.

It was all this that lay behind the decline. The crises in major sections of the economy have been accompanied by a heightened conflict of interest, if not always explicit conflict, between different sections of society, and particularly between capital and labour. As on previous occasions, too, a shift in international position has had its more detailed reflection in the internal geography of the country. Much of the rest of the book concerns precisely this.

                    *   *   *

One thing can be noted briefly now: the period since the mid-1960s has been very different from the shift in the international order which overtook the United Kingdom in the early decades of this century. In particular it contrasts with the thirties. For this is a different kind of change in Britain's place in the world. In the thirties the final end of economic dominance was signalled by the headlong collapse of a small number of particular, though very major, primary and secondary sectors. Since the 1960s it has not been the end of the Empire which has been at issue, but more generally the United Kingdom as a manufacturing economy. The decline has been far more widespread, encompassing most of manufacturing industry, and it has also had a different geography. The decline of the industries on which imperial dominance was built dragged down whole regions with it, but it left other parts of the country, notably the midlands and the south and east of England, relatively intact. This time the pattern is different. The very generality of manufacturing decay means that few areas have escaped entirely. But it is the old manufacturing specialists which have, inevitably, been hardest hit – the north-west of England, and the west midlands. In the period since the early sixties the latter region has plummeted down the regional rankings. It has left the core and joined the periphery, indeed the whole line between the two has been redrawn. Over this period, too, it has become clear that the old 'regional' level (in the formal sense of Standard Regions) is less and less relevant for drawing maps of industrial change, or charting relative prosperity and decline. From the mid-1960s to the mid-1970s the biggest disparities in employment decline were not interregional but between the cities and the non-conurbation areas (Fothergill and Gudgin, 1979; Keeble, 1980). The cities have suffered heavily, and for a whole range of reasons. It has not primarily been a result of the concentration there of old industries, though this has had some part to play. It has rather been because the cities tended to have the older and more labour-intensive capacity within any sector, and were therefore more liable to suffer from programmes of capacity-cutting and technical change, and from the fact that what new investment was available sought out the attractions of less urban areas. The decline in the cities, both within Development Areas (Newcastle, Merseyside, Clydeside) and in the non-assisted areas (London, Coventry), has again therefore not just been a simple parallel of the thirties; the economic changes to which this decline is a response are different from those of fifty years ago.

But job loss in the old basic industries of the Development Areas has continued at a high rate, although unevenly, throughout the period. In coal, in steel and in shipbuilding, huge declines in employment have taken place. As we shall see, this process has been of fundamental importance in the whole wider pattern of geographical change in industry as a whole. It has enabled the creation of a brand new reserve of labour, a reserve which has functioned in different ways at different times and in different parts of the economy. The continuing decline of the basic sectors has also remained a key component of political relations, again changing in its nature but almost always being significant.

*   *   *

The period since the early 1960s, then, has been characterised by national-level economic decline and stagnation, a persistent regional problem, an inability to rethink the conflict between a traditional international orientation and the present pressing needs of the domestic economy, and a long-term class stalemate. But it has not been a static stalemate, an equilibrium. On the contrary, the period since the early sixties has seen a shifting search for a solution at the political level. Different political alliances have been constructed, a variety of strategies have been tried, and regional policy and spatial policies more generally have risen and fallen in their importance and changed a number of times in their nature. The aim of the remaining chapters is to use this period, beginning in the early 1960s, to explore and illustrate some of the concepts and the approach outlined in the first half of this book. Three different slices are taken through the problem. The rest of this chapter examines changes in a number of industrial sectors; Chapter 5 takes a spatially-defined focus and looks at the impact of these changes in specific areas, and Chapter 6 examines variations over time.

The remainder of this chapter, then, explores the changing spatial structures of a few major sectors of the economy. Each sector has been affected by the shifting economic and political circumstances of the period, but each has been affected in different ways. The responses have likewise been different. The point of the discussions is not to present data but to reconceptualise it. Each discussion starts from an SIC definition of a part of the economy and explores what different kinds of capital operate within it. Each starts from changes in employment pattern and asks what spatial structures of the relations of production underlie these patterns. What is at issue is the way in which contrasting sections of British capital have been reorganising themselves into new spatial structures, each of which forms the basis for new kinds of geographical differentiation, and which together are an important element in the changing intranational spatial division of labour.

4.2   Electronics and instruments industries

The character of the industry

The group of products classified under the general heading of 'electronics' has been a focus of growth throughout the post-war period. Even after the mid-sixties employment in this field in the United Kingdom continued to expand quite rapidly, though by the early 1980s there was job-loss even here. Nonetheless the size of the industry in employment terms, and its relatively fast growth, means that it has been a significant element shaping the changing industrial geography of the United Kingdom over much of the period. It is also an industry which has gained world-wide notoriety both socially and spatially. Socially for the enormous contrasts which it encompasses, from the jet-setting microchip scientist/inventor/entrepreneur, male and flying Ambassador Class, to the young assembler of semiconductors, female, paid around 20 cents an hour (in the 1970s), and likely to lose her job in a couple of years, if the company has anyway not moved on by then, as her eyesight fails. At one end of the scale the celebration of individualism, at the other dispensability and infinite replaceability. It is a social contrast with definite spatial coordinates. It doesn't just stretch, it is deliberately spaced, from Palo Alto, California, to the Masan Free Production Zone, South Korea.

This is an international spatial structure, one of the classic cornerstones of the new international division of labour. And it is within that overall context that the spatial organisation of the electronics industry in any one country must be set. It is an international division of labour which has only really taken shape since the 1960s. 'It was not until 1966 . . . that world manufacturers began to appreciate the advantage of using Korea's abundance of cheap, diligent labour' (*The Times*, 26 September 1975; quoted in Froebel, Heinrichs and Kreye, 1980). Since then, each national geographical structure has reflected in its own reorganisation this massive reorientation of world production.

*   *   *

In the United Kingdom, the initial post-war growth of the group of industries known as 'electronics' was overwhelmingly concentrated in the south-east especially in Greater London, with a subcentre in the north-west of England, primarily around the Manchester region. As late as 1959, the earliest date for which precise figures are available, over 60 per cent of jobs in the industry were in the south-east of England, with the north-west trailing second with 8 per cent (Keeble, 1976). Such sectoral concentration mirrored that of other industries in the same period, and was part of the pattern of regional differentiation based primarily on sectoral difference. Since then, this pattern has begun to change, primarily intraregionally but also interregionally. While the south-east's share has fallen only slightly, other regions, in particular Scotland, have increased theirs. Within regions, and particularly within the south-east, there has been marked decentralisation (Keeble, 1976). While London's share has slumped, stretches of the outer metropolitan area and beyond have witnessed major growth, both absolutely and relatively. Two areas of major expansion since the fifties have been the New Towns of Scotland and the area between London, Southampton and Bristol. But a wide range of other areas, from the coalfields of south Wales to the coastal resorts of the south-west, experienced some expansion.

Behind these descriptive statistics lies a restructuring of British electronics in the context of world-wide reorganisation, and a shift in the industry's use of the British space. While employment continued to grow through the sixties and much of the seventies the industry nonetheless faced fiercer competition internationally from the mid-1960s onwards. Whole sections of it came under pressure to cut costs. The increasing vulnerability, particularly in the capital goods sections, brought a political as well as an economic response. The importance of this part of the economy both in increasing productivity over the economy as a whole and in being 'the new technology' gave it a political centrality which, although it varied greatly in importance, remained throughout the period. State intervention, exhortation and aid were important now in the further evolution of the industry, just as they had been in its birth. This combination of increased competitive pressure and State aid had a dual effect. First, it encouraged, over the late sixties in particular, changes in the structure and organisation of capital. Ownership was consolidated and there was a significant increase in the size of the major individual companies. This in turn enabled the financing of the second development: an acceleration of technological change within the production process itself, in response to the increased pressure to cut costs and especially to increase labour productivity. Together with the development of new products and types of components, this led to increases in the importance of standardisation and of mass-production. These were not brand new changes. They were reinforcements of existing processes (long-term technological change; the rise in importance of commodities and components which could be produced by mass-production techniques), but as a result of changed economic conditions they became more important.

Nor were these changes characteristic of the whole of the electronics industry. The word 'electronics' refers to the technological nature of the commodity produced, but the character of capital engaged in that production varies widely. To begin with, there are differences of product and of place in the economy. 'Electronics' covers the range from military equipment through computers for use in advanced production processes to TV games. These differences are mirrored in others. Military electronics and advanced computers are at the front-end of technological development, heavily research-orientated, fast-changing and with an emphasis on the unstandardised. At the other end, the manufacture both of consumer electronics and of components such as integrated circuits and semiconductors is geared towards large-scale mass-production and uniformity. It is not, though, just a question of product. There are also other considerable contrasts between firms 'in electronics'. The industry includes both some of the largest, most internationalised and most multisectoral manufacturing companies in the economy as well as operations of the 'two-men [*sic*]-inventing-something-exciting-in-the-garage-and-exporting-it-to-Japan' variety – the popular, and much promoted image of the entrepreneurial scientist. The differences which divide the sector revolve around product, the associated technology of production, the size and nature of capital involved and the degree of internationalisation of production. These characteristics cross-cut rather than simply map on to each other, but as a bundle they mark clear divisions within the industry known as 'electronics'. It was the big firms, their size itself consolidated in part in response to the changing economic environment, and with interests which were at least in part susceptible to mass-production, which during the sixties and early seventies were most able to reorganise both their production structures and their spatial structures.

Labour as a 'location factor': a social process

The acceleration of developments in the process of production in these companies reinforced what was already the changing nature of their demand for labour. In terms of production-line workers, there was some acceleration in deskilling and a reduction in the numbers of workers needed for any given level of output. At the other end of the social scale there was an increase in the importance of technical workers and workers in R and D. Electronics is a labour-intensive industry and it is undisputed that the search for labour is one of the dominant determinants of its location. These changes in production led to a shift in the balance of labour-related location factors. The distribution of skilled workers (skilled operative, not technical staff) became less important, while that of unskilled and semi-skilled workers became more important. At the other end of the spectrum, the distribution of highly-trained and highly-paid technical and scientific workers was of increasing locational significance.

The question of who does what job in the present organisation of the electronics industry has been firmly answered, as has the social status which is deemed to go along with each, status inside and outside the workplace reinforcing each other to produce a rigidly hierarchised social system of production. The technical, research and development work is overwhelmingly done by graduates: it is also, although this is in no way required by the nature of the job, almost always done by men. This is now so much a part of the character of the industry that it is taken for granted, simply assumed, by location analysts who begin with the existing structure of production. Thus Keeble, writing of professional electronics, argues that these parts of production 'are especially heavily research-oriented activities, producing ... products with rapidly-changing technology ... Many of their employees are *therefore* highly-skilled *male* research and development workers' (p. 192, my emphasis). It is also, of course, this group to which the highest status is attached, as witness the constant use in business and location literature of epithets such as 'the best staff'.

Most of the skilled manual workers, electricians, engineers and suchlike, are also male, in this case as an inheritance of the establishment of the virtual male monopoly during the last century over this kind of craftwork.

At the bottom end of the ladder, the assembly workers are equally assumed to be female. This is usually argued to be a result of the requirements of production because of women's supposedly greater 'dexterity'. 'A spokesman from Inmos admitted recently that the company would be offering "the sort of detailed, fiddly jobs that are traditionally done by women: they have a special aptitude for that kind of work" ' (Marks, 1980). As Marks points out, 'Female workers come at special prices too'. If dexterity really is the issue it seems surprising that not more women get to do the detailed, fiddly job of brain surgery. It is not, in the end, much to do with the requirements of production in a technical sense; it is much more to do with the fact that who does what job is part and parcel of the reproduction of social structures in society as a whole. Much the same applies to the low skill status attached to electronics assembly. Walker and Storper (1982) argue that semi-conductor assembly skills are often objectively higher than those required in car assembly. What is different about the labour process is that the tasks are less technically interdependent and high turnover consequently less of a preoccupation with management. Workers at this end of electronics really do lose their individuality as labour, become infinitely replaceable. The high levels of turnover combine with the lack of union attention to women workers' status to ensure that the official skill definition of the work will remain low.

Each of these parts of the labour force – different social groups – operates in different ways as a 'location factor'; the way it affects the location of industry is different in each case. Each social group, moreover, is unevenly distributed across the country – indeed if they were not they would not be operative locational considerations.

Take first 'the best staff', particularly those on the technical side, in research and scientific development. This part of the labour force is overwhelmingly concentrated in the outer metropolitan area of the south-east of England, stretching into Hampshire, East Anglia and west towards Bristol. Buswell and Lewis (1970) showed that in 1968, 63 per cent of electronics engineers in the United Kingdom lived in the south-east of England. There are other clusters, notably in north Cheshire, and in the Edinburgh area, but by far the largest concentration of these social strata was in England's 'sunbelt'. It is also to this area above all that the R and D part of electronics has gravitated. The interesting question is 'why?' What lies behind this clustering and the choice of these particular locations?

There appears for this part of the labour force to be an intimate and mutually-reinforcing relation between location and social status. Industries come to these parts of the country, cluster between the Solent and the Cotswolds, because that is where these people are. There are other reasons, too, which we shall take up in later chapters, but the simple presence of these parts of the labour force is of immense importance. This is not, though, a middle-class equivalent of taking work to the workers, believed to be a social principle behind regional policy. These workers are highly mobile; they are not stuck, nor are they moving about the country in search of employment. Work follows them, not vice-versa; to a large extent they choose their employer not the other way around. What is more, geography can play a part in their choice of employer. This, of all parts of the labour force, is the group 'most likely to be influenced in their choice of employer by the perceived quality of the local residential environment. In turn, then, it would seem logical to expect that this latter factor has influenced research-oriented professional electronics firms in their choice of locations for new laboratories and factories' (Keeble, 1976, p. 199).

In Chapter 2 we referred to the fact that workers in higher-status jobs tend to have better working conditions and more social amenities in every sense. One thing not so often recognised is how location itself can be part of the additional status and benefits which such workers derive. Living in Newbury, or rather just outside Newbury, makes you feel better, confirms your standing in society. In part this is a result of the physical environment itself, what Orwell called 'probably the sleekest landscape in the world', and its present fashionability, but this is also a group phenomenon, a process of social cumulative causation: the very fact that others of the same standing live round about is confirmation in itself of arrival at a particular status, and confirmation too of a set of values, reinforcing them and ensuring their reproduction. And the jobs follow.

What is more, the nature of the labour market for these social groups reinforces, beyond the social and residential considerations, the tendency to clustering. This labour market does not operate in terms of simple availability, of numerical supply and demand. Nor, certainly, does it operate in terms of cost. It is not low-wage research workers which are being sought. It is, in complete contrast, a very individualistic labour market. Particular people are sought, distinguished by their possession of knowledge, a monopoly established as a result of the very separation of conception from execution. The nature of competition in these industries reinforces the significance of this. Firms compete through technology and through quality, innovation and new products, at least as much as through price. What is being bought on the labour market is not just labour power but scientific knowledge. Poaching between companies is common. 'Some ... high technology companies ... have attempted to tie up their expert employees with contracts that prevent them from competing with their employer for several years after they leave' (Kehoe, 1982a). Legal battles are quite common. This, then, is a highly differentiated labour market creating a dynamic of competition in which it is necessary for both sides, employer and employee, to have detailed knowledge of the market; to be in on the scene. Scientific workers in electronics change jobs frequently. And they tend to belong to a community, a professional community, which extends beyond and cuts across the companies which employ them. These workers are the opposite of undifferentiated and replaceable 'supplies of cheap labour'. And because the social dynamic of this labour market is of this sort it can produce a geographical clustering of its participants. It is a vicious circle. Both for social reasons and as a result of the nature of the labour market, these groups, performing particular but increasingly important functions within the overall relations of production, both tend to cluster together in small and highly-defined parts of the country, usually well away from manual workers and from production as such, and have the power thereby to influence industrial location, the economic geography of the country. 'Despite powerful government pressure and financial inducements to move to the assisted areas, most electronics firms thus appear to have insisted on maintaining and expanding their research-oriented South East activities' (Keeble, 1976, p. 199).

Things are rather different for manual workers. The skilled manual stratum of the labour force, whose importance is declining, is mainly located where it was formed – in the old manufacturing areas and conurbations. Such workers operate as 'a location factor' mainly in terms of availability, and some groups at least are particularised in the sense that they have skills and knowledge deriving from long association with the industry. But it is rare these days for them to be an active location factor; most new investment in the industry is not looking for their kinds of skill.

In contrast to skilled workers, unskilled and semi-skilled workers are available almost everywhere, especially when there is a high general rate of unemployment, so it is not just simple availability, organisation and militancy of the workforce. And there is both actual and negotiable wage levels and the potential controllability, organisation and militancy of the workforce. And there is spatial variation in these characteristics. On the whole, wages are higher, the degree of trade union organisation stronger and things such as absenteeism lower where such workers have less history of employment in capitalist wage relations. There are therefore locational advantages, so far as access to this kind of labour is concerned, where there are reserves of new workers coming on to the capitalist labour market for the first time. A number of areas of the country have such reserves, in particular of female labour. The largest and most obvious of them was at precisely this period being expanded as a result of the accelerated decline of the basic sectors in the old mining regions, regions made additionally attractive by regional policy.[1] Other areas, too, had such reserves of female labour, especially smaller towns and tourist areas. The nature of these labour markets is different from that of the scientists and technologists. Here it is not a question of individuals but of 'reserves'. This is the kind of labour force which is advertised en masse, from Scotland to South Korea, from Cwmbran to Colombia. Moreover, precisely because here the dynamic of competition revolves about cost and degree of organisation, instead of clustering there may be some tendency to dispersion and isolation in an attempt to monopolise labour markets, to avoid competition from other companies and at the same time thereby reduce the bargaining power of the workforce. This need not be the dominant pressure; it need not always 'show up' in empirical cases. Factories in many of these areas indeed often cluster together on estates in order to take advantage of infrastructure without which the labour could not be exploited.[2] But the relative daily immobility of married women, because they usually have responsibility for the domestic sphere as well, makes them very vulnerable to the possibility of spatial monopoly, even by quite low levels of dispersion in terms of distance. Certainly it is in interesting contrast to the locational implications of the social dynamics at the other end of the electronics labour market.

'Location factors', then, have to be constituted and this happens both through the changing demands of technology and, particularly in the case of labour, through wider social processes within and outside the firm. Location factors should not be taken for granted; it is necessary to know why and how, at a particular point in time, certain things come to be geographical attractions for industry. This relates once again to the debate over the inner cities and to the whole mode of explanation implicit in the geographical form of blaming the victim. The issue is not the general adequacy or otherwise of an area or region, whether it is a success or a failure, but whether at any particular moment it happens to have what capital is looking for. And what capital wants might well, in any other terms, be an indication of failure – a cheap and vulnerable labour force.

Spatial structures of large firms

It was the already-dominant electronics firms which could take advantage of these inviting prospects – of the opportunities for profits offered by such a socially-differentiated national geography. Only the larger firms were able to incorporate fully this structure of spatial differentiation. Size, capital and particular developments in production technology were necessary to enable the classic electronics spatial structure to be established. Size sufficient to make possible a multiregional structure; capital for the new investment; and a technology of mass-production to enable advantage to be taken of the cheapest sources of labour.

In fact, a number of interregional spatial structures were established. In general terms, all consisted of the locational separation of control, research and development from those processes of production which required a skilled manual labour force, and from the increasingly important element of assembly work, defined as semi-skilled or unskilled. All are spatial structures, in other words, which include both a hierarchy of ownership and control and some form of hierarchy in the production process. At the bottom of this dual hierarchy are found assembly workers, low-level technical staff – such as testers – closely linked to production, and branch-level management. There is both external ownership and production dependence. Such facilities occur in most regions of the country but they are becoming increasingly and particularly important in non-conurbation parts of the industrial Development Areas, and in small towns generally.

What might be called 'the middle stage of production' has in fact a number of different aspects. First, there is the components manufacture of the 'classic' hierarchy, described in model form in Chapter 3, but there are also other structures. In some cases, for instance, the middle stage is concerned with production of products within the same line, often to serve the same function, but which are at a prior stage of technological development. The classic case of this is the staged development of telecommunications equipment, from electromechanical, through semi-electronic, to fully electronic (see Massey and Meegan, 1979; *Financial Times*, 20 February 1978; Lorenz, 1976). Production of the older products in this series still requires skilled manual labour, and these 'stages of production' are still characteristically located in the old centres of such labour, in particular the old centres of engineering skills – the north-east of England and some of the towns and conurbations of non-assisted parts of the country. The important characteristic of this latter part of production, however, is that it is declining. Investment in the new technology no longer requires such locations; being freed from its previous ties to skilled labour, new investment can now be made in the 'bottom-rung' regions of the hierarchy. This process is speeded up because of the overall lack of growth, for even while industry continues to update its techniques in the face of increasingly severe competition, it cannot afford in many cases to expand its output significantly. There just isn't the market. So the new investment in the new techniques in the new areas now has to be compensated for by closures of the old techniques in the old areas.[3] By this means, through what is really simply an accelerated process of scrapping, this stage of production – and consequently its demand for skilled manual labour in these areas – declines in importance.

The other aspect of the middle stage of production, however, continues to be important. This is the experimental/developmental first stage of production of a new product. It differs in a number of ways from the production processes just described. It is not declining, for it is at the new end of the process of technological change. Moreover, the labour requirements are rather different.

Much of the labour sought may in fact be of the assembly-line, semi-skilled type, but precisely because this is an experimental stage of production there is a requirement also for skilled labour, and the skills required will be not only of the 'old-fashioned' engineering type but also new technical skills. This difference in labour type combines with the need for contact with centres of R and D to influence the location of such facilities. Such production is then, very frequently, in or close to the 'top-end' regions of the hierarchy.

Finally, these top-end regions themselves are defined by the location within them of the upper echelons of all the hierarchies. They include the top managerial staff with their associated functions of ownership and overall control, the R and D workers with their functions of conceptualisation, and the early developmental stages of the production process itself, including assembly, craft and technical workers. As we have seen, within the United Kingdom this constellation of functions and social strata occurs above all in the south and east of England, with outliers particularly in the north Cheshire area (south of Manchester) and in the south-east of Scotland, especially around Edinburgh.

All these spatial structures of big firms in electronics share one feature, the locational separation of research from production. Such separation is not always simply a response to highly differentiated locational requirements. Spatial structures are established through social processes. In the early days of electronics many firms with a long history in electrical engineering, staid and worthy in their own fields but nonetheless on a loser, tried to keep abreast of the times by moving into electronics. Such companies had well established structures, their personnel were set in their ways, and the new growth was seen as potentially disruptive. In part this was precisely because it was growing, and at the expense of the electrical engineers, and in part it was because the whole ethos was different; old-time engineers faced electronics whizz-kids. The answer to the social problem was often spatial separation. Burns and Stalker (1961) document many such cases (one, indeed, where spatial separation was reduced to the effective and telling symbolism of building a brick wall through the plant!) in the Scottish industry of the 1950s. Nor was this socially-produced location strategy necessarily economically efficient. Indeed, it

often served to prevent the establishment of new relations between science and production which 'the laboratory' was supposed
to encourage.

There can be another social reason for spatial separation, too.
'Higher level' scientists and technologists have a completely
different relationship to the labour process from that of direct
producers. They dress differently, tend to come in late, possibly
stay on in the evening too, and don't have closely defined work
schedules, it's often not clear at any precise moment quite what
they should be doing, indeed there is often considerable latitude to
decide for themselves. This is exactly that degree of control over
one's work process to which Wright (1978) refers and which he
argues puts such employees in a different class situation from
ordinary workers. Certainly the contrast exists within the electronics industry in the United Kingdom and it has frequently been
socially problematical in management terms. The solution, again,
has often been spatial separation. 'The way out of these troubles
was seen by the heads of firms to lie in separating the new group as
far as possible, administratively and physically, from the existing
establishment. One firm planned to build a laboratory on the other
side of a large field, decided this was too close, and bought
premises in another part of the town' (Burns and Stalker, 1961, p.
141). The *fact* of locational separation can have its origin in many
different social processes. It can be functional also, for management, in management–labour relations

> Objections were raised to the laxity which prevailed among [the
> company's] development engineers over rules which members
> of production departments had to keep whatever their status –
> especially punctuality. Production managers objected strongly,
> as did development engineers, to the proposal that they share a
> new building. Their present establishments were miles apart,
> the development engineers in an elegant, pleasantly situated
> building, surrounded by lawns and gardens and attractively
> decorated and furnished. The production shops and managers'
> offices were, by contrast, crowded and makeshift. 'It's often
> been suggested,' said one production manager, 'that we should
> make up a party of our people and take them over to see around
> the labs – good idea to let them see what the firm is doing in that
> line, and so on. Well, that party hasn't come off and won't. We

daren't. What the eye doesn't see, the heart doesn't grieve over' (Burns and Stalker, 1961, p. 188).

So social differences within the workplace have in some cases been a significant determinant of locational strategy, and location in its turn has been a means of maintaining social differences.

The spatial structures of large capital in electronics are a varying mixture of technical division of labour, product cycle and product differentiation. In all cases, for 'top' and 'bottom' locations the implications are as discussed in Chapter 3, but the implications for the 'middle region' vary a lot. Where product differentiation is the organising principle of spatial form, the middle region of skilled manual labour tends to be the most vulnerable. These are the products which, along with their labour requirements, will soon be phased out, in this case not even to receive work on the next 'old' product, for its labour requirements will be different.

These are not forms of spatial organisation which simply re-plicate the international division of labour in electronics.[4] The Thames Valley is not Silicon Valley and assembly workers in the Development Areas and small towns of the United Kingdom earn more than 20 cents an hour. But the national spatial structure is clearly embedded in the international one; both balance and form reflect the national position. All stages of production are present. The existence of R and D marks it off from the industry in a Third World country, as does the manufacture of older products: the declining semi-electronic and electromechanical end of production. On the other hand many firms are 'headless' or at least half-decapitated. British firms have some research and advanced production in the United States. Some non-UK firms have only production facilities here, American firms in Scotland for example, and German and Japanese companies in Wales. The orientation of the different regions reflects the international position too. While parts of the south-east try to compete with Silicon Valley the regions with only assembly jobs may lose even them to a Third World Free Production Zone, or win production back only when there has been sufficient automation to reduce substantially the critical importance of labour costs, and therefore the number of jobs.

Spatial structures of small firms

But not all firms, by any means, could adopt this kind of spatial structure. There is within the electronics and instruments industries a range of companies which are different in two crucial respects from those so far discussed: in the character of the capital involved and in the nature of the dominant labour process. These companies are small, often entrepreneurial operations, and they do not on the whole use mass-production techniques. These two closely-linked aspects – capital organisation and labour process – together condition a locational strategy which is very different from the spatial structures just described, but which nonetheless reinforces some of their regional effects.

This is, *par excellence*, small capital of the venturesome, advanced-technology variety. In spite of its size it operates in an international scene. Its smallness is partly a reflection of the nature of the labour process. Much production of instruments and advanced electronics takes place on a small-batch basis, is labour intensive, and is geared to competition based less on cost than on technological characteristics. Production is often for specialised markets, often on the basis of customer specification, and requires development of and adaptation to a continually changing technology. There are few opportunities for mass-production and few also for economies of scale.

Labour requirements clearly reflect these characteristics. Software scientists, microchip people and technologists are very important. Manual workers, too, tend to be specialised and highly skilled, and the most significant aspect of this skill is adaptability. The work is non-repetitive, with a high degree of on-the-job control.

All this determines a very particular set of constraints on location. The small size of the firms means that it is difficult to locate research and production separately. The frequent one-off or small-batch character cuts down on the possibilities for mass-production and requires a much more intimate relation between research, development and operations on the shop floor. These things together immediately rule out a spatial structure of the multiregional, hierarchical, part-process variety. These companies are single-region affairs and usually also single-location. Further, the demand for skilled labour restricts the range of possible locations, concentrating them particularly, and once again, in the south-east of England. This applies not only to the research kind of skilled labour but also to the technically skilled shop-floor workers, who often do jobs which precisely involve the integration of conception and execution (Oakey, 1978).[5] Some evidence indicates that, although the south-east does not in fact always have slacker markets for such labour, it is often nonetheless perceived to be a better region for both skilled operative and administrative labour (Oakey, p. 207). The resulting concentration of these firms thus reinforces the region's existing dominance in the distribution of skilled and technical workers. And numerous studies show that this differential distribution of 'key workers' is real as well as perceived. One of the cases Oakey presents is of a small company (about 150 workers) which was trying to concentrate a previous hierarchically-structured location pattern. What is more, it was attempting consolidation in the lower end of the hierarchy, in a Development Area. A manufacturing plant at Camberley, Surrey, which had 20 per cent of the organisation's total manufacturing, and all the company's administration and research and development facilities, was closed in 1977, and the activities moved to an existing production plant at Runcorn. The Runcorn plant had been in operation since 1968 on a new government-built factory estate and had previously had 80 per cent of the company's production, but almost no administration (p. 275).

The decision to consolidate on the Runcorn site was governed by two factors – the smaller disruption to production and the availability of regional policy assistance. But problems arose in attracting skilled labour. First, only a small proportion of the 'highly skilled technical and administrative staff' could be persuaded to move north. Second, 'a shortage of "local scientific engineering and skilled manpower" (questionnaire response) that had been present since the Runcorn plant's initial establishment in 1968, having intensified since the Camberley relocation, had virtually forced the company to close the Runcorn plant' (p. 276). The plant did survive – with the help of the Temporary Employment Subsidy – but the example illustrates well the kinds of conditions which might keep in the south-east both that part of these industries which requires predominantly skilled and technical labour, and that part which consists of firms which, though they may have some processes performed by semi-skilled labour, are too small to establish a hierarchical spatial structure. No mention is made of any attempts by firms to train their own labour.

This, however, is an example of an attempted move to the industrial periphery. There is more evidence of successful moves by such firms to the rural regions bordering the south-east, and in particular the south-west of England and East Anglia. In these regions the environmental preferences of managerial and technical staff are more likely to be met (Spooner, 1972; Cornwall Industrial Development Association, 1977). Indeed, one of the complaints in the south-west is that too many of these jobs are taken by in-migrants – though clearly there are exceptions even here (see Note 5). The evidence is, however, that even in these regions such moves provide only a minority of incoming employment, the bulk of it being production work in branch plants. Moreover, although residential preference has been important in attracting such firms to the regions it has not saved them from a faster-than-average closure rate in recent years (Cornwall County Council, 1976b; Cornwall Industrial Development Association, 1977).

This part of the industry bears witness again to the negative social power over location of 'the best staff'. They could not be persuaded to go to Runcorn, and in St Austell there was a lack of artistic and cultural entertainments: the interpenetration of the economic and the social again. What has artistic entertainment got to do with making a profit in electronics? It is not a demand of the production process directly. But the technology being developed in electronics is based on a division of labour which increasingly separates conceptualisation from execution, and the social polarisation with which this is associated is in part the condition for, and in part reinforced by, ideological factors which go far beyond production. The kinds of social strata which occupy the top end of both managerial and production-technology hierarchies in these industries have been central to the rhetoric of economic strategy throughout the period since the sixties, though in vastly varying ways. In the sixties they were the linchpin of the State-backed white heat of technological, and managerial, revolution. By the eighties they were transformed, at least ideologically, into the dynamic entrepreneurs (the two-men-in-a-garage), to what would be left when the dead wood of British industry (and State intervention) had been cut away, when they would have space to breathe, expand, and save the economy. In both guises they manifestly failed, but their social status remained untarnished. The development of a particular social form and ideology of the technology of production is the precondition for a particular form of geographical differentiation. Equally, geographical form itself can help to reinforce the social divisiveness of a division of labour within production.

As it stands at present, then, the spatial structure most characteristic of this kind of smaller company is that of geographical concentration. All stages of production as well as of ownership and management are in general to be found in one area. And being able neither to establish a hierarchical spatial structure nor to decentralise the whole of production they were unable to take the same advantage of the existing form of geographical inequality. Clearly, therefore, it is not possible to generalise about the spatial structures of the technologically-advanced/means-of-production parts of the economy. For these firms, the characteristics of the labour process and of the organisation of capital were far more important determinants of locational structure.

Nevertheless, this spatial structure reinforces, although it does not replicate, the pattern of spatial differentiation implied by the locational hierarchies of production characteristic of other parts of electronics and related industries. It reinforces the concentration of supply and demand for particular kinds of skilled labour in the south and east, and it reinforces the concentration of ownership, and of upper management and control, in the same area. The locational structure of such firms thus contributes further to the reproduction of the differential distribution within Great Britain both of capital itself and of its immediate representatives, and of elements of those strata which Wright places between the working class and the petit-bourgeoisie.

4.3 Clothing and footwear

The character of the industry: increasing pressures

Employment in the clothing and footwear industry in the United Kingdom has been declining for decades. This is an old industry, grown out of domestic production of essential consumer goods,

rising to national significance in the nineteenth century, to undergo since the Second World War, and especially since the 1960s, a
radical shift in location away from industrialised capitalist countries of the first world. It is an industry which was early in, and has
been central to, the emergence of a new international division of
labour. The dramatic decline in employment has not prevented,
however, the evolution of new spatial structures within the United
Kingdom. Indeed, the pressures which have brought about decline
also lie behind those new structures. Decline is not necessarily a
process of stagnation or of simple closure; it can also involve quite
dramatic reorganisation.

'Clothing', then, is a very different industry, with a very
different history and place in the economy, from those we have
looked at so far. These contrasts mean that firms in the clothing
industry are subject to different economic pressures and also adopt
different locational strategies. Descriptively, the geographical
pattern of employment in clothing and the present changes in that
pattern are well known and undisputed. The decline in jobs
(though not in output) is long-term, though varying in pace. The
geographical changes are again long-term, but they accelerated
between the mid 1960s and early 1970s. The main shifts have been
from the traditional centres of London, West Yorkshire and
Manchester towards both rural areas and peripheral regions. The
change can thus be described on two axes: on the one hand from
major urban areas towards smaller towns and rural parts of the
country; and on the other from non-Development Areas towards
Development Areas.

This, however, is just a description of the two-dimensional
pattern. What lies behind it is a complicated set of changes, both in
the organisational structure of capital and in the relations between
capital and labour.

In order to examine this further it is necessary to look first at the
characteristics of capital in this industry. For the 'Clothing and
Footwear' Order of the Standard Industrial Classification is a
classic case where, because they produce the same kind of output,
very different kinds of firms are aggregated together under one
heading. In terms of the organisation of capital, the nature of
production relations and management, and the relation to technology and to the market, the clothing industry is split into a number
of different parts. At least two significantly different kinds of
capital operate within it.

An important segment of the industry is owned by small capital. But this is not the small capital of electronics and instruments production. As in those sectors, the survival and importance of small companies is in part due to the lack of economies of scale in production. But in total contrast to the instruments industry, this is here a result, not of the continuously advancing nature of technology, but of the fact that it is backward and relatively stagnant. The basic labour process in the clothing industry remains organised around the individually-operated sewing machine – conveyor-belt production is still unusual (NEDO, 1974a; Economists Advisory Group, undated). Although there are differences, this kind of labour process is broadly typical throughout the industry. The small firms, however, tend to be concentrated in those parts of the sector which are as yet least mechanisable and where long runs and mass-production are rare. This varies both between mlhs and between parts of the market (depending on the degree of 'fashion-orientation', etc.). The social nature of these firms is different too. In clothing, small firms tend to be in rather unentrepreneurial family-ownership and this in turn means that the technological backwardness is reinforced by the 'old-fashioned' nature of much of the management in the industry. A NEDO Report commented that it was of a character to manage a craft industry of low technological content, small capital investment and short turnover times, but that any attempt to raise technological levels and capital intensity would create 'large problems in management education' (NEDO, 1974c).

A report on the footwear industry came to much the same conclusion about the nature of capital and management there. Again in total contrast to the mushrooming new firms in high-tech sectors, firms in footwear tend to be old. 'Very few new footwear companies have been formed since the Second World War and the majority of the medium and large companies date from the nineteenth century' (Economists Advisory Group, undated, p. 95). This characteristic in turn has resulted in a relatively high average age of managements in family businesses, much of it in its second or third generation. 'An ageing structure of enterprise and management is, it appears, a general characteristic of UK industry, but it may be exceptionally pronounced in the footwear industry where, in the nature of things, technological change has been relatively slow' (Economists Advisory Group, p. 95). This is for the industry as a whole, but there are clear divisions within it:

'The general quality of management in the industry is poor except in the few very large manufacturers where it is professional, trained and competent' (p. 130). The lack of new management 'blood' is particularly marked in smaller, family-owned firms, and this is argued to be a direct cause of the introspection, lack of marketing energy and poor financial controls in many firms and of their failure to react to change. Social characteristics, in other words, affect economic behaviour. Indeed, they go deep enough to affect the companies' whole orientation to accumulation. 'Amongst the smaller family concerns, there is a pre-occupation with the task of making the business simply provide a living for its owner which shuts out all thoughts of new investment and a new aggressive approach to marketing and re-organisation...' (p. 130). Neither expansion nor rate, as opposed to amount, of profit features prominently on the agenda. The main concern is with stability 'Managements will not accept the prospect of reducing the scale of their operation in order to make the same percentage return on a reduced capital employed. This is especially so in the case of family concerns where such a change would mean leaving the original premises' (p. 130).

It could all hardly be more different from electronics. 'Small capital' in clothing does not consist of technologically advanced small firms, but of conservative family businesses in a nationally declining industry. This is the other side of the picture of the small firm as attractive employer and saviour of the economy. Characterisation by size alone does not adequately capture the real difference in social relations.

Finally, a significant proportion of these smaller companies operate on a subcontracting or outworking basis, making-to-order for manufacturers – or dealers who often go by the name of manufacturers but who perform only a commercial role (King, 1981, p. 9) – or retailers. In many cases, therefore, full economic ownership and control does not lie within the firm itself. This may again influence the company's dynamic. Certainly it will usually add a further degree of vulnerability to that which derives from smallness and relative backwardness.

But not all capital in the clothing industry is of this type. There are also larger, multi-plant companies, many of which are closely tied in with distribution (retail outlets, etc.), and which may be vertically integrated across production and distribution (see sources quoted here; also Leigh, 1975). This relation with the retail sector is very different from that of the small firms, which are often quite subordinate to it, and these different relations to distribution are an important part of the distinction between large and small firms in the clothing industry. The greater size of capital and greater market strength of retail outlets than of many of the manufacturers which supply them is typical of what might be called old-fashioned consumer-goods industries in the United Kingdom (Cowper, 1979; David, 1980; Churchill, 1981). In comparison with other countries the degree of concentration in retailing is quite high in the United Kingdom, and this has its effects not only on the consumer but also on the related manufacturing sectors. In the 1970s the retail sector took an increasing share of the profits from clothing manufacture.

Again, however, large firms in the clothing industry (and they include some of the largest in the country) are different from those in electronics. The advantages they gain from size are different. Certainly, large firms are more common in the more-easily mechanisable parts of the industry, and where mass-production is more feasible. They are, therefore, able to take some advantage of economies of scale in production, but even in these parts of the sector (for example, shirt production) such economies are relatively limited. The real advantages of size lie in the ability to dominate market relations, particularly with the distribution sector.

It is generally recognised that these two parts of the sector – small firms and large – have behaved rather differently in the post-war period, the former experiencing greater decline, the latter some expansion and greater mobility (primarily by establishing new branch plants in new locations). But behind this pattern lie a number of distinct processes. There has been some reinforcement of the structural division between the two parts of the industry, a relative strengthening of large capital, and an increasing identification of the different types of capital with distinct and different spatial structures.

*   *   *

Part of the cause of these changes stems from national and international developments. However, because of the sector's very different structural position within the economy, the effects of these developments on clothing firms were not the same as the effects in electronics and instruments. The recession hit different parts of the economy in very different ways. Over the long term, but particularly since the mid-1960s, the clothing industry has come under increasing pressure to cut its costs of production. Most obviously there has been competition from imports (from the Third World, from Comecon, from the United States) which could out-compete the products made in Britain largely because they were cheaper. Moreover, at the same time as the home market has been invaded by imports it has been slowing down in its overall rate of growth[6] (reports of Clothing Sector EDC).

If a company in an industry as labour intensive as clothing is going to respond to cost competition, that response is likely to be in terms of cutting labour costs. But at the same time that this long-term pressure on costs was building up so also was competition for the industry's traditional labour supply. In the 1960s, this supply was supplemented by immigration, but with political changes this source of new labour began to diminish also (Winyard, 1977). In most parts of the clothing industry over 70 per cent of the workers are female (the aggregate figure is just over 80 per cent), and the increase since the Second World War in the employment of women in the rest of the economy has put pressure on the availability of female workers. This pressure has come particularly from the growth of service industries, both State and private. There has been competition for this segment of the labour force. And it was a competition whose intensity, even existence, varied geographically, depending above all on the level of growth of employment in services. It has been strongest in urban areas and most particularly in London.[7] Since the War, wages for women in the clothing industry have stayed around the national average (for women) in manufacturing as a whole. This remained true up until the mid-1960s (Department of Employment Gazette; Department of Employment, New Earnings Survey). It was not low wages but the bad image of the industry which made recruitment difficult. The image of factory work as a whole for women, the particular reputation of this industry as a sweated trade, and indeed precisely as an 'old' industry, and the generally bad working conditions, put the sector in a poor competitive position in the labour market in relation to services in particular, but also to some of the newer manufacturing industries. Even the 'competitive' level of wages is largely earned, particularly by the women in the industry, on a payment-by-results basis.[8] This image problem is one of which management in the industry is acutely conscious, and it is one which applies to those 'young, unmarried females' and school-leavers on whom the industry has traditionally relied and who now prefer the relative glamour of being a secretary or a receptionist. NEDO (1974a) states the problem

> The supply of labour is thus of the utmost importance to the clothing industry. The industry recruits largely female labour in competition with the light engineering industry, distribution and the clerical trades. The industry requires as high or a higher degree of skill as any other employer of female labour without paying higher wages and the Department of Employment Gazette concluded in 1970 that, while the industry tended to gain recruits from the food, distribution and paper sectors, it incurred a net loss of workforce to the electrical and engineering industries and to 'professional and scientific services'. There is no reason to suppose that this competition for labour will decline in the future.
>
> Indeed the raising of the school leaving age may enhance the competition. The clothing industry tended to recruit 15,000 recruits annually direct from school and the raising of the school leaving age will remove one year's potential new entry for ever. Furthermore there is some reason to suspect that girls with a further year of education may be less likely to enter industry at all. Competitors such as banking and distribution services may be better able to pay the increased costs of recruiting and employing scarce young female labour (NEDO, 1974a, pp. 47–8).

It is the same in the shoe industry, particularly in the East Midlands where over the sixties and seventies there was increasing competition for labour from services and light industries, in both of which working conditions are seen as being superior (Mounfield, Unwin and Guy, 1982, pp. 198–205).

In certain areas, and including some of the industry's traditional bases, especially London, this 'image' problem was now added to by competition on the wages front. A study by the Clothing EDC, reported on in 1980, found low pay to be the major factor influencing people to leave the industry (NEDO, 1980), with boredom coming second. Pay was particularly significant in London – a reflection of geographical variation in competition for labour. This compares with an earlier study (NEDO, 1967) in which boredom emerged as the single major factor. Wage competition was relatively late on the scene. Indeed from the mid-1960s the disparity between wages for women in the clothing industry and in manufacturing as a whole increased dramatically. From 98.4 per cent of all-manufacturing average in 1965, women's wages in clothing fell to 89.4 per cent in 1970 and to 82.1 per cent in 1978 (Department of Employment data). This steep relative fall reflects the increasing pressure on the industry over this period; it also reflects the ways in which capital responded.

The search for new labour: two different strategies

This response mirrored once again the difference between large and small capital in the industry. The two behaved very differently. Many very small firms are more tied to the traditional and urban areas of production, both because they tend to be more geared into the fashion end of production (the existence of which is itself one of the conditions for the survival of small capital in the sector) and, more importantly, because their very smallness and their family nature means that they are less able to respond to changing cost pressures through geographical mobility. And it is precisely in the urban areas where these firms are concentrated that the most dramatic increases in pressure on costs have taken place (Department of Trade and Industry, 1973; Keeble, 1976). Small capital was thus often left stranded in the face of these rising costs – literally immobilised. Quite frequently it gave up the ghost, and died (Keeble, 1976).

For those small firms which survived it was necessary to reduce labour costs while remaining in the same general location. Extensive mechanisation and automation were impossible, both because such firms did not have sufficient capital or borrowing potential and because such small firms are precisely concentrated in the less-mechanisable parts of the sector. Other strategies had to be adopted. The work process was intensified, thus increasing its speed and also its monotony.[9] Further, unable to escape from these areas of increasing competition for labour, small firms turned to more vulnerable sections of the labour force, in particular to immigrants and older and married women, and forms of labour organisation such as homeworking (which in the late seventies was estimated, see King, 1981, p. 10, to account for 40 per cent of production in London, the highest level in the country). This reduced the bargaining power of the workforce and enabled the employers thus to hold down wages. Unable to change location to search for cheaper labour, they turned to other social strata in their existing areas and what came to be called 'the new sweated sector' grew up in London.[10]

*　　　*　　　*

Larger firms have been in a very different position, and able to adopt a very different strategy. First, they were often better able to survive simply because of the extra financial resilience given to them by size. Second, the fact that they tended to be in the more easily mechanisable and automatable parts of the sector, and that they had more capital to invest, meant that they were more able than were small companies to reduce costs by technological changes in the production process. This allowed them both to reduce the amount of labour per unit of output and to use the opportunity of the change in production method to introduce cheaper workers. King (1981) describes how technological innovation, by allowing the reclassification of jobs, enabled better-paid male workers to be 'bought out' with redundancy payments and women to be employed at a lower rate (Winyard, 1977; Disher, 1980). Such replacement also operated between different groups of women workers. When searching out new sources of female labour, management in these firms looked in particular for women with no previous experience of working in the clothing industry.

However, even among the biggest firms the labour-cost savings to be made by changes in production were not major, and other measures were also taken. In particular, these companies were better able to survive because, unlike the small ones, they were geographically mobile. Instead of being trapped in high-cost areas, they were able to take advantage of the changes going on at the same time in the geography of the female labour force. These big companies were unconstrained by the family ties of owners and managers, and they were large enough and had sufficient capital to take advantage of cheaper conditions of production elsewhere in the country. Socially, they were a completely different entity from the small companies, and their response was likewise different.

And the difference in geographical mobility mattered. The spatial pattern of cost and availability of labour was changing. While costs were going up in urban areas there was a growing female labour reserve available as a result of accelerated decline of male-employing industries in the Development Areas, and also significant reserves outside the major cities in smaller towns.[11] These alternative sources of female workers had numerous advantages for the clothing industry. First of all, the labour was cheaper. Keeble (1976), summarising the conclusions of the ILAG survey, reports that availability and cost of female labour were the main factors inducing movement by clothing firms between 1964 and 1967, and in influencing the choice of new location. 'The establishment of small clothing plants in many rural and peripheral areas to tap local supplies of underemployed women workers is a primary reason for the recent dispersal of the industry' (p. 179).

Such labour was not only available and comparatively cheap, it was also new to the industry. Keeble's (1976) analysis shows 'a very marked negative relationship with existing clothing employment', and the National Union of Tailors and Garment Workers (NUTGW) reported that the labour sought by these firms was mainly female, unorganised and non-traditional clothing workers. There was far less competition for it from other sectors than there was in major urban areas. This helped combat not just the problem of wages competition but also the unattractive image of the sector. If there is no choice, one cannot be too particular about working conditions. The importance of lack of competition is emphasised by the sample enquiry conducted through the Clothing EDC. This showed that lack of alternative employment was the most common reason for entering the industry and that the most common reason for joining a particular company was the convenience of its location (Clothing EDC, 1980). The latter reflects the fact that the largely female workforce is also tied to the routine of domestic labour – the sexual division of labour outside the factory influencing the geographical location of production. This aspect of recruitment must increase the attractiveness of small towns and rural areas where virtual monopoly positions over the labour force can be established by single firms. Of course, in some parts of the sector small-town location is a long-established tradition. Mounfield, Unwin and Guy (1982) document this for the shoe industry of the east midlands, bringing out clearly the importance of monopoly and distance from competition from other industries (pp. 185–8 and 197–8). The larger firms setting up new locations in the sixties were seeking similar advantages. In this context it is interesting that 'lack of alternative employment' was a particularly important factor in producing a labour force for the clothing industry in the West Country, a predominantly rural area (the other side of this process will be looked at in the study of Cornwall in Chapter 5). (In contrast to the situation in the West Country, in the East End of London significant numbers entered the industry because they wanted a trade – a clear indication of the social differences in the industry between the two parts of the country.) The advantages of small towns are reinforced by another aspect of the use of labour. Management in this industry has been accustomed, as is common with labour-intensive sectors, to lay workers off in a recession and take them on again with the first upturn in business. Competition from other industries means that laid-off workers are harder to attract back (NEDO, 1974a, p. 47; and NUTGW, undated). Such a strategy requires, if not monopoly control over a workforce, then certainly little competition. One factor in the choice of small labour markets 'revolves around organisational size. To put it bluntly, it seems that some firms not only regard small closing units of twenty or so women to be more "manageable", they are also thought to be less prone to militancy and easier to close or open during periods of depression or expansion' (Mounfield, Unwin and Guy, 1982, p. 125). Smaller, more peripheral, labour markets are ideal (as indeed, in the context of bigger cities, are homeworkers).

Like the small firms in the sector, then, big capital turned to more vulnerable sections of the workforce. Large firms, however, were able to change location in order to find it. Sometimes this was done by actual transfer, with a consequent loss of employment in the traditional and urban areas. Thus a Southwark Trades Council study notes sadly that:

Those parts of the industry not clearly tied to fashion have been moving out of the inner city ever since the war and the decline of employment in them in Southwark has been sharp. . . .

Just recently, in January 1976, there has been a major redundancy of approximately 200 workers when the Rocola-shirt factory closed in Bermondsey. This company is a subsidiary of Carrington-Viyella in which Imperial Chemical Industries has the major share-holding. It has moved its production to its Northern Ireland factory to enable it to pay even lower wages (Southwark Trades Council and Roberts, 1976).

But more frequently the new labour was reached by establishing new branch plants, in other words by the establishment or extension of a multiplant, multiregional spatial structure.

In this complex reorganisation of the clothing industry, then, geography played an active role in a number of ways. First, there was significant spatial variation in the nature and degree of competition between different parts of capital for particular segments of the labour force. Second, geographical mobility gave larger companies a wider choice in seeking out a cheaper labour force, giving them an option which could only increase their advantage over small firms in those parts of the market where they were in competition. Third, in their choice of new locations geographical dispersion and monopoly over local labour markets enabled these large firms to reinforce the vulnerability of their new employees.

Spatial structures of big firms

Let us look more closely then at the kind of spatial structures evolved by these larger multiregional and multinational companies in the clothing and footwear industry. How has big capital in this industry, an industry so different from electronics, attempted to gain maximum advantage from the existing form of uneven development of the British space?

First of all, multiregionality itself means that the spatial structure is one in which headquarters functions are carried out in one region while production in the others is subject to external ownership and ultimate control. There is, in other words, a hierarchy of ownership, supervision and control, a hierarchy of the relations of economic ownership and possession. Moreover, increasingly the location of headquarters is in London. This results both from the establishment of branch plants outside the southeast by firms already based there, and from another process which has been under way at the same time, that of takeover and merger.

This latter process has both reflected and further increased the strength of big firms in relation to small and has reinforced the dominance of London as a headquarters location. Leigh, whose study was of takeovers in the sector in 1973, provides evidence of how this process of centralisation is taking place largely by moderate-sized and larger companies taking over small ones (p. 12) and, in terms of the broader characteristics of ownership, that 'the major pattern ... is of public companies acquiring private limited companies, or, less usually, acquiring the subsidiaries of other public companies. No public companies were "acquired"' (Leigh, 1975, p. 5). Moreover, this pattern of types of firm is mirrored in a geographical pattern. Leigh reports that the picture is one of 'increasing "metropolitanisation" of the United Kingdom clothing industry by London-based firms' (p. 20). Such companies were at that period actively taking over smaller London firms as well as provincial companies. There was, on the other hand, little counter-provincialisation of the industry 'since provincially-based firms tend to take over other provincial firms, not metropolitan ones' (Leigh, 1975, p. 20).

Thus, a spatial structure in which London is the base of ultimate control over investment and production is increasingly important within the industry. In some cases this base is attached to production facilities in the same region, in some cases it is not. The production plants elsewhere are increasingly in rural and/or peripheral regions. This aspect of spatial structure is increasingly typical of the larger firms in the industry and, therefore, of growing importance in the sector as a whole. This is nonetheless a sector in which, because of its historic regional bases, quite a few larger firms still have their headquarters outside the south-east (Leigh, 1975).

In its multiregional nature the spatial structure of large firms in the clothing industry is very like that of their counterparts in electronics. In other ways, however, it is clearly different. It has already been mentioned that the technology in clothing means that the advantages to be derived from size are different from those in the automatable and research-based parts of electronics. In clothing, the advantages lie in areas other than direct production and R and D. This reflects itself in spatial structure. While this is multiplant and multiregional location it is not the multiplant structure characteristic of electronics. It is not a part-process but a cloning structure. So, as we have seen, while there is a hierarchy of administration and control, there is often no hierarchy based on a technical division of labour. This contrast in spatial structure affects interregional contrasts. In clothing there is little inter-regional difference in the social characteristics of production workers and because the branch plants are not embedded in a part-process structure they may be more differentially vulnerable to closure in economic downturns.

The low levels of technology and division of labour have other effects. This is not a science-based industry; there is no concentration of technical and scientific workers in the south-east. The management structure of the administrative hierarchy is flatter, and therefore again fails to contribute much to the congregation of highly-paid and high-status jobs around London. This also means, of course, that the higher proportion of headquarters 'in the regions' does not imply a large amount of white-collar employment there either.

The low level of development of the technical division of labour is also mirrored at the other end of the spectrum. Just as there has been no major separate development of scientific and conceptual functions so the production jobs are less reduced to repetitive execution. Clearly the clothing industry, like electronics, has contributed to the influx of jobs for women in rural areas and peripheral regions. Certainly, too, these jobs are not well paid. Indeed as we have seen the geographical shift itself has been part of the mechanism whereby women's wages in clothing fell behind those in manufacturing as a whole. It would be wrong, however, to see this as entirely unskilled or semi-skilled work. Certainly it has been the most mechanisable – and least skilled – sectors which have decentralised. And locational change sometimes went hand in hand with production change. But nevertheless in 1971 a good 20 per cent of employees even in the most mechanised sectors were female skilled manual workers. This is far above the proportion in any electronics sector. The same factors which make even mass-production garment assembly more difficult to automate than assembly in other industries (the need to engineer flexible, stretchable two-dimensional fabric into a three-dimensional shape) gives the actual job content of production work more of a craft character. The NEDO Review comments that 'the industry has the problems of a craft industry without the compensating benefit which other craft industries such as ship-building and house-building enjoy, of producing a high-cost article' (NEDO, 1974a, p. 47). It would seem, too, that even these higher percentages of officially skilled workers are an underestimate of real job content. For the clothing industry provides a good example of the cultural and ideological nature of the skill categories themselves. Phillips and Taylor (1980), analysing a study of the clothing industry by Birnbaum (undated), show how the classification of jobs varies, not according to job content, but with the sex of the worker. There is an identification of men with skilled and women with semi-skilled or unskilled status, and this in turn has been generated through the struggles of men workers to retain their dominance within the sexual hierarchy outside work. Throughout the twentieth century, machining in the clothing trade has been done by both men and women, but where it was done by men it was classified as skilled; where it was done by women it was classified as semi-skilled. Supposed non-comparabilities between men's and women's work were used to justify this distinction – the women worked in larger workshops, in a more subdivided labour process, machining men's garments, while the men worked in smaller shops machining women's garments. This discrimination has survived a whole series of redefinitions of the basis for skill classification – whatever definition was adopted, differences were always found and employed in such a way as to ensure skilled status for the men and semi-skilled for the women (Phillips and Taylor, 1980, p. 85). These distinctions cannot be rationalised in terms of the content of the work. Birnbaum argues instead that they arose out of the 'struggle of men workers from the Russian, Jewish and Polish communities to retain their social status within the family, even when excluded by their position as immigrants from the "skilled" jobs they might otherwise have done. Forced as they were to take on machining work usually done by women as semi-skilled, they fought to preserve their masculinity by redefining (their) machining as skilled labour. Within the clothing trade he concludes "the only way to become skilled was to change one's sex"' (Phillips and Taylor, 1980, p. 85).

In the clothing industry, then, there is not that development of technology and that acute dichotomisation of functions which so characterises major firms in electronics. And this conditions a different geographical form. In the clothing industry there are neither the high-status echelons of R and D nor the grindingly deskilled jobs of simple assembly. At the assembly end of the two industries it is the fact that the jobs are done by women rather than the real content of the work which reduces them both to the same social status. At the other end the clothing industry has no real equivalent to the scientists and technologists of electronics. The combination of industrial characteristics and different ways of using space, different spatial structures, leads to contrasting forms of geographical variation.

*   *   *

There are also indications of other spatial structures within the clothing industry. First of all, there are cases where different plants do perform different roles in a technical division of labour – where there is, in other words, a part-process structure. In the simplest case, each of the part-process plants performs different stages in the overall assembly of the product, but nonetheless has very similar employment structures. In this case, the fact that the technical division of labour has this spatial form does not show up in social differences between different regions. It does, however, have effects on intraregional linkages and interregional relations, for just as in the electronics hierarchy these plants receive their components (in this case half-finished garments) from, and send their product to, other plants within the same company.

In some instances, however, these interplant relations *are* associated with social differences in employment structure. This is mainly the case where cutting, performed by men, remains in the 'central' regions and assembly, performed by women, is decentralised. Evidence of this spatial structure exists in both footwear (see Chapter 3; also Massey and Meegan, 1982) and in clothing (NEDO, 1974a), but it is difficult to know, without more detailed enquiry, how general it is.[12] The rationale for such a structure is, however, clear. It was the cheap *female* labour which was the attraction of peripheral regions; indeed, both the Economists Advisory Group (undated) and NEDO (1974a) argue that male workers are not available in these regions. This is somewhat counter-intuitive, given the high and rising rate of male unemployment in the Development Areas. What the industries were looking for, however, were men already skilled as cutters and willing to work for an industry-wage which fell between 1950 and 1980 from 110 per cent of the male average weekly earnings in manufacturing to around 75 per cent (Department of Employment Gazette; Department of Employment, New Earnings Survey). There was, moreover, a way of dealing with the problem of male labour supply which was not available in the female-dominated machining process. For cutting is more easily automatable and it seems likely that, for the larger firms which could establish multi-plant structures, a shortage of female labour may have been solved by geographical shift and a shortage of male labour by automation. It is an interesting issue which merits further research, for it is another case where uneven advances in technology, long-established and ideologically-embedded traditions of who does what job, and changing locational surfaces (in this case changing patterns of wage levels) are all involved together in producing 'the regional geography of employment'.

The same process has been going on in the shoe industry, both between regions and between towns and adjacent rural areas. And it has not been confined to very large companies. In the Norwich area, competition from the service sector for female labour has pushed growing firms to look outside the town for small pockets of labour (Moseley and Sant, 1977, p. 70). In the east midlands new locations 'in rural centres where the local communities have provided a small but useful labour pool of married women' have been sought out (Mounfield, Unwin and Guy, 1982, p. 125). Labour has not been the only factor, but it has been critical. 'Market towns and villages, without any substantial industrial development or tradition of shoe-making, have been chosen in many cases: Corby, dominated by male-employing iron and steel, has proved a good centre, too' (Mounfield, Unwin and Guy, 1982, p. 125).

Finally, there is evidence of another set of interregional relations, this time at interfirm level between small and large companies. This is the much discussed issue of subcontracting. There are certainly examples, though again how significant it is difficult to say, of plants in peripheral regions being tied into such a structure. In the North East many of the smaller firms, particularly in the urban back streets of Newcastle, are directly subordinate to national retail companies (Benwell CDP, 1978b). This, again, has particular effects on interregional differences. While legally such plants are locally-owned, the real relations of control lie with a larger company elsewhere. Such small firms are different from those discussed earlier. In terms of the real relations of production and the dynamic of accumulation they are inextricably tied in to the large-capital part of the industry. In such cases, these apparently independent plants will suffer from the vulnerability to external decisions, as opposed simply to direct market forces, usually associated with cloned branch plants, and will develop few local linkages because they are already firmly tied into a wider structure of production.

The impact on national geography

All these spatial structures in clothing are different both in their form and in some of their effects from the spatial organisation of big firms in electronics.

At a wider level, though, the changing balance of spatial structures in the garment industry both reinforces and elaborates the form of geographical differentiation produced by the electronics and instruments industries. Most obvious are the different distributions of ownership and production, the former increasingly concentrated in the south-east, the latter increasingly decentralised to other regions. As has already been mentioned, this is probably less advanced in clothing than in many other sectors. In clothing there is still a fairly substantial degree of ownership in the traditional regions. However the firms which do still have 'provincial' headquarters are often those with a more traditional, less dynamic structure. Leigh's (1975) evidence on mergers points to this. Three of the largest firms in the sector were identified as having their headquarters outside the south-east, but none of these took an active part in the acquisition process he was studying. The regions where there is still a high degree of local control include Yorkshire and Humberside and the north-west, together with the east midlands and East Anglia. Overall, however, the evolving structure of ownership in the clothing industry, and its geographical dimensions, further contribute to the increasing degree of external control of production in the smaller towns and peripheral regions of Britain.

These regions, together with smaller towns in the country as a whole, have also seen an influx of clothing jobs for women, again mirroring the pattern of big electronics firms. The industry is another major contributor to the changing patterns of social organisation in those parts of the country.

Apart from external control and a predominantly female labour force, all the spatial structures of big firms within clothing share other things with those in electronics. Much of the early locational structure of the clothing industry was related to complex patterns of industrial linkage. First there were links with other sectors, particularly with the textile industry. These are now less locationally significant. The other intersectoral links are with the distribution industry. Much of the output of the clothing industry multiples (i.e. that part of the sector which is dominant in the decentralisation to the periphery) is already designated for specified retail outlets linked to the firm either by ownership or by long-term contracts. The second kind of linkage – the intrasectoral ones – is typical primarily of the smaller companies in the fashion end of the sector and again, therefore, does not apply to the decentralised production facilities. Indeed, the 'very marked negative relationship with existing clothing employment' (Keeble, 1976) must imply a low degree of reliance on local linkage to other clothing firms. The evidence therefore suggests that, as in the case of electronics assembly, these clothing factories will generate low local multiplier effects, and have little economic integration, in their recipient regions.

Links between work and community have also changed. As we have seen, some parts of the industry, especially footwear, have for long been established in small towns and rural areas. Here historically there has developed an interpenetration of factory and community life: 'Work and non-work roles and relationships are interlinked. The idiosyncrasies of the industry are widely understood in local communities ... work relationships in the factories are influenced, reciprocally, by the distinctive values of the ... small scale industrial communities in which footwear factories are principally located' (Goodman, Armstrong, Davis and Wagner, 1976, p. 59, quoted in Mounfield, Unwin and Guy, 1982, p. 188). Things are not quite the same around the new factories in peripheral regions.

The changes in spatial structure in the clothing industry are also reinforcing the problems of the cities. Jobs are being lost as a result both of closures, particularly of small firms and, to some extent, transfers by larger firms. And new jobs and new investment often go elsewhere. This has not led to significant levels of industry-specific unemployment in the cities, precisely because there is an already-established movement of workers away from this sector and towards others, but it has been accompanied by a worsening of the working conditions among those left in the industry. So in London and the south-east, the decline of the better-paid manufacturing sectors, and the worsening of conditions in others, are among the factors contributing to a polarised social structure which regional *per capita* and aggregate statistics totally fail to reflect.

In many ways, then, what is happening in clothing reinforces the pattern of geographical inequality being established in electronics, but in spite of the similarities there are also major differences, which it is equally important to note. Small and large capital in clothing is not at all the same as small and large capital in electronics, and this has implications both socially and for the structure of interregional differences.

Methodological reflections

What is going on in clothing and footwear is not just a change in a two-dimensional geographical pattern of employment but a reflection of the development of and changing balance between different ways of responding to spatial unevenness; a changing balance between different spatial structures superimposed on each other within the employment pattern of a single SIC Order. The contrast in spatial structure between small and large capital reflects different abilities to respond to the changing situation; two different dynamics. Moreover, the situation to which they were responding cannot be conceptualised simply in terms of location factors. At its broadest, these two different kinds of capital in the clothing industry were caught in the changing international division of labour and structure of accumulation. As well as facing increasing foreign competition in production, they also suffered from the international metropolitan concentration of the growing service industries and their competition for labour. To hold down labour costs the larger and more locationally-flexible companies sought out new reserves, some of which were simultaneously being added to by the further decline of those old basic sectors which had once formed a key element in a previous international division of labour.

To see this as a question of location factors alone is to underestimate both its breadth and its significance. It is also to underestimate the influence of geography itself as an active element in the process. Differential spatial mobility and ability to establish multiregional structures of production was an important part of big capital's advantage over small during this period. The former's ability to establish new branches in new regions can only have further worsened the lot of smaller capital.[13] And different spatial strategies went hand in hand with different strategies towards labour.

Further issues of explanation and of methodology are raised by the contrasts between large firms in the clothing industry and their counterparts in electronics. As we have seen, although the sociological characteristics of women's jobs in the two industries are very similar, the real job content is rather different. This has two implications. First, it means that the decentralisation of manufacturing jobs is not, as often implied, dependent on only one form of technological base, but can occur with a variety of different technologies and labour processes. It is as much dependent on *who* does a job (and therefore the nature of labour demand) as on real job content. Second, however, what this means in turn is that in each case a different causal structure must be involved. And indeed this is so. Large firms in electronics depended for their ability to decentralise on a change within production (including the development of new, mass-producible commodities) which would free them from previous ties to skilled labour. But there has been no such major change in production technology in clothing and footwear. It has not been this which has primarily governed its change in location pattern. In that sense the clothing industry could for centuries have decentralised to rural and peripheral regions. Although, therefore, it is important to know that it was the attraction of cheaper labour which induced this geographical shift, it is equally important to know why it happened *when it did*. Identification of a location factor in itself cannot answer this question, nor does the explanation lie in a change in labour process. As we have seen, the shift has been going on since the Second World War, though varying over time in its intensity. The question is why.

It has been the conjunction of four factors which has been primarily responsible for this timing. The growth in competition for female labour in urban areas is a long-term factor, though increasing in intensity after 1960 with the accelerated growth of the service sector. The emergence of a reserve of female labour in the industrial Development Areas is also a long-term phenomenon but again one which, in the post-war period, accelerated dramatically from the early 1960s. The third factor has been the greatly increased pressure on costs as a result of foreign competition, a pressure experienced particularly in the late 1960s and the 1970s. The fourth factor was the availability of regional policy incentives (and presumably especially the Regional Employment Premium). The ILAG Inquiry (Department of Trade and Industry, 1973) certainly shows regional policy to have been important in the mid-1960s. Such a constellation of factors indicates a very different *explanation* of decentralisation from that which obtains for electronics, and this is true in spite of the fact that the 'location factors' (cheap female labour and regional policy) were the same in each case. To limit industrial location theory to the identification of location factors is greatly to reduce its power to explain.

Moreover, with reference to the various forms of multiple regression which are so commonly used to string together groups of factors, it must be emphasised that the causes which together explain the decentralisation cannot be simply added up. They are mutually interdependent and interacting. To attempt an assessment of the autonomous influence of one of them is therefore to misunderstand the nature of the causal structures. In particular the effectiveness of regional policy was both dependent for, and reinforced in, its effectiveness by the existence of other conditions. Those conditions, and the way in which regional policy interacted with them, were different in different industries. In many parts of electronics a change in the nature of production was necessary for regional policy to be a relevant influence. For small firms in the same industry even that was not sufficient if the company was not large enough to become multilocational. In the clothing industry, as we have seen, the situation was different again. The question of this complex role of regional policy is taken up again in Chapter 6. Meanwhile we turn to the examination of another major sector of the economy.

4.4 Services

The industry: what are 'services' anyway?

Service industries have been given relatively little attention in employment studies. Yet more than half the economically active population of the UK now works within them. They have also often been thought of as subject to different laws from manufacturing industry, especially in consideration of the production process. Indeed, for long there was little recognition that there *was* a production process in service industries. But events have given the lie to these assumptions. From automation in the office to speed-up in the National Health and Social Security services, it has become abundantly clear that services are indeed produced and that the organisation of their labour processes is subject to many of the same pressures and changes as in manufacturing industry. And these changes in their turn have begun to have dramatic geographical implications.

Services, however, are clearly not homogeneous. Indeed they vary along all the dimensions discussed in Chapter 2. A clear conceptual distinction can be made between those services immediately geared to the reproduction of the labour force and those for which the market is other branches of industry. The first group, consumer services, includes most of the public services (health, education), much of the retail trade, and a vast range of direct consumer services from hairdressing through cinemas to religious organisations. Producer services, on the other hand, include business and professional functions such as advertising and market research, and much banking and insurance. Clearly, as throughout the industrial classification system, few services are entirely either consumer- or producer-oriented, but it is possible to make a broad and reasonably clear-cut division (Marquand, 1979, table 4.9). There is also variation in the nature of ownership. There are services provided through self-employment or by extremely small firms; in contrast an increasing proportion is owned and controlled by medium-scale and large private capital; finally, many consumer services in the UK are financed and controlled by the State. Just putting these divisions together with that between producer and consumer services gives a wide range of categories. As we shall see, there are still further subdivisions to be made – variations in labour process also have to be considered. All these dividing lines enable a clearer understanding of the spatial changes going on, the spatial strategies adopted in different parts of 'the service sector'. Because of our central interest in class and social structure we begin, though, with an examination of self-employment and family enterprises, for they are both an important element of service provision and distinctive in terms of their social organisation of production. As we shall see, once again social change and spatial change in this part of the British economy are clearly intertwined.

Self-employment and family enterprises

In comparison with many other Western European countries, self-employment and family enterprises are relatively unimportant in the United Kingdom, but both self-employment and very small firms (those with only three or four workers) are more important in the service industries than in any other part of the UK economy. Indeed the service industries broadly defined account for over three-quarters of all employers and self-employed people, most of the rest being in agriculture and in construction (Marquand, 1979, table 1.25). It is important, then, to examine these sectors in order to understand something of this aspect of the social structure of production in the United Kingdom.

For most of the 1960s and 1970s self-employment in the service industries remained fairly constant at just over a million people (including here – since the data will not allow their separation – both employers and self-employed). But as a proportion of self-employment in the economy as a whole that in services has tended to increase, going from 71.6 per cent in 1961 to 78.4 per cent in 1975.[14] This aggregate relative health and stability however, conceals important compositional changes. There has been a shift in sectoral distribution, a shift in the type of ownership and organisation of production and, integral to all this, a shift in spatial distribution.

Table 4.1 shows the change in sectoral distribution of employers and self-employed services from 1961 to 1975. Self-employment in Distributive Trades fell both absolutely and relatively and continued to do so right through the 1970s. Between 1971 and 1979 the number of grocery stores fell by 43 000 (41 per cent) and most

TABLE 4.1 *Changes in the sectoral distribution of employers and self-employed within services, between 1961 and 1975*

	1961 (000's)	1975	1961 (%)	1975
Distributive trades	526	425	51	42
Insurance, banking, etc.	32	52	3	5
Professional services	172	205	17	20
Miscellaneous services	296	335	29	33
Service (total)	1026	1017	100	100

Source: calculated from Marquand (1979, table 1.25).

of this reduction came from the independent sector, whose market share declined from 42.5 to 25.8 (*Financial Times*, 21 January 1981). In contrast, self-employment in all the other service sectors increased both absolutely and relatively.

Yet this is not simply a shift between sectors. It is not the result of 'entrepreneurs' pulling out of Distribution and going into other parts of the social division of labour in response to differences in the rate of profit. All self-employed people and owners of very small firms, according to Wright (see Chapter 2), are either petit-bourgeois (the self-employed) or occupy a class position somewhere along the dimension defined between petit-bourgeois and bourgeois class characteristics (the owners of very small firms). In the context of the United Kingdom, however, this classification and characterisation needs to be elaborated for it misses some important distinctions. There are, as we shall see, enormous contrasts within the group. And what has actually been going on is not just a sectoral change but a change in the internal social structure of these parts of the economy.

Self-employment in the Distributive Trades is primarily in retailing. These individual and family concerns have more in common with the small companies of the clothing industry than with the new, high-technology small-capital sector typical of electronics. This is 'the old petit-bourgeoisie'; individual proprietorships with little capital backing, maintaining a fairly precarious existence, in aggregate terms declining and constantly under threat from larger, corporately-organised capital. This is the corner shop, the independent chemist and the independent late-night food store. In a real sense this part of 'the service industries' is still undergoing penetration by fully-capitalistically organised concerns. Supermarkets increased their share of the grocery market from 44.3 per cent in 1971 to 59.2 per cent in 1979. The advance of the chain-store, the expansion of multiple-outlet retail concerns, and the growing organisation of these independent enterprises by group suppliers and the like, represent not simply the victory of big firms over small but a change in the dominant form of relations of production and capital organisation; a change in the internal class structure of ownership.

The kind of small firms and of self-employment which is expanding in the service sector is in stark contrast. This is particularly true in Insurance and Banking and Professional and Scientific Services (the composition of Miscellaneous Services is more mixed). Here we are talking about accountants, lawyers, those running private education and medical services, and research and development agencies. It is a mixture, in other words, of high-status professionals[15] and new entrepreneurial capital servicing expanding high-technology industries. In simple sociological contrast to the shopkeepers of the Distributive Trades, these people, above all, are graduates.

*   *   *

If, then, what looks like simply a sectoral shift is actually also a change in internal class structure, what does this mean for the changing pattern of geographical differentiation? First of all the spatial structure in all these cases of self-employment (and also of the smallest firms – for which precise regional figures are not available) is necessarily that of simple concentration. In all cases there is, obviously, local control. Geographical differences in self-employment derive from varying rates of growth and decline and from contrasts in social characteristics (status, income, etc.). Table 4.2 shows regional variations in self-employment as a proportion of total employment in the different branches. The first point to note is somewhat parenthetic and concerns column 1. In East Anglia, the south-west and Northern Ireland the proportion of self-employment in all services is noticeably (and untypically for the country as a whole) lower than the proportion in the whole regional economy (column 1 is higher than column 2). This is in all probability due to the high presence in those regions of self-employment within agriculture – the individual-proprietorship

TABLE 4.2 *Self-employment as a percentage of total sectoral employment, by region, in 1975*

	All self-employment	All services	Distribution	Professional and scientific
United Kingdom	7.41	8.2	13.57	5.53
South-east	7.47	7.48	11.47	7.12
East Anglia	9.71	9.02	12.12	5.88
South-west	10.20	9.36	14.17	5.56
East midlands	7.14	8.70	16.58	4.67
West midlands	6.34	8.45	14.23	5.11
Yorkshire and Humberside	7.05	9.09	15.81	4.25
North-west	6.86	8.90	15.64	4.82
North	5.31	6.53	12.20	3.24
Wales	9.02	9.14	19.51	4.22
Scotland	5.80	6.48	12.04	4.64
Northern Ireland (1974)	10.48	6.38	14.29	4.26

Source: Marquand (1979, table 3.11).

working-farmer element of what we have elsewhere termed 'industrial landownership' (Massey and Catalano, 1978). The only other region which does not follow the national pattern, of self-employment being dominated by the service sector, is the south-east, where the proportions are about equal. In this case the difference from the national average is more likely to be due to a higher presence of self-employment in manufacturing, thus confirming the analyses both of small firms in the clothing industry and of the geography of entrepreneurship in electronics.[16] Again, reflecting the historical structure of manufacturing and also the dominance of primary industries, in this case mining, it is noticeable that the north and Scotland have the lowest overall proportions of self-employment.

But what interests us mainly at this point is the considerable variation between services in different regions. Here it is the comparison between Distribution and Professional and Scientific Services which is important. Look first at the variation in self-employment in Distribution. What this reflects is primarily the degree of penetration of more advanced forms of capital, a low percentage representing a high level of penetration and vice versa.

The northern region has a long tradition of large co-operatives and the importance of small, independent traders is correspondingly less than in regions like the North West and Wales (Bennison and Davies, 1977, p. 9). Overall, the noticeable thing is the lack of bias of self-employment in Distribution towards the south-east of England. Indeed, the South East has the *lowest* proportion of Distribution operated on the basis of self-employment, and a Development Area (Wales) has the highest. 'In distribution, self-employment is remarkably high in Wales, and high in the east midlands, indicating the survival of the independent and suggesting relatively little penetration by national and larger local shops' (Marquand, 1979, para. 3.17).

The situation is precisely the opposite in Professional and Scientific Services. Here the south-east is far ahead in its proportion of self-employed, followed by East Anglia. The proportion in the south-west is just on the national average, and all regions apart from these three are below it, with the north having a particularly low level of self-employment in these services. There is thus a clear line across the country, from the Bristol Channel to the Wash, south of which there is a higher-than-national representation, proportionately, of these high-status, high-income forms of self-employment and north of which the proportion is lower, and considerably lower, than the national average.

If we now put all this together, how do the pattern, and the changes in it, relate to the forms of geographical differentiation already described? There are two aspects which are important: the social status of the jobs involved, and the degree of local control implied. The picture is clear in relation to type of employment. It is the south and east of England which has captured the bulk of the high-status, graduate-filled type of self-employment. The shift in the nature of self-employment in services, therefore, further reinforces the disparities in social composition which are implied by the uses of space in the industries already discussed.

The pattern of local control is more complicated. In the distribution trades, the degree of self-employment is still higher in many of the peripheral regions than it is in the south and east. But it is precisely this form of autonomy which is declining. Again, although the amount of self-employment is low in the south-east this does not mean that the distributive trades in that region are externally-controlled at regional level. For self-employment in this branch is being replaced by chain-stores and supermarkets, etc., the bulk of which are multiregional and have their headquarters in the south-east.[17] This disparity between regions is further emphasised by the dominance of the south and east of England in the fast-growing parts of self-employment.

There has, then, been a shift both sectoral and social in the nature of self-employment in services, and this has been integral to its changing spatial form. Further, the emerging geographical pattern, in its regional variations in occupational status, rates of growth (in terms of employment and in terms of accumulation) and levels of local control, reinforces many of the aspects of geographical inequality which have already been documented in the electronics and clothing industries.

Other consumer services: private capital and the State

The rest of the service sector is best dealt with by taking 'place in the economy' as the initial criterion of sub-definition – the distinction between consumer and producer services. It is this differentiation which most clearly segments the sector, coinciding both with contrasts in the nature of ownership and, through the very immediate relation to different markets, with contrasts in location. But, as we shall see, there are important subdivisions.

Take consumer services – that is, those service industries which are directly related to the living conditions of the population. This part of the economic system is controlled and organised in three different ways in the United Kingdom at the moment. The smallest part is that of self-employment and family-ownership, which has already been dealt with. Second, there are consumer services which are run straightforwardly as a basis for capitalist accumulation – that is, those in which private accumulation is not incompatible with the reproduction of the workforce to the levels determined by the history of interclass relations. Third, there are those consumer services where this politically-arrived-at level of reproduction *is* incompatible with the requirements of private accumulation and where services are provided by the State, frequently on a non-commodity basis. In the United Kingdom, much of the public-sector provision of such services derives historically from the fluctuating consensus of post-war years.

From the evidence available it would seem that it is only in certain consumer services controlled by the public sector that the geography of employment does not simply reproduce and reinforce the kind of spatial inequality which results from all the other spatial structures examined so far.[18] Such publicly-provided consumer services include educational and health services and also the operations of the local State.[19] In terms of wage earners, therefore, they are fairly heterogeneous. They include both high-status professional employees, such as doctors, groups such as teachers, social workers and administrative workers which have over the last two decades been undergoing a process of 'proletarianisation' in terms of working conditions and social status, and manual workers in, for instance, local government and the health service. All these groups have been important components of the post-1966 increase in trade union membership (NUPE, NALGO, CPSA) and their militancy and political stance have undergone an important transformation over the same period.

What distinguishes the geographical structure of such public-sector consumer services from, say, electronics is that this wide diversity of employment, in terms of occupation and status, is not organised into such a rigid spatial hierarchy. Indeed, each type of employment is fairly evenly distributed in relation to population (Marquand, 1979), certainly in comparison with all the other parts of the economy we have examined so far. Kirwan (1981) shows that this broad picture remained up until 1979, though with a slight weakening in the position of some of the Development Areas. In part, of course, this distribution results from the nature of the service itself (it has to be spread out for the services to be accessible). This is not, however, a sufficient explanation. Were the same services controlled by private capital it is unlikely that such a relatively even geographical distribution would have resulted. This is not to argue that there is equal provision of public-sector consumer services, nor even a truly equal distribution of the types of employment within them. There is not. There are more National Health doctors per head in the south-east than in other parts of the country. But there is an obligation on the public sector to a minimum level of provision regardless of the financial calculation at each location. This would not be so under private capitalist calculation. Were these sectors organised on the basis of private capitalist accumulation many parts of the country

might simply go 'unserved'.[20] The relations of production, therefore, and the associated nature of the financial calculations made,
have a direct effect on the geographical distribution of employment. That distribution cannot be accounted for purely by the
'technical' nature of the sector. Indeed, the private capital which is
operating within the same sectors (that is, private education and
private medicine) *is* much more biased in its distribution towards
the south and east of England.

Much of this relatively even distribution of employment in
public medical and educational services is, in most locations,
subject to 'external control' and the location of this control (the
administrative headquarters in the central State) is overwhelmingly in the south-east. But the meaning of 'external control' and its
effects depend upon the real social relations involved. As it is at
the moment the relations of external control in public-sector
services are clearly different from those in the private sector.
There is no relation of accumulation and so no geographical
pattern of appropriation of profits. Moreover, whatever the relation of external control as it operates now within the public sector,
it is open to reformulation (for instance in the direction of
increasing local democratic control) through political action. This
option is not available in the private sector. 'Public' ownership and
control is a necessary, though clearly not a sufficient, condition for
the transformation of such relationships. More will be said on this
later, but it is perhaps worth pointing out here that public
expenditure cuts not only produce an increase in unemployment
and a decline in services. Nor do they merely represent an attack
on one of the fastest-growing parts of the organised labour
movement: they also imply a reduction in jobs in one of the few
parts of the economy where the spatial structure of employment is
not massively reinforcing geographical inequality.[21]

*   *   *

Those consumer services which are produced on the basis of
private accumulation can now be dealt with quickly. What is clear
is that, in spite of having a more even distribution than, say,
producer services (see later), there are aspects of unevenness
which do characterise this distribution and some of which follow
the lines already described. Marquand (1979) is once again an
invaluable source of information and analysis. Her study showed
that 'there was nothing particularly even about the distribution of

many consumer services. Public services on the whole were evenly distributed, but areas varied widely in their endowment with private services' (para. 6.28). Moreover this inequality was fairly systematic: there is a marked tendency for certain metropolitan areas to be less well endowed than others with the whole range of private services. Finally, most of the metropolitan areas which are 'grossly deficient' in consumer services are in the Assisted Areas (para. 8.18). Even at an intraregional level, private consumer services are less evenly distributed than are public, being in general more biased towards location in larger centres (Marquand, 1979, table 4.9).

Putting it all together, then, in terms of the kind of job, and the location of ownership and control, privately-run consumer services increasingly conform to the general pattern of domination and advantage in the south-east of England. The long-term growth in importance of multiple-outlet consumer-service companies, and their increasingly interregional scope, has led also to the dominance of the south-east as a location for their headquarters. Relations of ownership and control are increasingly concentrated there. Because of the nature of their services this is a simple cloning branch-plant structure. The main distinctions in job type are therefore related to the hierarchy of ownership and supervision, and once again, though in this case there is no great number of 'higher-status' jobs, the bulk of them are in the south and east.

Producer services

Finally, producer services. The emergence of producer services as an important and separately distinguishable part of the economy has many sources. Banking and finance, the City of London, were the progenitors of British capitalism itself. The more recent emergence of a wide range of other producer services has been closely related to the development of both the technical division of labour and that within society as a whole. There are a number of rather different aspects to producer services. There are those relating to such activities as administration, control and marketing, and there are those relating more directly to production itself. The growth of service occupations of these varied types results from different, though related, developments. The growth of administration and associated functions derives from the increasing concentration of capital, from the requirements and possibilities of multi-plant location, from the increasing emphasis on and development of the marketing function, the increasing complexity of legal relations, etc. Those services more directly related to production, on the other hand, emerge with the increasing technical division of labour. The degree to which the different kinds of services are developed depends, therefore, on distinct conditions. The fortunes of banking and finance reflect the changing international organisation of capitalism. The growth of management-related services is especially responsive to the concentration of capital. Research and associated services reflect the development of technology in particular directions and the political centrality of technology-development itself.

There is also another distinction which can be made within producer services. In some cases they are internalised – provided by the firm which uses them – in others they are provided by separate companies. This distinction reflects the development of the technical division of labour giving rise to a further development of the social division of labour with the creation of new branches. What were once functions within the overall planned relations of an individual firm are now separate commercial entities bounded by market relations. Both (internal and external) services are quantitatively important and have been growing in employment terms in the United Kingdom.

Research and development, scientific and technical workers, are present in almost all industries, but their biggest concentrations proportionally are in chemicals and in the whole range of engineering industries. Quite a lot has already been said in the study of electronics about the kind of reasons behind the geographical separation of R and D within a firm's overall production activities, and about the factors which govern its location. The overwhelming preponderance of detached, but internal, research and development is within the south and east of England. Westaway's examination of major firms (1974), Firn's study of a particular region (1975), and Crum and Gudgin's complete survey (1977), come to the same conclusion. The last-mentioned authors suggest four main reasons for this concentration of corporate research laboratories in the south-east. These four reasons are:

(1)   the region's industrial structure favouring high R and D industries whereas that of other regions is either biased towards low R and D industries or towards industries whose R and D has to be located at production sites
(2)   the existence of a large potential supply of scientific and technical personnel in the south-east
(3)   the contact advantages of being near head offices and scientific centres, and having easy communications both to production sites and abroad
(4)   the past history of the acquisition of suitable sites (para. 334).

The list is interesting, if depressing. The first reason relates precisely to the concentration of industries such as electronics, which we have already discussed. The second and third reasons point to the self-reinforcing nature of this concentration, once under way.

But, as Crum and Gudgin indicate, there is a distinction, not only between high- and low-intensity R and D industries, but also between those where the R and D facilities are separately located, and those where research and development takes place at production sites. The latter situation is particularly characteristic of the engineering industries, and it obviously leads to a very different kind of geographical distribution: 'Such units tend to be small and scattered throughout the London area, the Midlands and most of the development regions' (Crum and Gudgin, 1978, para. 326). Since most internal research and development is of this type, it might indicate a counterbalance to the centralisation in the south-east of these 'high-status' jobs.

But things are not so simple. The very fact of geographical location – at production sites or separated from them – is an index, both of the nature of the R and D being undertaken, and of the kinds of employment involved. The R and D at production sites is primarily development work (the 'D' of R and D), more intimately connected with production itself, less 'theoretical' and less long-term. It also involves rather different kinds of staff. Scientific and technical workers can be subcategorised into research staff, production engineers and draughtspeople. It is the first (research staff) which are most likely to be located away from production at detached R and D sites. The second two are more often located alongside production. We already saw indications of this distinction in the study of electronics. The overall result is that the major over-representation of such workers in the outer metropolitan area around London, and in other areas in the south-east and south-west, is in the research occupations – scientists, general engineers and technicians. Production engineers and draughts-people are also more-than-proportionally present in these areas, but for them the deviation is only half as large. Moreover, several other areas, outside the south, have high proportions of draughts-people, particularly the old shipbuilding and heavy engineering areas (Crum and Gudgin, para. 85).

In other words, although areas outside the south and east are better represented in these professions as a whole, more detailed analysis reveals important distinctions. And the social character of these distinctions is clearly reflected in geographical differences. The higher-status jobs are both more distant from direct production in terms of the technical division of labour and more distant from it geographically. They are also more likely to be in the southern parts of England. There is again, in other words, a clear and mutually-reinforcing relationship between aspatial and spatial divisions of labour. In this case the greater the degree of separation of conception from execution, the greater is likely to be their geographical separation too.

Moreover, this is only research and development within manufacturing firms and therefore embedded in the division of labour within those firms. The evidence available, however, indicates that research and development which is separated off into a distinct branch of production is even more geographically concentrated, and again into the south-east. The data in Table 4.3 are taken from the study by Buswell and Lewis (1970) and show clearly both

TABLE 4.3   *The percentage of UK research establishments in the south-east of England, 1968*

Industrial firms	45.2
Other private firms	77.4
Research Associations	43.4
Government and nationalised industries	54.9
Total	50.2

Source: Buswell and Lewis (1970).

the general concentration in the south-east and the higher degree of that concentration in those parts of research which are organised into an independent branch. These figures are for 1968, but the cumulative nature of the location of research means that such an advantage, once attained, will not easily be lost. The difference between industrial and other private firms is wide and indicates that the development of the geographical distribution of employment in these activities may depend in part on the future relationship between the developments in different aspects of the division of labour. But whatever this precise balance, the rapid growth and geographical concentration which has so far occurred in research for industry is undoubtedly contributing to the further dominance of the outer-metropolitan south-east of England in the distribution of high-income, high-status jobs.

One reason frequently mentioned for the higher concentration of autonomous research services in the south-east is their attraction to the headquarters of major firms, for it is through these headquarters that research contracts are assigned. There is thus a link between the two types of producer services in their spatial concentration. The fact that detached company headquarters are also biased in their location towards the south-east, and that the degree of detachment and bias increases the larger the company, is therefore doubly important. First, it reproduces the difference in job type and in the presence/absence of control functions between the south-east and the rest of the country. On this, the evidence on the relation between managerial location and managerial function is important. While all managerial and professional occupations show some concentration in London and the south-east, there is a clear geographical split between control and executive functions. It is the former which is more often centralised and the latter more often located at production sites. Second, the concentration of upper-echelon control functions in the south-east further encourages the location there of autonomous producer services. The spatial concentration of headquarters of major corporations is clear (Parsons, 1972; Firn, 1975; Goddard and Smith, 1978) and is increasing with the increasing centralisation of capital (specifically centralisation here rather than concentration; it is mergers which appear to be the major mechanism). As Marquand (1979) points out: 'The consequences for the service sector are serious since branch plants draw significantly fewer of their services from within the region than locally-owned plants, with subsidiaries in an intermediate position. (The same is not true of purchases of material input.)' (para. 3.61). Crum and Gudgin (1978) summarise what they see as the main reason for this spatial concentration. They write

Detached head offices are located in the south-east because of:

(i)   the positive advantages of agglomeration that accrue to chairmen [*sic*] and managing directors because of the potential for extensive contacts, at a senior level, with personnel in other companies, government, finance, and from abroad

(ii) the need of finance directors to be near the City

(iii) internal linkages within firms that make it desirable that head offices should include a minimum number of non-production functions that require extensive contacts with the chairman [*sic*], managing director, and finance director. Many of these functions also derive benefits from the possibility and ease of contacts with experts in the London area

(iv) the span of responsibility of senior personnel dictating that immediate subordinates should be close at hand, except in situations such that there is a break between control and executive action

(v)   the superior facilities provided for both UK and international communications (Crum and Gudgin, 1978, para. 392).[22]

This list of factors also gives some indication of why *independent* firms producing administrative, marketing, legal services, etc., are also concentrated in the south-east. For this group, one can add to the reasons for the location of internal headquarters services the need to be near those headquarters themselves.[23] Once again, the mutually-reproducing nature of the various components of this overall concentration is very clear. Once under way, private-market mechanisms are unlikely to stop it. The SIC Order Insurance Banking and Finance is notably both the Order most clearly falling into the category of external administrative producer services and the Order which is most highly concentrated into the south-east of England (Marquand, 1979, tables 3.1 and 3.2).

This industry, of course, with its history in the early days of merchant capital, was one of the initiators of the whole self-reproducing cycle; it is now, along with so many others, caught up in the inexorable circularity.

An emerging spatial structure

These burgeoning new branches of the economy, the result, among other things, of the technical division of labour within manufacturing, are now beginning themselves to develop an internal technical division of labour with a characteristic spatial form. There is, broadly, within these industries a division between on the one hand high-status, highly paid, non-routine jobs in the upper echelons of control and professional functions, and on the other hand routine clerical work. Increasingly within the larger firms this technical division is taking on a geographical form, with the high-status jobs remaining in London and/or the south-east and the more routine work, providing only low-status and low-income jobs, being decentralised. Nor is it only private firms. A number of departments of central government have adopted a similar pattern. This is, once again, a spatial structure which divides the sexes. It is also a spatial structure which incorporates both a hierarchy of relations of economic ownership and possession and a technical hierarchy of production. It is therefore different from the cloning structure adopted by large clothing firms. But it is also different from that in big firms in electronics. For this is a different technical division of labour. Here virtually all the employees are white-collar, non-manual workers and the division is a fairly straightforward twofold one. The mixture of managers, professionals and scientific workers at the 'top-end' of the hierarchy is, however, very similar in class location to those in the upper echelons of the hierarchy in electronics, and in sharp contrast to the ranks of clerical workers.

As would be expected, big companies have a higher tendency to decentralise. This is in part because size makes multiple location easier, and smaller firms may find the pull of the south-east for the control and professional functions and staff greater than the savings to be made elsewhere on the routine jobs. For in almost all cases of decentralisation, whatever the size of firm, a head office is retained in London. In other words what is occurring is not just a geographical shift *in an industry* but the development of a *new use of space*. Again, while many moves are only short-distance ones, remaining within the south-east, it is the bigger companies which tend to decentralise their routine functions over longer distances. In contrast, the few 'whole moves' which do occur (in other words where no central office is left in London, and thus no split spatial structure is established) tend to be precisely the shortest-distance ones, remaining in the regions around London (Marquand, 1979, para. 5.36).

The reasons for this spatial structure themselves indicate some of the effects it is likely to have. There are three main groups of location factors involved, and to some extent they mirror those for the tertiary sector within manufacturing. First there are the additional costs of a London location, encouraging the decentralisation of those functions which 'can' be decentralised. The evidence is that both rent and wage costs decline with distance from London – for up to about 60 miles from the city centre. This, then, is a push factor. But it operates differentially. The second factor has already been mentioned – that of the necessity for 'contact networks'. It is one of the most accepted axioms of locational analysis that high-status people, faced with the long-term orientation decisions (which their functions at the apex of the relations of economic ownership and possession imply) require frequent face-to-face contact with similarly high-status people. This, then, is a real 'linkage' reason for clustering, as opposed to the social mechanisms discussed in the context of research scientists in electronics. But such economic reasons presumably apply more to the managerial than to the production hierarchy. The latter (the high-flying technicians and research workers) are perhaps more able to operate their residential preferences. In their case it will be the more social-class and internal labour-market aspects of location which fuel the cumulative causation. This may also relate to the different intraregional distributions of managers and scientific staff. It is the managers who tend to be most highly concentrated in conurbations. Within the south-east it is the scientific and technical workers who have the greater tendency to be in the more rural stretches of the 'sunbelt' and the outer metropolitan area rather than in London itself.

Thirdly, in the establishment of these spatial structures there are the non-cost aspects of the routine clerical workers. The LOB case study found that 'almost all firms appeared satisfied with their moves. Staff morale was almost always higher and absenteeism lower; productivity had often improved. Few difficulties were found in recruiting clerical labour locally' (Marquand, 1979, para. 5.38).

Putting all these factors together, of course, means precisely that it is the low-status jobs which are decentralised, precisely those parts of the operation which require, and generate, few local linkages and which include few functions of control. What remain in London and the south-east[24] are the high-status jobs where wage cost is not the main criterion, the overall control of the relations of ownership, and the contact-generating functions which both enable an advantage, once-gained, to become self-reinforcing and which give to a regional economy precisely that internal coherence which is being destroyed in other regions of the country. Marquand sums up the potential effects in the areas recipient of decentralised office work: 'It is important to bear in mind the disadvantages to the receiving community of relocating large blocks of routine office work there. It is unlikely that there will be many local service linkages, and there will not be many additions to the higher-level job opportunities in the area. However, there will be additional employment, particularly for women' (Marquand, 1979, para. 5.52).

Thus, all components of the private-sector service occupations confirm the south-east as the location for the bulk of high-income, high-status social groups. Table 4.4 is simple confirmation of this aggregate pattern. The boxes indicate the category of office worker in which each region is most highly represented (no regions except the south-east are actually *over*-represented in any category). The pattern is clear. Moreover, Kirwan (1981) confirms, on a slightly different basis, that this geographical bias continued through the decade. His calculations show how only the primarily publicly-controlled Education, Health and Welfare sector disrupts the consistent pattern of over-representation in the south and east and under-representation in the Development Areas.

TABLE 4.4 *Employment-based location quotients for office occupations, 1971 (England and Wales)*

	All office jobs	Clerical	Managerial	Other (mainly professional)
Greater London	1.51	1.53	1.47	1.61
Outer south-east	1.00	0.97	1.03	1.08
South-east	1.31	1.31	1.30	1.40
South-west	0.88	0.86	0.82	0.88
East Anglia	0.79	0.82	0.85	0.79
East midlands	0.81	0.81	0.88	0.80
West midlands	0.88	0.85	0.98	0.90
Yorkshire and Humberside	0.79	0.81	0.86	0.66
North-west	0.92	0.99	0.92	0.82
Wales	0.74	0.76	0.62	0.70
North	0.76	0.81	0.66	0.70

Source: Marquand (1979, table 3.12).

5
The Effects on Local Areas: Class and Gender Relations

5.1 The general and the unique

The view from the vantage point of production was provided in Chapter 4. What about the view from particular local areas? What kinds of changes have the developments outlined in the previous chapter meant for them?

One common feature of at least parts of all the 'sectors' examined in Chapter 4 was the decentralisation of 'jobs for women', and it is primarily this theme that we take up here. It is a process which has been going on since the Second World War, but it has varied in importance in different periods, and in particular was quite strong between the mid-1960s and the mid-1970s. It has involved both intraregional decentralisation away from conurbations, and interregional shifts to peripheral areas. And, as we have seen, it has involved a range of different industries. Other examples, such as light engineering, could be added. This influx of jobs, in other words, represents the common effect in particular areas of a whole complex of new spatial structures.

What, then, has been its impact? What follows are two studies of contrasting areas. This contrast is important; it shows that what at one level may be perceived as 'national' changes may vary greatly in operation and in impact between different parts of the country. The effects of this new round of investment are indeed very different in the two cases, for although both types of region are now being drawn into a similar place in an emerging wider division of labour, their roles in previous spatial divisions of labour have been very different; they have different histories. They bring with them very different class structures and social characteristics, and, as a result, the changes which they undergo, as they are drawn into a new division of labour, are also different. In the schematic and formal terms used in Chapter 3: in this process of the combination of 'layers', any one particular layer, or round of investment, may produce very different effects in different areas as a result of its combination with different pre-existing structures. What we see here are national processes in combination with and embedded in particular conditions producing the uniqueness of local economic and social structures.

The emphasis here is on the relation between industrial change and social change. As we have already argued, employment structure cannot in itself provide a complete explanation of local class characteristics. Broader social structures of community, changing patterns of consumption (see, for instance, Cooke, 1981a), changing national ideological and political climate and the marked patterns of geographical cultural differentiation – all of these will combine with changes in the social relations of production in determining both the overall pattern of class structure and the more detailed internal characteristics of classes. The concern here, therefore, is not to explain class formation but merely to draw out some of the implications of recent processes of industrial change which are one contributory factor in local class composition and recomposition. What this also allows is a bridge to be established between 'industrial' and 'social' geography. Finally, these sketches are not meant to characterise whole regions. Rather, they are studies of kinds of labour market areas which typify parts of the wider regions. Indeed, one important element of social restructuring has been the internal spatial reorganisation of these areas themselves. Class restructuring has not taken place on a given and continuing spatial base. 'Regions' and coherent local areas are not pre-given to analysis, nor are they unchanging. They are continually reproduced in shifting form as part and parcel of the kinds of processes looked at here.

5.2 The coalfield areas

The pre-existing structure

On the industrial periphery of the UK are areas where production in some of the basic industries of imperial Britain has for long structured the overall pattern of economic life. The focus here, although it broadens to consider the wider regions, is on the declining mining areas, the towns of the coalfields of south Wales, the north-east of England, and central Scotland. The slightly shifting spatial focus reflects the changes going on. Certain characteristics and processes can only be examined at the wider regional level. More important, the mining areas are no longer as self-contained in terms of population and employment as they once were, and the influx of new industries has been a prime cause of this opening out. Spatial reorganisation is an important aspect of industrial reorganisation, and 'regions' are a product of such processes. In these areas industrial change has broken down a pre-existing coherence and homogeneity. The 'localities' with which the analysis starts do not have the same validity or boundaries by the end.

The areas differ in detail both in the sectoral balance of new employment, and in its effects. Although mention will be made of some of these differences, the emphasis here is on the broad structure of similarities. If there is one focus more than another, it is the valleys of south Wales.

These mining areas have evolved, as a result of their role in the previously-dominant spatial division of labour, very specific and coherent structures of economic and social relations. They were dominated by, and often developed by, the coal-mining industry. The decline of Britain's imperial position, and the collapse of the coal-exporting industry therefore entailed the beginning of their long-term economic decline. The pattern on which the newly-emerging role of these areas is being imposed, in a new complex of uses of space by industry, is thus a relatively simple one.

$$*   \qquad   *   \qquad   *$$

The most characteristic element of the class structure of these areas, in terms of numerical importance and of geographical distinctiveness, has been the working class. The very fact of single-industry dominance has been one of the conditions for creating a degree of coherence both in the internal structure of the working class and in its organisation. In most of the small mining towns the majority of those employed in capitalist wage relations have for over a century been employed in the coal-mining industry.[1] This comparative homogeneity of economic structure was reinforced in its class and organisational effects by the nature of the industry itself. In mining, the work experience of the bulk of the workers is similar, the detail of hierarchical structures is relatively underdeveloped, and a number of the potentially divisive differentiations which do exist (such as between surface and face workers) are less effective in their divisiveness because individual workers may well experience both at different stages of their working lives.[2] All this has had a number of effects. First, the working class itself, within the mines, was relatively undifferentiated. It was the kind of situation which Friedman (1977, p. 53) refers to as producing 'resonance' between workers – a basis for solidarity. Second, there were relatively few within the industry in these areas who could *not* be defined as working class. The division of labour was not developed sufficiently to form the basis of any significant element of those strata whose functions include middle-range management, the maintenance of capitalist discipline and mental as opposed to manual work.

Moreover, this dominance of a single industry was reinforced in its effects by the nature of trade union organisation within that industry. The history of sectoral unionisation which has included an important syndicalist component (see *The Miners' Next Step*, Unofficial Reform Committee, 1912) together with a very high degree of union membership, meant that a high proportion of those in paid employment in the community were in the same union. Moreover, even before nationalisation of the coal industry, this similarity of union membership was reinforced within individual communities by the fact that there would often be only a single employer to fight. The potential effects of such conditions are indicated by Lockwood (1958) and Sayles (1958), who find that worker resistance is greater in coherent communities dominated by one factory or one industry. In this case it was both. Indeed, the growth of unionisation in mining was mainly through strong district associations which were frequently jealous of their autonomy (Beacham, 1958, p. 146; Francis and Smith, 1980). Not only, therefore, were these communities highly proletarianised, but also their potential for organisational and political unity was high.

Of course, while these conditions may make organising easier, they don't guarantee a particular response. Trade union coherence and militancy also require active political organisation. The inter-war history of the South Wales Miners' Federation was in fact a constant battle against *dis*unity between workers of different companies and pits (see the Beacham reference above) and between the Federation and the 'scab' union. There have, too, been long periods of relative quiescence and submission (Allen, 1982; Cooke, 1981b). Coherence of industrial structure in itself guarantees nothing. Nevertheless, these geographical areas and the unions associated with them have, both symbolically and actually, throughout this century been centres of strength for the trade union movement in the United Kingdom.

It has, however, been an organisational strength of a particular kind. It is economically militant. In 1974, of course, it led to the resignation of the government; but the record over the longer period is equally notable. Beacham (1958) reckons that from the thirties to the fifties miners, a mere 4 per cent of the economically active, accounted for over one third of the losses caused by industrial disputes in Great Britain.[3] But this is also a unionism which is defensive of status within the working class, a status based not so much on craft skills and higher wages, as, say, with engineers, but on closed-shop solidarity and a clear identity of job. The National Union of Mineworkers was a leading union in the fight for the closed shop, and was one of the first to win recognition of the principle from employers (Beacham, 1958, p. 146). It is a status which has a basis, too, in pride in the physical toughness of the work. This is a pride which refers itself to masculinity, a characteristic based not only on the nature of the work but also on the complementary lack of paid employment for women. This, as Beynon (1973) says is 'the solid, traditional heart of the British labour movement' (pp. 70–1) – with all its positive collectivism, its militant strength, and its social conservatism.

These characteristics were not simply a product of what might be called 'purely economic', still less 'locational', mechanisms. Even the single-industry nature of these areas, and consequently their relative coherence, was also the result of social and political processes. First, the lack of paid work for women. All these areas had, and in varying degrees still have, very low female activity rates (with the exception of the large towns and the conurbations, which are, in any case, off the coalfields). In the colliery towns the rate was sometimes extremely low. The increase in paid employment for women began in the Second World War, but even in the mid-1960s in some towns it was as low as 20 to 25 per cent (Department of Employment and Productivity, 1970). This seems more than anything to have been a result of the nature of the work done by the men (in particular the fact that it demanded large inputs of domestic labour, and the fact that it was often shift-work) and of the primacy accorded to that work. As Humphrys (1972) points out, women's 'place was clearly seen as being in the home looking after the breadwinner' (p. 30). Secondly, there seems in a number of cases to have been an active policy of keeping out alternative employment for men. The dominance of these local labour markets by single industries was not simply a result of location factors. The National Coal Board, for instance, seems to have guarded rather jealously the monopoly of the male labour force which it held in the north-east (Hudson, 1982). Thirdly, very little competition for this labour was generated locally by the rise of indigenous firms. This, again, is a characteristic which these older coalfields, of south Wales, of the north-east of England and of Scotland, have in common. It is also, as we shall see, in part a product of the class structure associated with the dominant industries.

In all these ways, then, in the lack of job opportunities for women, in the lack of alternative jobs for men, in the lack of a locally-owned 'small-firm-sector', the coal industry (and in the broader regions other industries such as steel) determined the conditions of existence of other (actual or potential) parts of the local economy. And those conditions were determined by mechanisms both economic and extra-economic. There were other effects, too; on the potential (or lack of it) for local financing (Humphrys, 1972), on the establishment only of sectors very directly related to the main industries, and even on the spatial structure, which itself was a constraint on incoming capital (the export-orientated north-south communications system of the Welsh valleys is a very good example). It is in this sense, rather than just numerically, that the coal industry has dominated the employment structure of these areas.

*   *   *

Compared with the overwhelming preponderance of the working class, other classes have been much less important. There has been, however, quite a significant and fairly long-lasting traditional petit-bourgeoisie. Such a class seems to have existed in all the older coalfields but it was particularly strong in the Welsh valleys. The existence of a large number of smallish, relatively isolated communities, together with the influence of the physical structure on communications, encouraged a relatively high level of local, and locally-owned, services (Humphrys, 1972, p. 28). Sometimes the union itself would be involved in running local community services, particularly in welfare, education and recreation (Department of Employment and Productivity, 1970; Francis and Smith, 1980), but there was also a significant degree of private local ownership. The extent to which this traditional petit-bourgeoisie has hung on varies considerably between areas, but the structure of small communities has again increased its longevity. Segal (1979, p. 214) points to both the smallness of the local population bases and the limited purchasing power and range of demand as discouraging not only the development of local consumer-goods production but also the entry of fully-capitalist retailing chain-stores and the like.

In contrast to this presence of the traditional petit-bourgeoisie, there has been a very low level of development both of a new petit-bourgeoisie and of small entrepreneurial capital. As we have seen, the lack of the former is in part due to the absence of any significant managerial hierarchy or independent technical functions within the dominant industries. The lack of any important development of small capital seems to be related to a whole complex of causes. Certainly, cultural factors have played some part, but, as Humphrys points out, it 'seems reasonable to speculate' that the supply of investment funds and entrepreneurial talent within the region has also been largely affected by the nature and organisation of the dominant industries (p. 31). The dominant industries in this case include not only coal-mining but also metal manufacture. The same arguments apply to heavy engineering, more important in the north-east of England. The influence of these industries (or actually of their social organisation) has varied both between regions and over time. In south Wales, the semi-colonial nature of much of the early development of capitalism had its effect. In the early days, the siphoning-off of the available investment funds and the domination of much of the development by English capital (Lovering, 1979) were of particular importance. And the characteristics of the industries themselves have not been conducive to the formation of such strata. Both the occupational structure and the large size of individual works, together with the fact that single works often dominated whole labour markets (Gudgin, Brunskill and Fothergill, 1979) have in this sense been negative influences. These latter influences have also been important in the other coalfields. Segal (1979) provides a detailed analysis of the characteristics of the past industrial structure which have contributed to this aspect of class formation in south Wales, west central Scotland and the north-east of England. He summarises them under three heads: the nature of the traditional products and the associated labour processes, the nature of the individual companies engaged in the production of these commodities, and the geographical settlement pattern which was associated with the industries (pp. 214–5).

Finally, in none of these coalfield areas, nor in their wider regions, is there now a local capitalist class of much significance in terms of commitment to industrial production within the areas. Again, the picture varies a bit from region to region. In south Wales, this characteristic is more accentuated than in the other coalfield areas, certainly in part as a result, once again, of English domination. This was particularly true of the metal industries; the coal industry itself had a greater presence of Welsh capital, and its structure seems to have had much in common with that elsewhere (Carney, Lewis and Hudson, 1977). The decline of the coal industry, however, changed the 'regional' nature of that capital. In coal production private capital was replaced by State ownership, enabling the former to continue to accumulate by further diversifying its investment, both outside the sector and outside the region. In south Wales indeed what was once big capital seems to have abdicated any connection with the region even more than has been the case in the other coalfield areas. In the north-east of England, without a colonial aspect to its development and with a greater presence of engineering in the wider region, there was a greater initial presence of a genuine local ruling class. But here, too, there has been a long process of diversification, out of the initial sectors on their decline (and not only with nationalisation), and out of the region (see Benwell Community Project, 1978a). It now retains neither the coherence of its former hegemonic role within the region (and the real strength of that former role is well documented by Benwell CDP) nor the high level of commitment of its own investment resources to that region. The point is that these regions tend to have a capitalist class which is regionally much less distinctive than is their working class. For the working class this differentiation is both a source of strength (in terms of regional coherence) and a potential source of weakness (in terms of insularity, for example). Capital – at least, large and medium capital – has achieved a far greater degree of supraregionality. It would be wrong to suppose that there is nothing 'local' at all about capital in these areas, as the Benwell Community Project pamphlet *The Making of a Ruling Class* points out for the north-east of England, but in purely economic terms it is now increasingly merged into international capital.

*   *   *

All these characteristics have in turn formed one basis for the development of others: electoral domination by the Labour Party, a labour movement whose demands focus on State intervention, and a politics of regional consensus. Labour support among miners is greater than among any other group of manual workers. A number of the 'variables' which, in the past, have been said to produce a Labour vote come together here: the traditional industrial occupation, the self-contained communities, the intergenerational similarity of work, the high level of unionisation (Blondel, 1977, p. 64). The NUM has a major role in the Labour Party. In 1970 it was only the eighth biggest union in the country, but it still had as many candidates and MPs as the engineers' union, the AUEF, which was four times larger. The fact of geographical concentration has certainly been part of the explanation for this continuing influence (Blondel, 1977, p. 210).

The dominance of the Labour Party in these mining areas has been associated with a particular kind of old-style Labour (and labour-movement) politics – a politics very much based around demands for State intervention and State control. Coal, and indeed most of the major industries of the wider regions, have, on their decline, been brought under State ownership. The regions themselves are often spoken of as 'nationalised'. Strong demands have also been made on the State from these regions for welfare provision to stave off the wider effects of decline (Carney, Lewis and Hudson, 1977; NALGO, 1978) – a demand for State action which has for long included as a major component a claim for specifically regional assistance.

With such a large and strong working class addressing itself mainly to the State, what of the political role of the remaining local representatives of capital? Unable to pursue their interests through local electoral politics, an avenue blocked by the dominance of Labour, they have, especially in the north-east, built up an influential role in regional plan-making and in regional para-State institutions and the like (Segal, 1979). The Northern Industrial Group of the 1940s was the birthplace of the North East Development Association and of many lines of policy which continued into the 1970s. The old regional families have dominated the non-elected State machinery and important regional institutions. 'These include several official and semi-official industrial development bodies, the New Towns and Newcastle University. In this way Tyneside's old ruling class has been able to implant within official thinking its own definition of the problems affecting the region, and advocate solutions that best suit its own material interests' (Benwell CDP, 1978a, p. 63).

Thus, the leaders of local industry, even if retired from their ownership of the region's major sectors, retained an important political influence. Moreover, this local hegemonic role was frequently endorsed by at least the leadership of the trade unions in the region. What was effectively constructed was a politics of consensus about 'the needs of the north-east'. And such a consensus was necessary if a policy in many ways determined by locally-based capital was to be implemented by local authorities which were firmly in the hands of the Labour Party (Carney, Lewis and Hudson, 1977, p. 65). In Wales, a not-dissimilar consensus has been constructed (Rees and Lambert, 1979). Here, however, the notion of 'the region' as a simple and non-contradictory entity is based more on nationalism than on the presence of a locally-hegemonic ruling class. In considering the 1967 White Paper, *Wales: the Way Ahead*, the nearest thing that Wales has to a national plan, Rees and Lambert suggest that it is a clear expression of the 'regionalist consensus' which had developed by the early 1960s about the nature of the Welsh regional problem, the goals of Welsh economic development, and the means for their achievement: 'It is a "consensus" in that it cuts across the divisions of Welsh society, embodying both organised labour and capital, and the political parties' (p. 10). The numerical dominance of one class has been an important basis for this. Cooke (1981b) talks of 'the mystical image of a classless society which has traditionally served a variety of political interests so well' (p. 1). And the content of the policies focused on good old-fashioned State intervention: 'The "consensus" clearly held that State intervention in the form outlined in *Wales: the Way Ahead* could solve South Wales' remaining problems' (Rees and Lambert, 1979, p. 14).

The impact, or 'the combination of layers'

It was into this context that came the female-employing, low wage branch plants discussed in Chapter 4. It was a new phenomenon. Women's employment in these areas has been increasing since the Second World War (which seemed to provide the necessary economic stimulus and ideological rationale to begin the process of raising the traditionally low female activity rates), and coal-mining has been declining, in employment terms, for much of this century. But the process has accelerated, and with it the starkness of its impact, to reach a peak between the mid-1960s and the mid-1970s.[4] Neither are these the only new sources of jobs in these regions; Chapter 4, after all, looked only at a few sectors. However, they do probably form the most important component of the industrial changes going on in these areas, particularly in terms of social impact.

In the wider regions a number of other manufacturing industries continue to be important (apart, that is, from steel, shipbuilding, etc.). Chemicals and vehicles are good examples. Both provide a range of jobs – including skilled and well-paid ones – for men, but they also share the characteristics of the spatial structures discussed here in being subject to external control and generative of few intraregional linkages. And examination of employment numbers throws doubt on how important these industries will be in job terms. Table 5.1, taken from a trade union compilation of 'the most important Welsh industrial investment projects announced or carried through during 1977' (and thus including these sectors of heavy capital investment), shows how even major projects can result in little new employment. A quotation from a *Sunday Times* survey (9 March 1980) helps put the bare numbers in that table in some kind of context: 'Alan will almost certainly be sacked from the Port Talbot mills on the principle of last in, first out. "I'm going to try for a job in the new Ford plant at Bridgend – they surely can't close that." He'd heard there were 2500 vacancies –

TABLE 5.1   *Industrial jobs created in Wales, 1977*

	£m	Permanent jobs created
BSC Port Talbot	835	−1000
BP Chemicals, Barry	33	0
Texaco and Gulf, Milford Haven	350	200
Ford, Bridgend	180	2500
Dow Corning, Barry	18	−600
Duport, Llanelli	20	0
Alphasteel, Newport	70	850
Total	1506	1950

Source: NALGO (1978, table 4).

and 15 000 applications to fill them.' Even in the broader regions, therefore, the new jobs for men are fairly limited.

That context helps account for the international and interregional competition which is let loose every time a car firm hints that it might be thinking of establishing a new facility. Employment in car manufacture is, then, important, as is employment in a number of other industries generating jobs of a similar type. The increasing participation of women in the wage labour force was not the only thing going on. Socially, however, it was of crucial importance.

So what have been the effects on the social structure of these areas of the combination of the continuing decline of the old use of space with the increasing importance of their insertion into a new spatial division of labour?

*   *   *

First, this shift in economic role and structure has not had negative effects on, nor been opposed by, the remains of regionally-owned medium and large capital. Indeed, as we have seen, such capital has been important in forming the plans and policies which enabled the entry of the new forms of production, and it has participated in, and to some extent benefited from, the process by its involvement in the financial and property sectors. Benwell Community Project (1978a) documents the role of the old local bourgeoisie in building societies, and land and property dealing and development in the north-east. So the previous strategy of diversification has enabled capital not only not to be harmed too much by the decline of the industries in which it was originally involved but also (to the extent that it has not abdicated altogether – as in south Wales) to benefit from the next role to be played by 'its region' in the national and international division of labour. Moreover, to the extent that this capital is still involved in industrial production within the wider regions it is more a question of its participating in the process of multinationalisation than of being harmed by the entry of new, much larger, capitals. The kind of labour which it requires, still being largely male, is not suddenly boosted in its bargaining power by increasing demand. The incoming multinationals seek a higher proportion of female labour, while the bargaining power of the men is kept slack by the continuing redundancies from the basic industries. Moreover, to the extent that this capital had formed itself into a local 'establishment', it has not been unseated from this position either. In all these regions the professional and institutional infrastructure and the prominent positions in political and civic affairs, although by no means so dominated as in the past by the 'leaders of local industry' (Benwell CDP, 1978a) have certainly not been taken over by the new managerial personnel of the incoming sectors.

This lack of attachment to the region on the part of the new management strata (and consequently the lack of challenge to the old hegemony) is related once again to the organisation of production – to the satellite and production-only status of much of the incoming industry (they don't need the local university), the associated lack of senior management, to the fact that individual managers see the job – and thus the region – as only one step in a career structure, and to the greater diversity of the incoming new industries (Segal, 1979, pp. 217–8). So, while it is certainly true that the whole notion of a local establishment being dominated by anything called 'regional capital' is on the wane, to the extent that such a phenomenon does continue to exist it is still firmly in the hands of the capital based in the previous spatial division of labour.

*   *   *

In contrast, what remains of the traditional petit-bourgeoisie *has* suffered a decline, in particular as locally-owned shops are pushed out of the market by big retailing firms. This, of course, is not a new process, and it is one which is at different stages in different regions. In south Wales, Humphrys (1972) identifies the 1960s as the decade when the invasion really took off (p. 56). In so far, then, as the old petit-bourgeoisie can no longer reproduce itself as a class and in so far as it is being replaced by the wage labour of chain-stores, there is a process of proletarianisation going on. But this is not an aspect of change of which too much should be made; it is extremely small in scale.

The effects on other non-working-class strata have, however, been considerable. The incoming industries exhibit a more advanced division of labour in the sense of the separation of control from production. They have longer hierarchies of administration and control; top managers can be distinguished from a whole series of middle ranks. It is, however, mainly middle and lower management which is based in these areas. The combination of this increasing separation of functions with the growing centralisation of capital means, as we have seen, that more and more regions are subject to external control and the coalfield areas are no exception. The combination of their pre-existing economic peripherality and their lack of attractions either environmental or cultural – for upper management – means that the functions of real economic control of the means of production, and some of those of possession, are carried on elsewhere. This is true of all the incoming sectors in that they are all largely subject to 'external control'. Further, in those industries where there is also a production hierarchy, it is the more 'professional' functions, those with higher status and greater individual job control, which can be, and are, centralised away from these regions. In terms of Wright's analysis these people would precisely fall into the category of semi-autonomous employees, occupying a contradictory location between proletariat and petit-bourgeoisie. The upper echelons of the managerial hierarchy on the other hand occupy a contradictory location between proletariat and bourgeoisie, though with a far greater affinity to the latter than to the former. The development of the division of labour, which means that these functions come to be performed by separate groups of people with identifiable social-class characteristics, has enabled also the geographical separation, and removal, of the elements of conception and control.

The functions of low-level technocrats and low and middle management *have*, however, tended to locate within these regions of direct production. To a large extent this geographical location is necessitated by the nature of their functional relation to the process of production. What it is important to note here, however, is that the very fact of the separation-out of these functions through the developing division of labour has contributed to a blurring of the former starkness of the capital–labour confrontation in these regions. Thus, there has been a growth in these regions of middle management and technocratic strata through the very emergence of separate functions.

Here the question of 'regionalisation' comes in. These middle managers and technocrats are less likely to live on the coalfield itself. Spatial reorganisation within these areas, and their integration with the wider region, is part and parcel of social reorganisation. In relation to South Wales, Rees and Lambert (1979) write. 'The division and polarisation between the valley communities and other parts of South Wales have a clear class dimension. Hence, it is arguable that the changes that have taken place in the nature of the economy in South Wales and the consequent shifts in population have resulted in what may be termed the "embourgeoisement" of the settlements of the coastal plain. It is here that those parts of the State administration which have been moved from London are located; it is here that the many immigrants of managerial and executive level who have come with UK or multinational firms to work for a spell in the region find homes' (pp. 33–4). Given the functions which they perform, middle management and production-based technicians, unlike top management and strategic R and D, cannot remove themselves entirely from the region, from the place of actual production. But *within* the region, the separation-out of these functions has been accompanied by geographical and social separation. The relation between social distance from actual production and geographical distance could not be clearer.

The absolute increase in the wider region is important to note, for it is often claimed that one of the main problems of the wider regions of which the coalfields are a part is their lack of white-collar, managerial and technical jobs. As we saw in Chapter 3, this is to miss the point. What has happened is that the pushing forward of the division of labour has both increased the absolute number of such jobs in these regions and at the same time, because of the removal of the top-level functions, increased the difference

TABLE 5.3 *Age-specific activity rates for men, 1971: a comparison between regions*

	Age: 40–44	45–49	50–54	55–59	60–62
Wales	98.0	97.1	95.5	91.9	78.7
Assisted areas*	98.2	97.7	96.6	94.2	84.1
Great Britain	98.3	98.0	97.2	95.3	86.6

* Comprising the North West, North, Yorkshire and Humberside, South West, Scotland and Wales.

Source: *Welsh Economic Trends*, no. 4, quoted in NALGO (1978, p. 4).

the male activity rates for the older age groups have declined, but also that even among those still considering themselves to be economically active (or potentially so) the unemployment rate is higher and increasing faster than for other male age groups.

Finally, of course, what is really wrong in an immediate sense with the new jobs is not that they are for women but that they pay low wages and involve little interest or job control, and this applies also to a growing proportion of the jobs which are taken by men.

The basic industries of these regions, and not only coal-mining, have since the early 1960s been subject to intense pressure to increase productivity. Those who have kept their jobs have often seen considerable changes in the nature of the labour process and in work practices; changes which in turn have involved a shift in the skill composition of the workforce, often towards deskilling, and with a related loss of autonomy. But the changes experienced by those who have found jobs in other industries have been even greater. Few of the previously-dominant industries in these areas, even in the wider regions, employed Fordist forms of organisation of the labour process. This is obvious in coal-mining and also in steel, but it is true also of the heavy engineering industry, which has been based around the production of small numbers of large-scale, often individually-specified commodities (Massey and Meegan, 1979). Such forms of production involve far greater individual control over the job than do those of the newer, incoming industries where production is more often based on conveyor-belt or related principles, and with a fairly high degree of subdivision of tasks.[6] There is therefore under way a process of conversion of the workforce of these regions to the greater discipline, and the reduced autonomy and job control, of the modern factory. Report after report discusses the 'problems' of 'attitude to work', of absenteeism and high turnover, the difficulties of the 'acclimatisation' of ex-miners. Figure 5.1 gives a good indication of the kinds of social processes this entails; the quotations are taken from a government study of the redeployment of miners after a major closure. And it is not just the workforce which has to acclimatise; management, too, is new to the job, or at least to the region. Figure 5.2 is taken from another survey, this time undertaken by the Rubber and Plastics Processing Industry Training Board. It points to the problems created not only by a workforce new to factory discipline but also by a management only recently arrived from outside the area. What confront each other in these factories are workers used to greater independence, collectivity and individual job control, and a mangement, unused and sometimes insensitive to local attitudes, anxious to make its mark and be off.

This, then, is the other end of the increase in professional, technical and craft functions in the south-east of England and adjacent regions. While at one end of the social spectrum of the employed population these jobs are increasing in importance, at the other they are mirrored in jobs involving only repetitive tasks. The changing technical nature of industry, and the greater degree of division within the labour process of the new industries, are not only producing new ranks of these 'semi-autonomous workers', they also involve the removal of such autonomy and individual control over the labour process in regions where such things were once important aspects of work, and important bases of solidarity and organisation (Cooke, 1981b).

These, then, are some of the changes in the structure and composition of the working class to which the changing balance of spatial structures within industry has contributed. This changing balance has also disrupted the level and type of labour movement organisation. First, instead of the focus of the economically-active community being around one industry and one company there is now a disparity both of branches of production and, even more particularly, of employers. The individual plants are often smaller. The basis for coherence and solidarity which existed in the single-industry/single-owner mining towns is disappearing. Friedman (1977) has pointed to the difficulties for working-class organisation which such heterogeneity of work-experiences may produce.

Although ex-miners were by no means the only, or main offenders, some employers thought that pit work tended to bring about its own attitude to days off. Thus it was understandable, and not particularly reprehensible, that men would hesitate to go to the pit if they were not feeling really well, not only because of their own health but also because of the element of danger involved if their own work were below par and caused any hazards to their workmates. Another reason for absenteeism at pits was probably the need to arrive in time for the cage which would not be usually running if men arrived half an hour late for work. It was, one employer said, necessary to emphasise to ex-miners that if they came in a little later for a good reason, ('chest cases' were often unwell in the morning) the only penalty imposed would be a small loss of pay. The more serious aspect to absenteeism among ex-miners appears to be a long standing tendency to take the occasional day off, but employers referred to the need for a firm approach to this early on in the man's new employment.

Comments on particular visits

A.   *Autolifts and Engineering Co. Ltd., Stanley, Co. Durham*

5.   Mr. Aaronson spoke highly of the training potential and performance of the ex-miner employees. They had settled down well as welders, semi-skilled and skilled machine tool operators and precision fitters and he thought that some of the camaraderie of the pit had transferred to the floor. He had himself fostered this aspect to working relations. There had been the occasional case of the older, less fit worker, who was finding his new work and life difficult. However, quite apart from the humanitarian aspect, it had been well worth trying to re-settle such men since they had often been

integral workers at the pits in their time, and had considerable standing and influence with the other ex-miners.

6.   There was, however, some problem about absenteeism, although Mr Aaronson thought that its incidence lessened as the men settled down. Mondays off were the initial difficulty.

B.   *Elliott Bros. (London) Ltd., Cowdenbeath, Scotland*

1.   This firm, a major employer in his mining area, is concerned with the manufacture of two types of products, control valves and computers, with a separate labour force for each: ex-NCB employees are employed more on valve manufacture, where they make up about 24 per cent of the total employees (CSS). Only 8 per cent work on the computer side, where many of the operations are done by women. The firm's Personnel Manager, Mr. Forsyth-Brown, pointed out that about two-thirds of the ex-NCB men were trades-men, since there were NCB engineering workshops at Cowdenbeath.

2.   Those ex-miners without special training had had the choice of taking a GTC course, or having their training with the firm, beginning on an unskilled basis.

On GTC training, Mr. Forsyth-Drown thought that the cources, although short, served a valuable purpose in acclimatisation to industrial life-especially for men like ex-miners, who needed some form of transitional period. If they later went on to work in other trades (or even did not get any jobs, for a time) their GTC training would not have been wasted, in that it exercised their 'learning processes' and so made them more amenable to subsequent training or re-training within a new industry.

FIGURE 5.1   *The acclimatisation of labour*

216

4. The firm placed great importance on personnel selection, and at all interviews both the recruiting department and the Personnel Division were represented. No special age limits were set, but the age-factor was regulated. The interviewers looked, essentially, for the right attitude in an applicant: the technical demands of the job were not excessive, but it was vital that he really wanted to do it. Ex-miners, particularly, needed to realise that they could not, at once, step into work paying NCB rates on the grounds that their family commitments made this necessary or that 'They' had rightly put industry here to provide ex-miners with a high level of wages. But there were instances of ex-NCB men who had done very well indeed: thus two senior despatch and stores employees had come from the pits and one ex-face worker, now 28, had made such brilliant progress that he was now on the sales staff. He has shown, clearly, that he had the right attitude to work and been willing to take advantage of the opportunity offered.

5. On absenteeism, Mr. Forsyth-Brown thought that pit work differed from factory conditions. A miner might well be a hazard to his 'mates' if he came to work when not feeling well and again, there would be no point in his arriving late at the pit, since 'the cage' would have gone down without him. On these, and other, points, ex-miners needed to be 'educated' and the firm took great trouble, and spent a great deal of time, in holding discussions with their workers on a variety of subjects. It was necessary for management to appreciate that many new workers, including the ex-miner element, were not used to factory life, and if a firm, but understanding approach was taken from the outset, absenteeism, and other problems, could be lessened. Ex-miners were, however, by no means the only, or chief category as regards absenteeism and were reasonably 'stable' employees: only 18 had left the firm since 1964, mostly for understandable reasons of health, or self-advancement.

C. *Aladdin Industries Ltd., Pontardawe, Wzles*

2. Mr. Marshallsea thought that ex-miners missed the challenge of the pit and, above all, the freedom to move about. Many found difficulty, at first, in being 'tied' to a machine, and the days were long. There was no significant difficulty about taking the odd day off, but miners were, perhaps, more likely to go sick around holiday periods.

Conclusions

The essential factor is the will to work.
Employers generally speak well of ex-miner employees, with, however, the one difficulty of absenteeism. There seems to be some long-standing tendency of miners in this respect but, as some firms have mentioned, the attendance record has improved with time and good management control. All in all, therefore, it seems that with good planning and, above all, with far-sighted training arrangements, employers coming to 'mining' areas can rely on good service from ex-miners.

Source: Selected quotations from the Department of Employment and Productivity (1970).

The problem of labour and industrial relations in South Wales is fairly
well-known.... Where a problem exists, it is frequently described in terms
of 'attitude' to work, and subsequently considered in terms of absenteeism
and labour turnover.
'Attitude' is a matter of subjective assessment.... However ... the
difficulties could perhaps have been better anticipated in the translating of
the skills and relationships associated with the traditional industrial activities
of this part of the Principality into the industrial hierarchy patterns of more
'modern' industries.
Absenteeism is looked upon by many managements as having social
overtones, relating to the meeting of personal needs within a particular and
close community.
High labour turnover* is brought back into the context of 'attitude', and
explained in terms of the work content and the absence of any sense of
'belonging' such as was characteristic of, say, coalmining.
Such problems are more apparent in the 'valley' areas, where new industries
are being introduced through a variety of governmental and
quasi-governmental arrangements, than in the established main centres of
industrial activity such as Cardiff or Swansea. This suggests that the
problems are essentially temporary in nature. However, they justify the
drawing of serious attention to the fact that companies moving from an
English region into the development area of Wales should not assume that
the production efficiencies and costs achieved will be comparable with those
they had previously considered their norm....
  Having recognised the problems associated with labour,... management
may frequently not have been as adaptable, perceptive and accommodating,
as the situation merited. Further, that management might well consider
what measures it could take to improve its own understanding of these
particular problems.

FIGURE 5.2 ... *and the acclimatisation of management*

* 35% per annum for South Wales, compared with a 25% average for Great Britain
  (Department of Industry, 1978).

Source: (Department of Industry, 1978).

A particularly glowing report of one aspect of the success for
capital of this whole process of reorganisation in these areas was
given in the *Financial Times* survey mentioned earlier. It discussed
the Fife coal-field and in particular Glenrothes; the militancy of
Scottish miners has already been noted. The *Financial Times*
reported: 'One very good reason for industrialists' high opinion of
the Fife town is the almost uncanny strike-free record in Glenrothes. Industrial relations in new towns are generally better than
in older metropolitan areas, but Glenrothes' officials are con-

vinced that their record is second to none in Western Europe'
(Drummond, 1978).

Of course, one of the initial attractions of these areas for these
industries was the existence, alongside the reputedly militant
males, of a completely unorganised female potential workforce. It
has already been pointed out that the female activity rate in these
areas was previously extremely low. A large proportion of the new
workforce has thus had no previous experience of capitalist wage
relations and, at least in recent decades, male dominance has
excluded women from many forms of public and political activity.
No basis of union organisation exists, therefore, and the fact that
these new workers are female compounds the difficulties, both
because of the problems for women of doing two jobs and
attending union meetings (for while women may be doing an
increasing share of the breadwinning, men do not seem to be doing
much more domestic labour), and because of the traditional lack
of commitment to organising women workers in the trade union
movement as a whole. The high level of long-term unemployment
weakens trade union organisation still more, acting as a visible
threat, its existence reverberating through the rest of the community.

Finally, the increasing degree of external – particularly multinational – control poses new and different problems for working-
class organisation – the feeling of negotiating with ghosts, that
those on the other side of the negotiating table have little more
control over, or even knowledge of, decisions than have the
unions. It is a situation which not only poses new difficulties for
trade union negotiation and action but which also again reflects the
changed status of management in the region, the removal of its
real control, its reduction essentially to functions of administration
and direct supervision. Again, however, it is worth remembering
that external control as a legal form is not new. There has been
external control through nationalisation in the coal industry for
years. Legal form, however, is not everything. As was argued in
Chapter 4, external ownership which is also public ownership in
principle gives the potential for local control and democratic
forms. Such indeed were the hopes of many in the industry when it
was nationalised. Those hopes did not materialise. The combination of this with the drastic job reductions and rationalisations
which have subsequently been pushed through has engendered a
significant political shift – a profound disappointment with the

actual effects of public ownership, and a lack of resonance now of the traditional calls for nationalisation and State intervention (Coventry, Liverpool, Newcastle and North Tyneside Trades Councils, 1980). One of the centrepieces of the Welsh TUC's strategy in the early 1980s is a proposal for workers' co-operatives.

It is clear that the context for trade union organisation in these areas has changed dramatically. What is not yet clear is how successful this will be from industry's point of view. Certainly some of the old bases of male, economistic trade-unionism have been attacked, and that is important for capital's way out of the crisis. It is also true that initially weaker workers have been taken into the workforce. But all that industrial change can do is to alter the preconditions for organisation. It remains to be seen how much longer the new workers will remain unorganised and unmilitant.

*   *   *

Meanwhile the areas have changed in other ways. Their spatial form has been substantially reorganised and the old spatial coherence of the local economies has broken down along with the social homogeneity. What were once socially and economically homogeneous areas within the broader regions may become more varied; what were once economically isolated communities may be integrated with their surrounding area. The spatial structure of even quite small areas may undergo substantial reorganisation. The internal, local spatial structure of a particular region is just as much precondition and product of economic development as is the broader geographical structure. In the valleys of south Wales the once coherent and closed communities of the pits have for long been undergoing a process of integration into a different, more complicated and heterogeneous network of spatial relations. Much of this internal spatial restructuring started with the decline and reorganisation of the old industries, particularly coal and steel. In these industries, attempts to increase productivity have involved both concentration into larger units and often fairly substantial intraregional shifts (for instance, in steel, towards the coast). Much of the New Towns policy, an important part of the strategy of spatial reorganisation, has also been associated with the decline and 'rationalisation' of the older industries.

The location pattern of the incoming industry has also been very different from that of the old. Humphrys (1972) points to two main elements in this pattern in south Wales. On the one hand, the large factories lie isolated on greenfield sites outside the towns: spacious, single-storey, windowless boxes housing modern flow-line manufacturing techniques. On the other hand, the smaller factories cluster together around the shared infrastructure of bleak trading estates. It is an industrial landscape shared by many Development Areas.

The most favoured location of the newer industries is close to a motorway. In Wales, by the mid-1970s, 70 per cent of all the overseas-owned establishments had been set up within ten miles of a motorway (Davies and Thomas, 1976, p. 57). Contact with 'the outside world' is more important than links within the region.[7] It is an evident reflection of the growing role of these areas as a place of production of consumer-related goods for the UK and the EEC. Many of the new manufacturing industries produce consumer goods or components of consumer goods for mass markets. But less than 4 per cent of the total British population lives in south Wales; the major markets are in the midlands and south-east of England. Inputs and components, too, often come from outside the region. The 'transport demands of the new industrial economy could hardly be more different from those the inherited transport network grew up to serve' Humphrys, (p. 66). The completion of the Severn Bridge – carrying a motorway – in 1966 was symbolic of this changing relation between the economies of the areas which it linked.

In all this restructuring of spatial relations within the region, the State, both central and local, played an important role. The industrial estates (the publicly-owned ones), the motorways and the New Towns were all State organised and financed – though they provided private industry with some lucrative projects. In a more general way, too, this provision by the State of the new, and massive, conditions of production was already (apart, that is, from regional policy incentives) a considerable subsidy to private industry. Hudson (1979) has documented the process – the reorganisation of spatial form through the State's use of 'devalorised capital' – for the case of Washington New Town in the north-east of England. Very similar shifts, disruptions and desertions (and accompanying political battles) have also taken place in south Wales – the move from the valleys to the valley-mouths and the coastal plain being the most obvious, and at the broadest level, and closely paralleling the west-east shift in the north-east of

England. Cooke (1981a) points to an increasing geographical as well as social polarisation in Wales.

Apart from providing a more appropriate spatial structure and new physical infrastructure, the New Town strategy has been a means of reorganising the labour force in a way which would meet the requirements of the new and changing industrial structure. Housing policy can also work to this end. In the north-east, for example, the distribution of new stock – mainly in Washington New Town – particularly affected new households looking for a place to live for the first time, and the pattern of in-migration and of Development Corporation lettings contributed to a bias towards younger people. Between 1968 and 1972 over 50 per cent of male 'heads' of in-migrant households were aged 34 years or less (Hudson, 1979, p. 47).[8] This is in stark contrast to the average age of redundant miners. The patterns of new housing and of job opportunities may be mutually reinforcing in excluding older redundant men from further 'economically-active' life.

So the spatial reorganisation of these regions provides new conditions for accumulation not just in a physical infrastructure sense but also through the part which it plays in social restructuring. It is a phenomenon which Rees and Lambert (1979) and Rees and Rees (1981) refer to in their discussions of south Wales. It is also part of the breakdown of previously-definable subregions and localities.

For local populations all this has often meant either residential change or having to travel much further to work, or both. Many of the older settlements have become essentially dormitory towns. A new economic and social subregionalisation emerges. From a situation where most people lived close to work and even walked there, there is now a complex pattern of commuting. The study of Ryhope colliery found that, while the colliery was still open, 67 per cent of people working there lived less than a mile away, and another 15 per cent between one and two miles, that for 90 per cent of people working at the colliery travelling time was less than 15 minutes, and that 81 per cent walked to work. Hudson (1979) describes some of the complexities of the commuting pattern which has now evolved. And the situation is similar in other old coal-fields. The *Financial Times* reported 5000 people travelling each day into Glenrothes. In south Wales it is a pattern which has been emerging for some time. In the whole of that region 'The area with the largest net outflow of workers daily ... is the Rhondda, where it amounts to a staggering 9,370 workers daily ... One out of every three workers living within the Rhondda travels elsewhere daily to work. It will be remembered that the Rhondda has also experienced the largest loss of population over the 1931–66 period' (Humphrys, p. 94). Disaggregation of the socio-economic group and industry of these outcommuters (see Table 5.4) makes clear that this is not much contributed to by movements of miners themselves. It is overwhelmingly to manufacturing and service jobs.

With this social diversification and spatial dislocation has come a breakdown, too, in the old, predictable politics. The long-held hegemony of the Labour Party machine and the ideology of labourism is under challenge.

In Wales this began as early as the 1960s with the growth of Plaid Cymru. Here 'devolution' and nationalism had been developing as elements of the regionalist consensus since the 1960s; they were 'not a sudden phenomenon born of 1970's crisis' (Rees and Lambert, 1979, p. 23). And in the ideology of that nationalism 'the valleys' played a central role: 'one of the central themes of the Public Inquiry on the proposed New Town at Llantrisant was the extent to which the development would destroy what was assumed to be the "way of life' characteristic of the industrial valleys. The possible destruction of this "way of life" was viewed as self-evidently deleterious to Wales's national development (Inspector's Report, 1974)' (Rees and Lambert, 1979, p. 15).

In this context the economic changes from the late 1960s onwards were of particular significance, and the spatial restructuring which they entailed, the shift away from the valleys, undermined one of the central elements of the ideological basis of consensus. Both continued decline and spatial reorganisation pointed to the failure of the existing policies and politics to achieve their stated aims. While the rhetoric insisted that the modernisation of the region as a whole 'should occur in locations aimed to restore the economic and social vitality of the valleys' (Rees and Lambert, 1979, p. 15), that apparent political aim was sacrificed to the kinds of spatial restructuring required by a motorway-based, externally-reorientated form of accumulation.

In all these areas 'modernisation' has failed for much of the population. But it is not just the policy of modernisation which has

TABLE 5.4   *Workers living in Rhonda in 1966 but working else-where*

Socio-economic Groups	
Employers, managers and professional workers	430
Intermediate and junior non-manual workers	2350
Skilled and semi-skilled manual workers	6570
Unskilled manual workers	1270
Others	920
Industry Groups	
Primary (Orders 1 and 2)	1540
Manufacturing (Orders 3–16 inc.)	4830
Construction (Order 17)	1950
Services (Orders 18–24)	3190
Unclassified	30

Source: Humphrys (1972, p. 94).

failed; so also has the form of politics on which it was based. 'Labourism' has neither prevented further decline nor offered a positive way out. While the old defensive militancy is being sapped, there is less in the way of new socialist politics to replace it. Indeed, some aspects of that old strength are now themselves the problem 'by 1966, the major obstacle to the advance of socialism in Wales had become the organisations, the traditions, the practice and the populist grip of institutionalised labourism whose connection with socialism had become as mythical as the Mabinogion' (Williams, 1981, p. 17). And all this both draws on and increases the impact of the social changes now under way . . . the increasing differentiation within the working class, the rise of middle management and related white-collar strata. It is fertile ground for new politics and a politics which, given the experience so far, might reject the label 'socialist'. Of Wales, where the changes are perhaps the most dramatic, Thomas (1982) writes: 'The South Wales valleys are actually existing labourism. Nothing has brought socialism more into disrepute in Britain, except perhaps the experiences in some parts of northern England, than the "socialism" of the Labour Party in South Wales. . . . This is not a case of a proud and utopian socialist mythology falling into disillusion, it is rather the actual destruction of the socialist idea itself by the practice of labourism' (pp. 34–5).

5.3 A different kind of 'periphery': the case of Cornwall

The pre-existing structure

The old coalfields are, however, by no means the only areas which have been experiencing growth through decentralisation of these kinds of economic activity and these kinds of jobs. Cornwall, too, has been on the receiving end of the process. And here the social structure into which the new industries have been implanted could hardly be more of a contrast. Instead of the combination of State ownership, big industry and working class, Cornwall has much more significant proportions of small industry and self-employment, and a much lower importance of large industry and highly-organised, relatively well-paid male working class. All this, of course, in some measure again results from the very different role which this part of the country has played so far in the UK economy, in other words its previous location in a wider territorial division of labour.

The class structure of Cornwall is not dominated by an industrial proletariat. In sectoral terms, its historically-important industries have been agriculture, mining and tourism. Only the second of these, together with some small presence of shipbuilding and engineering, form a basis for the *kind* of unionisation which exists in the coalfields, and even then these industries have been on a far smaller scale.

Moreover, while Cornwall is like the old coalfield areas in having had historically a very low female activity rate, the reasons for it have been very different. The Cornish County Structure planners (Cornwall County Council, 1976b) analyse this in detail and argue that the most important explanations are: first, a straightforward lack of work opportunities, second, the availability of seasonal work during the summer (which they argue is probably a factor reducing the willingness of married women to seek year-round employment), third, the fairly high overall level of unemployment, and fourth, the geographical nature of the County. This last, the distribution of much of the population in villages and small towns, is argued to be 'perhaps the most important factor affecting married female activity rates' (p. 99). It lengthens the average journey to work and this in turn particularly affects women as a result of the restricted public transport facilities and of their having less access to the 'family' car. It is, therefore, often more feasible for women 'to help on the farm, take in summer guests or to be less well off and stay at home' (p. 99). For similar reasons this geographical structure reduces not only the number but also the range of jobs within easy access. The continuing influence on activity rates of these problems of accessibility is confirmed by the variations within Cornwall between urban and rural areas: 'Rates were up to 8–9% lower in rural areas than in the towns in 1971'. It is a clear example of the interaction between geographical forms and patriarchical structures. It is of course probable that, precisely because of the higher proportion than nationally of small capital and self-employment, particularly in agriculture, more women were involved in economic productive activity than the statistics show. But this kind of work has been declining dramatically – between 1961 and 1971 the number of female workers actually registered in agriculture declined by 12 per cent (while nationally there was an 11 per cent increase) (Cornwall County Council, 1976b). So the labour-reserve which was one of the attractions to incoming industry was 'produced' by a very different social history from the apparently similar labour-reserve not that many miles away in south Wales.

It was, moreover, a reserve with different characteristics. A married woman in this region was less likely to be 'just' a wife and housekeeper to a 'breadwinner' and more likely to be involved in some form of non-domestic labour; keeping a bed-and-breakfast boarding house, maybe, or doing (paid or unpaid) work on the 'family' farm. In both the coal-fields and Cornwall one of the attractions to industry has been a reserve of labour which – so management hopes – will be relatively cheap, but above all non-combative. In both these areas the reserves are in large measure composed of women. But the vast variety of ways in which patriarchy works, and in particular its geographical variations, means that the processes by which such characteristics are produced, and therefore the indices on which they can be measured, also vary widely. While many married women in Cornwall may not have been confined to the home and to domestic labour, and may even have appeared in official statistics as 'economically active', they have nonetheless rarely been working in capitalist wage relations and even more rarely within any labour process likely to provide the basis for solidarity and workplace organisation. In the Cornish economy, especially that part in which women were directly involved, a kind of petit-bourgeois self-sufficiency and independence had been the order of the day. Such social characteristics are very different from those of the coalfields, but they lead to a crucial similarity – they provide what seems like infertile ground for trade union organisation.

Cornwall also differs from the old coalfield areas in having been historically a low-wage economy. This appears to be the result of industrial structure, low relative wages within that structure, and the availability of seasonal work. Seasonal work provides extremely low (annual) wages to those who have to rely on it altogether, but it can also have the effect of subsidising other wages, so that people can supplement the income from their regular employment by temporary or part-time jobs. On the other hand, if the pay from their main jobs were higher, the need for this might not arise (Cornwall County Council, 1976b, p. 40). Such employment may, in other words, mean that wages in other sectors can be held down. Depending on the number of people who have *only* seasonal work, it could also produce a divergence between average wages per job and average income per head. It is parallel to the subsidisation of wages in capitalist firms by subsistence farming in peasant areas.[9]

Finally, the structure of the ownership of production is different in Cornwall. Neither locally-based big capital nor State-ownership is of much significance. In contrast, small capital and self-employment are far more important than in the coalfields. As a proportion of the population, self-employed people are 2.5 times more important in Cornwall than nationally, and Cornwall has been and still is much more dependent than the economy as a whole on profits from such sources and from professional earnings (Cornwall County Council, 1976b, p. 41), much of it coming from agriculture and from tourist-related activities.

The impact, or 'the combination of layers'

Until the 1950s, the manufacturing basis of the Cornish economy was in decline, but in the mid-1960s this long-term trend was reversed and manufacturing firms began moving into the County. The in-migration reached a peak in 1969 and 1970, but in the mid-1970s was still well above the figure for the mid-1960s. The new employment is very similar to that arriving over the same period in the coalfield areas. Two-thirds of it is in branch plants, which in turn are the element most heavily biassed towards female employment (about 60 per cent). Many of the manufacturing jobs are in instrument and electrical engineering, and new jobs in services have also been important.[10] The largest factories (in employment terms) have gone to the towns (themselves small), but the biggest impact has been in rural areas.

So what, then, of the effects of the entry of these new forms of employment, and how do they compare with the impact in the old coalfield areas?

Descriptively, some of the implications have been similar: the size of the population engaged in wage labour has increased, again primarily because of the incorporation of more women (almost all of them married women) into the workforce, and unemployment in some areas has increased.

But it is the differences which are striking.

In the first place, the implications for the working class are far less dramatic. There has here been no existing and well-organised working class whose economic base is declining. The extension of the workforce, and particularly its extension to more women, and in low-paid jobs, has therefore not resulted in the same contrasts: it has not produced the same bases for conflict, it has not been associated with such a lowering of wages (relatively – see later). The structure of unemployment is also changing in a different way. While in the coalfields an increasing proportion of unemployment is among older men, without jobs for long periods, perhaps permanently, in Cornwall male unemployment has also been significantly boosted by in-migration (Perry, 1979, p. 5). There is less implication in Cornwall, therefore, of the changing structure of unemployment undermining a previous base of trade union strength. Indeed, in Cornwall the dichotomy between working class and capital has if anything become more clear-cut as the growth in wage labour has been accompanied by a continuing decline of the local petit-bourgeoisie and small capital. Even the growth in tourism has been of a capitalist variety, much of it focusing on self-catering holidays and employing unskilled and transient workers (CIDA, 1977, p. 12).

The structure plan report covering employment and income

(Cornwall County Council, 1976b) comments on this changing balance between social groups and points out that the trend over the 1960s was for income from profits and professional earnings to grow much more slowly in Cornwall than in England and Wales, whereas the other sources of income, such as earnings from employment, grew at a similar rate (p. 41).

There are, however, changes going on *within* the structure of self-employment and small capital. While some of the older-established 'native' self-employment is on the decline, there has been a significant influx of 'small entrepreneurs'. This is what most differentiates the new industry in Cornwall from that in the coalfield areas. It is worth pausing for a moment, therefore, to examine its impact. How much is this group going to contribute in the future to the development of a locally-owned basis of accu-mulation, and to the growth of the local capitalist class and the extension of the working class? The answer, on all counts, seems to be: not much. First, in terms of its current employment of workers, this group is unimportant in comparison to the branch plants established by bigger firms (Cornwall County Council, 1976b; Perry, 1979). Moreover, although the combination of decline of old and influx of new has indeed produced a change in the nature of self-employment and small capital, it is not a straightforward shift from traditional petit-bourgeoisie to profit-maximisation and accumulation. A study of the 'independent small-firm manufacturing sector' in the county distinguished be-tween different types of small firm on the basis of whether they were local or immigrant and whether they were new or existing companies. What is interesting is that, although there were certainly contrasts in attitudes to growth, *none* of the groups conformed to the classic model of capitalist accumulation. Certain-ly, the traditional sector tended to be of the 'simple-reproduction' variety, but the new entrants do not live up to the fashionable image of the striving entrepreneur either. Thus

Differences in the groups' attitude towards growth were ... discovered. Established local entrepreneurs tended to show satisficing rather than optimising behaviour and to be people-rather than profit-oriented. New local entrepreneurs were craft-rather than market-oriented. Owner-managers of incoming complete transfers, attracted by a combination of regional aid in a pleasant environment, were not strongly growth-oriented, and were the group most conscious of capital-transfer problems on retirement. The new incoming entrepreneurs came closest to the stereotype of a profit-maximising entrepreneur, but even this group contained many redundant or disenchanted executives from larger corporations, strongly attracted to Cornwall by the environment.

Thus something of a semi-retirement culture prevailed, but, of course, the typical small firm everywhere stays small, and there is no reason why it should expand just to suit the wishes of regional planners. Boswell's (1972) studies of small firms in the Midlands, (assumed to be one of the more growth-oriented regions) led him to conclude that only about half of them were expansion-minded: our survey would suggest a proportion that was a good deal less for Cornwall (Perry, 1979, pp. 19–20).

It is worth at least considering whether the very fact of such a response to this kind of environmental attraction (as opposed to the more 'social', and economically more central, environment of the 'sunbelt') on the part of owners of capital might imply a relative lack of interest in profit-maximisation. In Perry's survey, *all* the new entrants had first got the idea during a holiday visit to the County.[11] Certainly, this group is unlikely to become the basis of an extension to a local, truly capitalist, class; still less the basis for locally-controlled accumulation. Similarly, the implications of this kind of entrant for employment *growth* in the future, and therefore a further expansion of the working class, are not major. Finally, and for all the same reasons, it does not provide much basis for self-reliant regional growth. Indeed, even worse, it was precisely this kind of in-migrant which was most subject to fluctuations in employment as a result of changing macroeconomic conditions (Cornwall County Council, 1976b). In particular, they were more subject to decline in the recession of the 1970s than were branch plants. Certainly, a strategy based on these kinds of firms is unlikely to be a viable basis for regional economic resuscitation.[12]

This consideration of the nature of in-migration points to another contrast between the changes going on in Cornwall and those under way in the coalfields. In both, as we have seen, there is a growth of the 'new middle class', taken at its widest, but the composition of this expanding social stratum is different in the two cases. In particular, too, they are different in their relation to the region. In Cornwall, the group consists importantly of the self-employed and small employers. They are defined in terms of their relation to the ownership of (small-scale) production. The growth of this group in Cornwall is, moreover, very much a reflection of its desire to be there. It has been attracted by the characteristics of the region itself. The situation in the coalfields could hardly be more different. Here, the dominant elements of the new white-collar middle class consist of middle management in large corporate and State organisations. Very often they, too, have been drawn in from outside. But in this case it is rarely a voluntary move, rarely a result of the attractions of the region; all too often the region is merely a transient, and often unwanted, staging-post in a climb up the corporate hierarchy.

But the main difference in impact between the two regions is that, while in the heavy-industry areas capital has not been adversely affected by the entry of the new industries, in Cornwall it seems to have witnessed the process with some horror. The most important bone of contention concerns competition for labour, and specifically wages. Cornwall has for a long time been a low-wage area, and the Structure Plan Reports bemoan the fact that the jobs being created there in the 1960s have done little to change this. One of the recommendations of the Plan is to create conditions to make it easier for women to do paid work. The Cornwall Industrial Development Association is the main, and vocal, representative of locally-based capital, most of it small, and including some already-established in-migrants. Its reply is unequivocal. It agrees that women have to travel further to work than men. This, in CIDA's opinion, 'seems ... to conflict with the natural preference of the people' (p. 49). It agrees with the Council that the difficulty women have in getting to work is unlikely to be overcome 'unless either earnings increase so that more wives can afford their own transport [!], or public transport services are increased without large fare rises'. This, thunders CIDA, 'is precisely the kind of spurious "growth" which we seek to avoid. The problem, as we see it, is *not* to bring in more female-intensive factory jobs; the problem is *to take work to women to carry out at or near home*' (p. 49). In other words, the aim should be to open up the labour market rather than add to the demand for labour and so push up wages. What seems to be going on here, in other words, is a tussle over spatial form, in which the ideology of the family is invoked, but which is actually about who taps a labour supply and how. Internal spatial structure is important in this conflict. CIDA rejects all notions of growth poles, 'growth triangles' and industrial estates – all, presumably, designed to collect together sufficient labour and provide adequate infrastructure for relatively large incoming plants. In contrast, the demands of local industry are for opening up access to the in-situ labour markets of small villages.

The argument also takes place over aggregate supply–demand relations. The Structure Plan recommends that more opportunities should be provided for people to increase their earnings and, quite explicitly, that the pressure of demand for labour should be increased. All this goes down very badly with the Cornwall Industrial Development Association. The findings of the Structure Plan are based on a detailed analysis of the causes of low pay and in particular of the relation between pay and activity rates, as it might operate in Cornwall. The analysis points out that in Cornwall both female activity rate and average female wages are relatively low. It shows that it is possible for employers to offer lower wages than in many other places because there is a higher proportion of women potentially able to work but not actually working, and hence less pressure of demand for labour (p. 45). In reply, CIDA, in a substantial document on regional policy and the Cornwall Structure Plan, mounts a sustained attack on branch plants employing women and owned by big capital. For while it argues strongly for more high-level technical and administrative employment, more unskilled and semi-skilled jobs represent to CIDA only more competition for labour. Unlike the dominant elements of capital in the heavy-industry regions, these industries are still locally-owned and based. They have not been nationalised, they have not diversified geographically, they are more likely to overlap in their labour requirements with the incoming industry, and they are just not large enough to compete. They argue that

> What our planning seeks to avoid is this: individual decisions by one group of people unwittingly upsetting the environment of other people . . . if we encouraged the inflow of new Companies

with high 'multiplier' effects, this would put great pressure on the local labour market (possibly causing some other firms to become unprofitable), more people would be attracted in to fill the jobs at enhanced salaries, and in a recession the problems would all be magnified as the process went into reverse (CIDA 1977, p. 102).

The provision of more jobs and/or higher wages and salaries can only add to the already-strong pressures arising from inwards migration and are not therefore prime objectives. Indeed, it is doubtful whether Cornwall could *ever* have a high wage economy: it would lead to a loss in profitability and additional unemployment, and hence would be self-defeating (p. 119).

Other reservations about attracting new industry also find expression. CIDA is unreservedly pro-market and wary of State intervention. Keegan (1980) characterises the regional CBI (South West) as the most right wing of the CBI's regions: 'the land where they still believe in the phoenix'. Moreover, given what has already been said about the nature of small capital and the new petit-bourgeoisie in this part of the country, it is not surprising that environmental issues play a role in local politics. Cornwall had the only county council with an Ecology Party member. What is ironic is that such considerations are probably more important to the in-migrant (but already arrived) self-employed and small entrepreneurs and also, of course, to some professionals, such as estate agents, than they are to long-established local capital. Indeed, CIDA's initial formation (in 1974) was in part in response to a focus on environmentalism and conservation which had tended to reflect *all* industry in a bad light (Wight, 1981). Environmental arguments are, however, nonetheless useful things to mobilise in the overall resistance to too much incoming new industry. By the turn of the decade CIDA was building links with the conservationists, arguing that "it is not so much a question of industry versus the environment; it is more a matter of large scale versus small scale. Policies which encourage developments on a small scale would meet the aspirations of all interests" (quoted in Wight, 1981).

CIDA's own recommendations, unsurprisingly, concentrate on

policies to encourage the development of existing and locally owned businesses. In brief

(i)   Our primary concern is to encourage the effective development of *three natural 'basic' industries* which are already key components of the local economy ...

(ii)   There is a whole range of indigenous *local services* and other industries which have developed naturally without any long-term need for artificial financial support ...

(iii)   We believe that the best way to promote the economy of the region is to promote the products of the region. We place particular emphasis on actively promoting the sales of craft industries in international markets ...

(iv)   Priority should be given to activities which fill identified gaps in the local economy, by *import substitution*, by recycling and by *better use of local resources* ...

(v)   There is a particular opportunity to be developed in taking work to women to be carried out at or near to their homes ...

(vi)   We *reject* the policy of deliberately attracting a general inflow of up-country operations, whilst welcoming those which decide to set up locally without the need for artificial aid (pp. 4–5).

Local electoral politics here are dominated by the right, in the guise of Independents. The Labour Party hardly gets a look-in. Yet here local State and local capital, on the issue of industrial development strategy, are opposed. Local capital sees the County Council as an arm of the central State, interventionist on behalf of big capital, and pursuing a strategy called 'modernisation' which is in fundamental opposition to the interests of established local employers. The contrast with the coalfields is complete.

6
Class, Politics and the Geography of Employment

6.1 Spatial structures and spatial divisions of labour

A major change is under way in the geography of industry and employment in the United Kingdom. A number of things are going on at once: the continued reproduction of the old form of the regional problem with the seemingly endless decline of employment in sectors such as coalmining; the new, and presently accelerating, collapse of manufacturing employment – a result of both the slowdown of the international economy and Britain's declining manufacturing role within it; and the increasing importance within the national geography of different kinds of spatial structures. All in all, a new spatial division of labour is in the making.

This new spatial division of labour is the outcome of a whole series of changes affecting different parts of the economy in different ways. Some of this is already clear from previous chapters. The overall pattern of change has been contributed to by the decline of some industries, the growth of others and the development of new spatial structures in yet others. The new geography of employment reflects a whole range of different spatial structures and it is their combination which produces a new spatial division of labour over the country as a whole. Chapters 4 and 5 have looked at only a few of these spatial structures, and have deliberately concentrated on certain aspects, but even there we saw that the general feature of the decentralisation of jobs for women was underlain by a range of different causal structures and a variety of distinct spatial structures. The emergence of a new spatial division of labour at national level does not imply that each individual part of the economy itself reflects that pattern. Just as the economic response to recession has varied between different parts of the economy so has the locational response.

The changes discussed in the preceding chapters are not new, though the period since the early sixties has seen their strengthening. Nor do they represent continuous, uninterrupted processes: even over the twenty years which our analysis has spanned there were major variations over time in the strength of each of the different components of the broader geographical shift. These variations in part reflected changes in the economic situation over that period. But that was not all they reflected, for there were also, over the same period, major changes in politics, in political alliances and in national ideology and temperament. So it has not just been changing economic circumstances which have been important but also changes in the way in which these economic pressures were filtered, moulded and translated through the prevailing political and ideological climate.

The end of the long boom saw both the widening of cracks in the national economy and the re-emergence of regional inequality as a political problem. Since then there has at the political level been a shifting search for a way out, both of economic decline and of the impasse of political class stalemate. A number of different economic strategies and political and ideological offensives have been tried. Each has been constructed in rather different economic circumstances, each has been built upon a rather different social base. From our point of view what is significant is that each has also been associated with the advance of different aspects of the long-term shifts in the shape and form of uneven development in the United Kingdom. And in each of these contrasting economic-political conjunctures, 'geography' and uneven development have played a different role.

The first major section of this chapter analyses this shifting political and economic climate and the role of geography within it. The period as a whole is divided very broadly into three: first, there was the attempt at modernisation through structural intervention, from the early sixties to the early seventies. This was followed by the relative political eclecticism of the mid-seventies, a period of 'holding the fort', but with a gradual shift within it, heralding the third subperiod, in which a social and political philosophy of individualism, competition and the market has been associated with the dominance of a strategy, in economic terms, of private-sector, market-based monetarism.

The section deals with each of these periods in turn, and

analyses the economic, and some of the political, determinants of this shifting pattern of change. It also points to the different role of 'geography' in each of these contrasting economic and political conjunctures. What emerges clearly is that, not only has each of the strategies adopted in these different periods failed to 'rescue the British economy', on anybody's terms, but each has contributed – though in different ways – to perpetuating forms of geographical inequality.

By looking again at the economy and society as a whole, picking up the story we introduced at the beginning of Chapter 4, and attempting to take seriously our earlier strictures that 'the economic' does not arrive raw at the factory gate, these analyses pull together other aspects of the backcloth to the shifts in industries (investigated in Chapter 4) and in areas (see Chapter 5). For as we have said, the 'layers' within which particular localities are embedded are not only economic; they are also political and cultural. Cornwall, and the coalfields, also went through these wider political changes, and the internal transformations which they have registered, and which we looked at in Chapter 5, must be read also through this prism.

These analyses step back and look at the economy as a whole, and at changing patterns over the country as a whole. They thereby perform another function, of filling in the partial picture we have painted so far. This provides a basis for the second major section of the chapter to pull together the threads and consider what can be learned about the particularities of the broad class structure of Britain, the changing composition of the working class, the character of its capital, and most particularly to consider how that changing social structure relates to the changing class geography of the country.

6.2 Uneven development and national politics

Modernisation

The period from the early 1960s to the early 1970s was a very particular phase in British economic and political history. Economically, the relative decline of Britain was now obvious; there was clearly a need for action on the economy. This was, moreover, a period when the world economy was still growing, and when there was still therefore much more room for manoeuvre than there was to be after 1973–4. Politically, too, the period was distinctive. Both main parties had a commitment to structural intervention in industry. The 1964 election was fought around the question of which party could most speedily modernise the production base of the economy. It was probably the period when the British State came nearest to holding together a consensus. The economy was to be saved by advanced technology, modern management and 'rationalisation'. In return there was to be a measure of reform. It was a strategy founded on an attempt to construct an alliance between big, private, 'modern' capital and Labour's base in the manual working class and, in part, the technocratically orientated 'middle strata'. To that extent the heart of the period was that of the Labour administration from 1964 to 1970, but as a whole it runs from the earlier Conservative political and ideological shift towards intervention, 'planning', and incorporation of the unions, for example through the establishment of NEDO, to the utter collapse (after the Selsdon interlude) in 1973–4.

This attempted 'alliance' was not between the whole of capital and the whole of labour. As far as capital was concerned the leading participants came primarily from big private interests in manufacturing industry. A succession of their more eminent representatives passed through State and para-State organisations. Arnold Weinstock, chair of GEC, epitomised the period. His style, uncompromisingly profit-maximising and without commitment to industrial sector, region or workforce, contrasted sharply with that in much of the rest of British industry and was proclaimed by business and government alike to be the type of management which could save the economy. The emphasis was on size and modernity. Small, 'old-fashioned' capital was marginal to the strategy, and indeed there is evidence of opposition from that part of capital, at least to specific measures (see, for instance, Jessop, 1979, p. 33). The Machine Tool Trades Association, small old capital *par excellence*, successfully opposed the MinTech scheme to introduce a Machine Tool Industry Board under the Industrial Expansion Act (*Economist*, 20 July 1968, p. 60 and 12 October 1968, p. 86). Nor was the modernising strategy given the wholehearted support of the banking sector. Indeed a degree of public conflict occasionally surfaced between banking and manufacturing – for instance in the latter's dissatisfaction with its financial and investment relationship with the City, in the oft-referred-to battle between the Department of Economic Affairs and the Treasury, and in the arguments over the property boom of the early 1970s and the notion of unproductive investment (Samuels *et al.*, 1975; Massey and Catalano, 1978; Jessop, 1979). This – capital's arm of the alliance on which the modernisation strategy was based – was new. The direct representation of manufacturing industry in the State (for instance in the shape of the DEA) was an innovation. And as Jessop (1979, p. 28) points out, until the formation of the CBI was sponsored by the Labour administration in 1965, there was no single peak organisation to represent industrial capital in Britain.

The attempt to incorporate the working class in the strategy for modernisation also included the appointment of 'its representatives' in State and para-State organisations, this, again, being a relatively new phenomenon (Jessop, 1979; Purdy and Prior, 1979). Harold Wilson celebrated this innovation (which had actually begun under the Conservatives) by delivering himself of the following:

> The TUC has arrived. It is an estate of the realm, as real, as potent, as essentially part of the fabric of our national life, as any of the historic Estates.
>
> It is not easy for many within a movement that grew out of revolt to accept all the implications of a role that now is creative, consultative and, in the central economic struggle in which this nation is involved, decisive. Influence and power carry with them the duties of responsibility. Never has this been more clearly illustrated than in the historic decision of the Trades Union Congress, fifteen months ago, to accept the need for an incomes policy which would relate the planned growth of wages to the achieved growth in productivity; which, indeed, went further, in that individual unions, many of them of great power, agreed to surrender to the central organization some part of the historic sovereignty for which they had battled for over a century (Wilson, 1974, p. 674).

The hope in particular was that the union leaders – and thereby the membership – would co-operate by bearing the immediate burdens of technical change and restructuring – in other words, of 'modernisation'. In return, there was to be a strong element of social democratic reform. Just as State intervention in industry was seen in this period in a positive light across much of the political spectrum, so also, and particularly in the Labour Party, there was a commitment to the expansion of the Welfare State. Consistent with the faith in technology (which was presumed to be neutral) and organisation (which was always seen as coming from the top down) this took the form largely of a major expansion of the State sector and a range of reforming, ameliorative measures, ameliorative in many cases precisely of the negative effects for working people which 'modernisation' was to bring in its train. The introduction of a redundancy payments act in 1965 was a classic case in point.

The third element of the social base on which this strategy drew was a large section of the white-collar strata. Industry was to be revitalised by modern management and technology, and social problems were conceived as being amenable to solution through education and 'rational', technocratic planning. The Centre for Environmental Studies was one of a wide range of institutions established during this period (including also the SSRC, London Business School and the Open University), and its early attempts to come to grips with urban and regional problems were, typically for the period, concentrated on building mathematical models of spatial interaction. (This was also, remember, the period when geography's self-definition as a discipline centred on the construction of 'a science of the spatial' in the context of a quantitative revolution. Intellectual and socio-political philosophies fitted perfectly together, and fed off each other.) In such an atmosphere technocrats, business-school managers and significant elements of the educational and social science community were central to the rhetoric of building the new Britain.

The economic strategies which characterised this period clearly reflected the alliance on which they were based, and reflected too the balance of power within it. The emphasis was on modern production industries, on size and on high technology, and there was an explicit underplaying of the private service sectors. Within the emphasis on production industries there were two main foci. First, there was to be financial restructuring and technological updating of private manufacturing, and particularly of modern capital-goods sectors. This strategy was directed primarily to those sectors where big capital was already dominant (computers, electrical engineering, cars) and the changes reinforced that dominance. There was NEDO, MinTech, the DEA, a National Plan. Productivity bargaining was introduced and the Lancaster House Conference on productivity took place amid a fanfare of publicity. The Industrial Reorganisation Corporation began its life by restructuring major sectors, smoothing the way to the centralisation of capital, providing funds for investment. It, too, concentrated on the big and the modern. And it was both characteristics which mattered. The distinction was not simply between big and little capital. Small companies in high-technology sectors and with a reputation for 'dynamism' were supported. Nuclear Enterprises, at that time an independent firm, was certainly small in employment terms, and was owned by two brothers. But it was hardly an old-fashioned family firm. It was fast becoming a force in a highly international industry. Said the IRC: 'We are taking a couple of entrepreneurs and backing them' (*Financial Times*, 6 December, 1967). In total contrast, small old-fashioned capital in long-established industries was completely external to the strategy. In face of the small capital in wool textiles, the IRC gave up. 'In industries where there is little movement, the IRC is helpless. The wool industry is a good example. The majority of firms in this extremely fragmented sector are small and family-owned. Their posture is defensive and their interest in modern management methods slight' (Smith, 1969, p. 93). But the emphasis on size was inescapable: wider economic pressures, quite apart from government stimulus, were pushing towards concentration and centralisation. There was a merger boom, especially among already-large firms (Whittington, 1972), and there was a significant increase in plant size. The strictures of the Monopolies and Mergers Commission were spirited away (McClelland, 1972); competition, it was confidently asserted, began abroad. There were relatively high levels of investment, much of it replacement investment (Treasury, 1976) indicating an updating of techniques rather than a simple extension of capacity. Indeed, the rate of growth of output began to slow while, precisely up until 1973, the ratio between the rate of growth of labour productivity and the rate of growth of output was high (Singh, 1977). All this showed up in the employment statistics. The fastest rate of employment growth (number of jobs per annum) in manufacturing was in those capital-goods industries based around new technology, particularly electronics.

The second side of the strategy towards production industries was 'rationalisation' of the heavy basic sectors. There were programmes for shipbuilding, the Devlin Report on the docks and steel was nationalised, but most of all there were massive closures and reorganisation in the pits. Much of this, and the huge job losses which it involved, was carried through with the effective compliance of the trade union leadership, though there was resistance in some industries, such as steel (Cooke and Rees, 1980). Overall, this period saw a faster annual level of job loss in these sectors than was seen either the first half of the sixties or the rest of the seventies.

The strategy was also clearly reflected in the changes in the service industries. The growth of service employment slowed, in part possibly due to Selective Employment Tax, itself a reflection of the policy emphasis on manufacturing, but there were considerable differences in the rate of employment change between different parts of services. Two sections dominated the growth in absolute terms and grew faster during this period than in the years either before or after: these were producer services and the State sector.

Producer services completely dominated private sector growth in service employment, and this was a reflection of what was going on in the wider economy: a commercial-office boom and a property boom (Marquand, 1979, para. 1.9), mergers and reorganisation in manufacturing (para. 6.20), and – very importantly – the spread of the computer (para. 1.15). The social class implication of this was that the growth in employment in these producer services 'was almost entirely a growth in higher level managerial and professional employment, as was much of the growth in office employment in the secondary sector too ... [suggesting] major changes in organisational structure and behaviour accompanying the growth in office employment in the 1960s' (Marquand, 1979, para. 1.15). It was a clear reflection of the broader changes going on in the economy and of the emphasis on modernisation and technology. So, too, was the enormous growth in State employment, in this case being at least in part a reflection of the reforming social-democratic element of the modernising alliance, part of the *quid pro quo*.

Private consumer services slowed in their rate of employment growth, however, and small private-capital services, particularly in distribution, declined. Although data are difficult to come by, it seems likely that from 1964 to the early 1970s there was a high rate of merger activity in the service sector also (Bolton Committee, 1971; Marquand, 1979). Putting this together with what we know of the service industries from Chapter 4, it seems likely that at least part of this was associated with the accelerated decline of petit-bourgeois ownership in distribution and miscellaneous services with the further extension of larger capitalist firms (Marquand, 1979, para. 1.53 and ch. 7). (Certainly distribution was the only part of the service sector which experienced an absolute decline in self-employment over the whole period between 1961 and 1975.) As in the rest of the economy, then, these differential changes within services clearly reflected both the overall economic changes and the different elements of the dominant political and economic strategy.

*   *   *

'Geography' was integral to all this. It was not just that national-level processes were differentially mapped on to the British space but that geographical differentiation, distance and locational mobility themselves moulded, sometimes even enabled, the social and economic changes which took place. The particular character-istics of the period meant that locational mobility was a potent weapon in the hands of management. In manufacturing industry this was, overall, a period of job loss, but it was a period of peculiarly 'active' job loss. Employment decline frequently took place in the context of major investment in new technology (Massey and Meegan, 1982). Such a situation provided ample opportunities for dividing the workforce, the combination of locational flexibility with economic slowdown being crucial. Thus 'geography' played an active role in the frequent coincidence in the early part of the period between technical change, or related means of increasing productivity, and locational shift. Locational change and changes in production process were often part and parcel of each other. The category of 'in transit' losses of employ-ment (Massey and Meegan, 1979) is important here in highlighting the fact that the number of jobs gained at the 'destination' end of such moves was often well below the number of jobs lost at the 'origin'. Moreover, in many such cases it was not just a net loss of jobs which was at issue but also a change in the nature of the workforce. The very fact of distance and of the possibility of locational change could often make such 'restructuring' easier for management. Above all, it frequently confused the issue. In this period new techniques, and changes in labour processes, were often introduced into the production of existing levels of output, rather than being embodied in extra capacity. This had two effects. First, if the changes were introduced on site, in an existing factory, the investment itself appeared to be responsible for the loss of jobs. 'Technology' became the enemy. New investment came to be feared as probably leading only to reductions in employment. Second, the new investment in the new techniques of production might take place in another region – in a peripheral or non-conurbation area, for instance, whereas the existing capacity was in the city. However, because this was taking place in a period of slowdown, because it was not possible substantially to increase output, the new investment in the new processes had often to be compensated for by closure of the existing factory. In this case, the issue again often came to be defined in terms of competition between different areas – those about to be made redundant in the inner cities could only too easily interpret the situation as the regions of new investment 'taking their jobs'. Had the new technique been introduced as an extension to capacity it is unlikely that it would have been fought by the unions. Indeed, it would probably have been welcomed as providing new employment. Such a situation will typify periods of growth. The real problem, of course, was neither 'technology' nor the competitive demands of workers in other areas, but the continued efforts to increase productivity when the rate of output growth was slowing down.

In other ways, too, geography was central to the period. Regional considerations and regional policy[1] were important aspects both of the construction of the political alliance of this period and of the attempted solution to the economic and political problems which presented themselves. The end of the long boom had seen the re-emergence of the regional problem as a political issue. The onset of economic problems was heralded by falls in employment in the basic industries in the early 1960s. Indeed, the very return of a Labour Government in 1964, and the full establishment of the political strategy of this period has to be seen in this context. In 1963, the Conservatives had taken firefighting measures to quell potential discontent in the worst-hit regions (the north-east of England, and Scotland). It was the beginning of the re-establishment of regional policy. In 1964 the Labour Party was returned to power with an electoral base primarily in what were to become the Development Areas and with significant promises in both the Manifesto and the Queen's Speech of a commitment to regional policy.

The strength of the Labour Party in these regions (see Chapter 5) was thus an important support of the national-level alliance while, precisely because one side of that alliance had a strongly-coherent regional basis (at least in terms of labour-movement leadership), regional policy was an important component of holding together the national politics. Both sides of this equation were to be particularly important given the serious job losses which subsequently resulted from the rationalisation of some of the core-sectors in these regions, and in particular of coal-mining. There was a real potential conflict here. On the one hand the electoral and organisational strength of the government lay in peripheral regions which were already suffering above-average, and increasing, levels of unemployment. There was real pressure, from regions such as the north-east, for action. On the other hand one of the central aims of the Wilson government in its attempt to modernise the economy was to rationalise the heavy basic sectors. As we have seen, this programme resulted in massive losses of jobs. Some 48 000 jobs were lost in the pits in Durham in just four years between 1964 and 1968. And these industries, and consequently the job losses, were concentrated precisely in the regions of Labour's base and electoral strength. Regional policy, and the promise of other jobs to replace those fast disappearing, was part of the means of acquiring the compliance of trade union leaders. Major closures in particular areas were frequently compensated for by a grant of Special Development Area status. The existence of alternative employment had always encouraged a high level of voluntary redundancy from mining, which would clearly ease any rank-and-file objection to the rationalisation. In other words, at the start of this period not only were there already calls for a regional policy, but a commitment to such a policy was to be even more necessary if the cutbacks in the basic sectors were to be pushed through. The support of the labour movement – or at least its leaders – in those regions was therefore important to economic policy-making at both national and regional levels, and in its turn, regional policy was important in gaining that support.

The significance of regional policy, however, even at the beginning of this period, also had another aspect. This concerned the reserves of labour in the old heavy-industry peripheral regions. These reserves included not just the unemployed but also the reserves of labour implied by the low activity rates in the regions (see Chapter 5). In the 1950s one of the pressures towards regional policy had been concern about the inflationary effect of geographically-differentiated pressure on the labour market (see Chapter 4). By the next decade, however, the problem was initially perceived as being one of potential 'absolute' shortage: one of the main constraints on national economic growth was expected to be a shortage of labour. The National Plan of 1965 predicted an annual rate of growth of output of 4 per cent, and the chief obstacle to the achievement of this was thought to be potential 'bottlenecks', of which one of the most important was expected to be that of labour. A 'manpower gap' of 800 000 was calculated, and regional policy, by evening-out unemployment and activity rates, was to provide half of that extra labour. At precisely that time, of course, the accelerated decline of the heavy industries, itself a product of government policy, was substantially adding to these reserves of labour, both male (through unemployment) and female (through freeing women on to the labour market). Development Areas, where regional policy incentives were available, were defined broadly, to encompass not only areas of high unemployment but also potential foci for growth, and spatial reorganisation within them (see Chapter 5) made conditions ready. The quotations in Figure 6.1 indicate the argument and also the importance of regional policy in this respect. The earlier role of helping to damp down inflationary pressures was also mentioned, but now in a secondary position. The summary of the role of regional policy added: 'At the same time a more even spread of employment throughout the country will help to avoid regional pockets of excess demand setting the pace in driving up costs and prices while there are still unused resources elsewhere' (p. 11).

Regional policy, in other words, was to be used to create space for the projected growth. Looked at another way, what this meant was that regional policy, by increasing the supply of labour, would be one instrument in breaking the increased economic power which workers had gained during the expansive growth of the previous period. In relation to 'the working class' the policy was thus quite contradictory. It was both a pay-off to a particular section of that class (a section defined spatially – the party's

---

The reserve of labour in the less prosperous regions

7. Over the last 10 years an average of 420,000 workers have been unemployed in the United Kingdom at any one time; and the incidence of this unemployment varies considerably between regions. If the unemployment rate in the less prosperous regions could be reduced to the average for Great Britain over the last 10 years (which is also the actual rate in 1964) some 100,000 more people would be employed in those regions. The main increases would be in Scotland (37,000) and Northern Ireland (28,000), and the North-Western Region, Northern Region and Wales would each gain 12,000. (In this calculation the national average unemployment rate has been taken as a convenient measuring rod; but other standards could be used, such as the lowest regional rate.) It would be imprudent to assume that the whole 100,000 addition to employment could be achieved by 1970; but with effective policies to increase employment opportunities in the less prosperous regions, it should be possible to reduce the numbers unemployed by some 50,000 during the plan period.

8. There are also some (among old people and married women, for example) who might be willing to enter or remain in the working population in certain circumstances. Activity rates of older men (the proportion of the group which is in the working population) have been declining, particularly with the spread of state and private occupational pension schemes, and the forecasts in paragraph 2 assume a continuing though slower decline. If this were halted, and 1964 activity rates maintained, there would be about 50,000 more men in the labour force in 1970. The forecasts of working population already involve a continuing increase in activity rates of married women above the age of 35; but they still assume that some 3 million married women between 45 and 65 will not be in the labour force in 1970.

9. Activity rates in the country as a whole are higher now than in 1943, at the height of mobilisation of manpower resources in the Second World War. They are also higher than in the United States and among the highest in Western Europe. But the differences between activity rates in the different regions give some indication of the scope for drawing extra people into the working population if employment opportunities were more equally distributed. Some of the differences in regional activity rates are due to variations in the proportion of the population in each region which can be regarded as potentially economically active; and the calculations in Table 3.1 make an allowance (in the second column) for those who are retired, being educated or in institutions. The third column of the table then shows that if activity rates in the regions where they are below average could be raised to the national average, the addition to the labour force in Great Britain would be around 320,000. Practically all of this increase would be made up of women. In addition 40,000 extra people might be drawn into the working population in Northern Ireland if activity rates there could be raised to the national average. It would

not be practical however, to expect to bring the whole of this extra 360,000 into the labour force by 1970. It would be a substantial achievement to get half way towards this goal.

Regional activity rates 1961([1])
Great Britain

TABLE 3.1

	Activity rate([2])	Active persons plus specified inactive([3])	'Labour reserves'([4])
	Percentages		Thousands
South East England	61.0	70.2	–
South Western	55.8	66.3	85
Midland	64.6	71.9	–
North Midland	61.4	69.5	–
East and West Ridings	61.5	70.0	–
North Western	62.9	72.0	–
Northern	57.8	66.1	83
Scotland	59.9	68.1	54
Wales	55.2	64.7	97
Great Britain	60.7	69.5	319

([1]) Employed people expressed as percentages of population aged 15 years and over. Derived from Census of Population.
([2]) Including employers, self-employed, H.M. Forces, and unemployed.
([3]) Including students, retired people and those in institutions.
([4]) Number of additional people who would have been in the working population if the activity rates in the second column were raised to the national average.

10. It may be concluded that, in addition to the possible reduction of unemployment by some 50,000, some 100,000–200,000 extra people might be drawn into the United Kingdom labour force if a major effort were made to raise activity rates in the less prosperous regions. The addition of these extra workers to the employer labour force would raise the expected increase in potential employment from the 390,000 persons shown in paragraph 2 to about 600,000.

11. The regional policies that are being developed to assist both in raising activity rates and in absorbing the regional pockets of above-average unemployment are described in Chapter 8. But in all regions there are some people, particularly among older people and married women, who may not be registered as unemployed but would welcome the opportunity of a job.

FIGURE 6.1 *The role of regional policy in the National Plan*

Source: HMSO, 1965, pp. 37–8.

political base in the regions) and at the same time it was a way of undermining the economic strength of labour more generally, but a strength which, given the geography of the previous decade's economic growth, was spearheaded by workers in the midlands and south-east.

Nor were the other determinants of regional policy simply a question of the requirements of 'capital' as some undifferentiated whole, or of some aggregated notion of 'accumulation' at national level. Regional policy was, rather, a response to the requirements of particular parts of capital. Not only was big capital expanding faster than small up to and over this period, but it was also more likely to be able both to shift geographically – or to set up branches in new locations – and to use the kind of reserves of labour available.[2] This was not, then, some kind of 'trade-off' between potential social and economic roles for regional policy, but a combination of the requirements of different parts of the social structure, the result of the historically-specific configuration of the ruling alliance. The rationale for regional policy has to be understood as a combination of responses, to social and political pressures, and to economic requirements.

Further, we have already seen in Chapter 5 that the regional bases of this alliance took a particular form. It was not just a question of country-wide alliances between social groups but of a whole series of structures, often with fairly coherent regional-level existences. Chapter 5 referred to the construction of a politics of consensus in certain regions. These were 'regional' structures in terms of both their social bases and their aims. They were constructed to address regional problems, but they were also fundamental to national-level strategy. It was through them that acquiescence was won for the modernising strategy at regional level; for the spatial, social and economic restructuring of these areas. All of this was crucial to the national strategy.

Fairly quickly, however, the 'economic' aspects of the role of regional policy underwent a shift. While much of the original argument for regional policy (in the first half of the 1960s) was couched in terms of expanding the supply of labour, by 1966 unemployment over the country as a whole was starting to rise steeply. While, given the continuing political commitment to international competition in open world markets, it was certainly necessary for industry to cut costs, and true that this could be aided by both moving in search of cheaper labour and expanding the overall supply, there was no immediate prospect of some kind of 'absolute' shortage of labour. Instead of output marching ahead by 4 per cent a year, its rate of growth fell off. The problem for the potentially expanding sections of capital became one of retaining – and if possible increasing – competitiveness rather than one of finding sufficient elbow-room to grow. In this context regional policy played a role in what came to be called 'restructuring'. For individual firms, investment grants (as opposed to the previous system of depreciation allowances) were especially useful in the context of liquidity problems and relatively low profits. In that context, regional policy and the changes in industry were mutually reinforcing. On the one hand changes in production could be a precondition for advantage to be taken of regional policy; on the other hand the grants available through regional policy could encourage or even enable those changes by subsidising the investment in the new processes of production. But not only did the economic role of regional policy change over time, its impact also varied between sectors. Most obviously, it was simply more important in some sectors than others as a factor in locational change. But more than this, regional policy combined in different ways in different industries with other developments taking place at the time. The *way* it actually operated was also different. Not all industries were 'restructuring' in the same manner. In clothing, for instance, there was no major reorganisation of production processes which enabled decentralisation. Here it was more a question of competition for labour (Chapter 4). In other sectors similar decentralisation took place without regional policy playing any role. This was the case in services (although SET may have had a differential effect). In the service industries as a whole, while overall growth was relatively low, there was still some growth and it was precisely in those parts (except for local authority services) which are less locationally tied to local population (i.e. producer services, central State, etc.). It was during this period that the spatial separation and decentralisation of clerical work began, much of it at this time going to Wales. So each of the three major sectors examined in Chapter 4, all of which decentralised jobs – and similar jobs – over the period, did so with very different relationships to regional policy.

It has been argued elsewhere (Massey, 1979) that 'the effects of regional policy' cannot be treated as a matter simply of the geographical distribution of numbers of jobs. This analysis of the late sixties and early seventies shows just how complex and changing its role, and consequently its effects, can be. But it also argues that regional policy in this period cannot be discounted as having had *no* effect. It was not simply a free lunch for big companies. In some individual cases that undoubtedly was the situation, but overall the role and place of regional policy was far more complex. Regional policy was an integral, if changing, part of both the economics and the politics of the period.

Table 6.1 pulls out some of the more specific characteristics of employment change during this period. While none of the general trends is new, or confined to this period, it is also clear that there was at this time a particular condensation of many of the different elements in the overall, much longer-term shift between national-ly-dominant spatial divisions of labour. Other changes reinforced this shift. While all the evidence suggests that the merger boom did not lead to any spatial centralisation of production it did involve increasing locational detachment of head offices and their concen-tration in the south-east. The high level of inward foreign direct investment reinforced the changing employment pattern. As Dicken and Lloyd (1980) show, the period 1963–71 was one of considerable evening-out between regions of employment in foreign-owned enterprise, reducing the previous dominance of the central regions.

All these changes reinforced the kind of long-term tendencies discussed in Chapters 4 and 5. The secular switch between spatial divisions of labour was in full swing. But the changes also occurred under a very particular set of economic and political conditions, and this influenced their aggregate effect. Although the old basic sectors were declining very fast there was also more potential for decentralisation than in either the period before (when there had been no regional policy) or the period after (when there was so much less room for manoeuvre in the economy). Thus, in compari-son with the later 1970s this period saw continued growth in those parts of manufacturing (new means-of-production industries and consumer-goods industries owned by big capital) most likely to be able to decentralise, and continued technical change which in itself, because it often involved substantial new investment, pro-duced potentially mobile employment. This was also a period of fast growth in local authority employment – the only sector of

TABLE 6.1 *Some employment characteristics of the modernisation period*

Aggregate employment change	Geographical characteristics
Decline of old basic industries fastest, and proportionately most important; mainly a result of rationalisation.	Major creation of additional labour reserves in peripheral regions.
Fastest decline of old means-of-production industries; a result both of capacity closure and of technical change.	Serious losses of jobs, especially for male skilled and semi-skilled, in conurbations and nineteenth-century industrial areas.
New means-of-production industries provide main source of new jobs outside services; partly a result of emphasis on productivity and technology.	Growth of R & D and technical occupations, particularly in the south-east. Also some decentralisation of assembly-type jobs for women.
Continued, though reduced, growth in consumer-goods industries owned by big capital.	Some continued decentralisation of employment, including jobs for women, to peripheral areas.
Fastest rate of growth in State services.	Central State: high status jobs in the south-east. Local authority employment, professional and manual, more evenly distributed.
Fastest rate of growth for producer services and period when producer services most important proportionally.	Important growth in high-status professional, technical etc. jobs in south-east.

employment which did not simply reproduce either the old or the newly-emerging patterns of geographical inequality. It was also a period when there was not only an active regional policy but one which – for the reasons already mentioned – had a heightened potential for effect.

So this period of modernisation, rationalisation and public-sector welfare produced the famous 'convergence' of centre and periphery on the classic indices of inequality. But the same period, too, saw the most pronounced shift over the country as a whole between one spatial division of labour and another. Another kind of geographical inequality looked set to replace the one which had been dominant for half a century.

*   *   *

The disintegration of the economic and political basis of this period took place gradually and unevenly. At the political level the alliance itself broke down, and conditions worsened economically. The political alliance broke down both because of its internal nature and because of the economic conditions which it faced. It is often argued that each side of the alliance collapsed because of its lack of internal coherence: that it was an alliance of 'peak organisations' (Jessop, 1979). The whole conception of reform (and indeed of 'socialism') was a 'from-the-top-down' affair, transmitted through the organs of the State. Thus on the trade union side the rank and file of the movement had little influence or control. The incorporation of trade union leadership in the State was accompanied by the growth of activity at shop steward level, and by an increase in unofficial action and factory-level bargaining. The strike-rate increased markedly in the later 1960s (Westergaard and Resler, 1975). All this was highlighted by the Donovan Commission and was probably the major preoccupation of the White Paper 'In Place of Strife'. This period saw 'a major ... change in trade union attitudes. Before 1968 ... the trade union movement put its trust in economic reform being handed down by the Labour government from above' (Hodgson, 1981, p. 75; Hughes, 1968). The Wilson government did much to dispel, at least for a while, that illusion. Grass-roots militancy increased – and the Labour leadership set about attacking it. This was the late sixties, and the more general revival of socialist political culture, and of radical movements based around groups other than trade unions, saw little attraction in the Labour Party.

There were also other more material reasons for disenchantment among those whose jobs were affected by the policies. Unemployment continued to grow apace, incomes policies were imposed and there were attacks on previously-established union rights. Technological change in industry, being introduced so late, when economic growth had already begun to slow down, provoked fierce opposition, as did – more obviously – closure and rationalisation. Arnold Weinstock became a *bête noire* of the labour movement.[3] Regional policy had contributed to the movement of jobs to Development Areas, and those regions' relative unemployment rates were indeed falling, but absolute rates (which are, perhaps, what matters more) continued to rise. Moreover, the fact that such a high proportion of the incoming jobs were for women, of whom in turn a high proportion had previously not been 'economically active', meant that the unemployment was not reduced by an equivalent amount. This, and the fact that the jobs were often lower-paid and less demanding of industrial skills, meant that they provided little direct relief for redundant miners and steel-workers (see Chapter 5) – those, in other words, for whom regional policy had apparently been part of the bargain. The labour-movement side of the alliance, under such a combination of circumstances, could hardly be expected to hold up. In 1969 Wilson's reception at the TUC conference was frosty; in 1970 the Labour Party lost the election to a government with no basis at all for such an alliance (and indeed which went to the country in 1974 with a challenge – which failed – against the regional 'core-sector').

Moreover, manufacturing industry also refused to react in the politically-desired manner. Not so much antagonism as inertia characterised its response. The more dynamic sectors continued the predilection for investing abroad, and indeed many of the policies of the period reinforced this orientation. The IRC, by encouraging size and international competitiveness, produced contradictory results, as international competitiveness, for the companies, meant not so much exporting as investing abroad (Singh, 1975; Massey and Meegan, 1979). The conflict between the traditional world role and the modernisation of the economy had not been grappled with, and the net result in so far as manufacturing industry was concerned was to reinforce it, by strengthening those sections whose influence on policy put in second place the health of the UK internal economy. Later, EEC entry did much the same (Gray, 1982).

There was, moreover, more straightforward opposition from other parts of capital. Banking capital, the fraction more used to holding power, had throughout been more ambiguous in its relation to the strategy (Jessop, 1979, p. 102), and its opposition was part of the eventual undermining of the policy. By 1967, with devaluation, the contradictions should have been obvious. But 'the fatal persistence in the belief that no choice was necessary gravely undermined the modernisation strategy of the 1960s and wrecked many of the reforms which it launched' (Gamble, 1981, p. 102).

With such uncertain adherents the strategy could not survive the worsening economic situation. While some restructuring had been achieved, the economy continued to decline. The political stalemate had not been broken.

Muddling through

The rest of the 1970s was a period of greater variability, in terms both of economic strategy and of the social basis on which it was built. The period began with the inheritance of the Wilson and Heath governments. There was, in the early years, a high level of grass-roots union militancy and a union leadership which, until 1975, inclined towards the left. While much of this renewed activity remained still within the old defensive, sectionalist terms (Hodgson, 1981), there were also more positive experiments, particularly during 1974, with Tony Benn at the Ministry of Industry. Labour's Programme 1973, with its emphasis on multinational capital (the meso-economic sector) and the problems of trade, represented the beginnings of a recognition of the persistent conflict between internal economy and international role (Gamble, 1981). There was also increasing recognition of the need to shift the locus of power within industry through an extension of industrial democracy.

None of these initiatives, however, was to last or bear fruit. The economic strategy of 1973 was transformed beyond recognition from an assault on international capital to powerless 'Sector Working Parties', one 'Planning Agreement', and a gradual slide into monetarism. Some of the longer-term themes were continued: modernisation (though now more muted), continual financial pressure (epitomised by the IMF drama) and the attempts to gain agreement from the unions to policies which inevitably, in the short term at least, meant higher unemployment and lower wages. But the overall political climate was different from that of the sixties.

This difference was reinforced by, and interacted with, other contrasts. Most importantly, the wider economic situation was now spectacularly different. This time the attempt to 'do something about the British economy' was being conducted against the background of a world economy which gave far less room for manoeuvre.[4] In the first half of 1975 output in the eight largest

OECD countries fell at an annual rate of 5 per cent and world trade fell at a rate of 14 per cent, and although there was some recovery, it was slow and patchy. By early 1977, at least 20 per cent of existing productive capacity in the OECD as a whole was standing idle (Coates, 1980, p. 36). All this, combined with the more muted modernisation policy, showed up in the fall-off in investment and in the rate of growth of productivity after 1973 (Singh, 1977). It also had a wider effect on policy. The Labour government, adopting an emphasis on holding back inflation, was by 1975–6 beginning to cut back on the growth of public expenditure (and what this meant was expenditure on welfare and related services – State aid to industry increased).

This period was also different from the sixties in that the emphasis was now less exclusively on big, manufacturing capital (in spite of the clear analysis in Labour's Programme 1973). The National Enterprise Board, which the party's Programme wished to see establish some degree of public ownership in the largest companies, instead (with a shoestring budget and politics the opposite of radical interventionism), concentrated its main efforts on small and medium-sized businesses (Coates, 1980, p. 116). The large companies with which it dealt were lame ducks rather than the commanding heights of the economy. There were also schemes which applied to, and which were taken up by, small 'old-fashioned' capital. There were the sectoral schemes introduced under the earlier 1972 Industry Act and designed to promote investment and modernisation and/or rationalisation. These were by no means all, or specifically, directed at small capital, but many such sectors were involved, including wool textiles (on which the IRC had refused to act), clothing, ferrous and non-ferrous foundries and machine tools. In clothing, for instance, a special Clothing Industry Productivity Resources Agency was established, and firms in the industry were eligible, as part of the Industrial Strategy, for the special scheme of assistance under Section 8 of the Industry Act. Similarly, the qualifying size of new investment for the Accelerated Projects Scheme and its successor, Selective Investment Scheme, were set relatively low. Inner city policies, too, tended to lay considerable emphasis on small firms and the end of the period saw the heady but relatively short-lived enthusiasm for the United States findings of Birch (asserting the importance of employment growth in small firms), while there was a general shift in all areas of subnational economic policy towards 'indigenous growth', an emphasis which had much the same implications. This shift towards smaller firms had a number of bases. In part it was a straightforward extension of the programme of modernisation, in part it was a response to the patent inability of large capital, given existing policies and the worsening economic situation, to generate sufficient jobs. It was also further reinforced in 1978 when, during the 'Lib–Lab' pact, the Liberals insisted on a greater emphasis on the revival of small businesses. Certainly, as we shall see, it was to have spatial implications.

There were two other ways, already implied but worth noting explicitly, in which this period differed from the sixties. First, there was a less wholehearted attack on the basic sectors of the peripheral regions, less of an attempt to modernise and rationalise them. Second, from 1975 on there were cutbacks in the rate of growth of public expenditure and also in the rate of growth of employment in the State sector. These changes, too, were to have geographically-differentiated effects.

These political and economic differences between the seventies and the sixties were reflected in changes in national employment structure. Table 6.2 highlights some of the major directions of employment change in the seventies, and indicates their broad geographical characteristics. The picture which emerges is that, while the rate of decline of the old basic sectors in the Development Areas slackened, there were also fewer potentially-mobile jobs to replace them. In particular, those sectors which had been providing jobs in the previous period – new means-of-production industries and big capital in consumer goods – moved from net growth to net decline. Employment decline in itself, of course, does not prevent locational shift (see the example of the clothing industry in Chapter 4) but in this case the likelihood of such shifts must have been reduced by the cutback in capital investment. It was a less 'active' period of decline. Certainly it seems possible that the potential for decentralising even assembly work was reduced. At the same time, however, the faster decline in employment in manufacturing as a whole, the major losses in consumer goods, and in particular in those consumer-goods sectors dominated by small capital, left the urban areas and older industrial regions particularly vulnerable. The shifting international division of labour, and the declining manufacturing base of the United

TABLE 6.2   *Some employment characteristics of the mid-1970s*

Aggregate employment change	Geographical characteristics
Decline of old basic industries, and old means-of-production sectors continues, though at a slower rate.	Continued loss of jobs in older industrial areas, Development Areas, courbations.
New means-of-production industries begin to lose jobs.	Combined with slower rate of technical change – see text – less jobs available for decentralisation.
Consumer sectors dominated by big capital begin to lose jobs.	ditto
Consumer sectors dominated by small capital lose jobs at increasing rate.	Serious losses in urban areas and in areas of industrial specialisation.
Producer services still growing, but more slowly, and proportionately less important.	Less rapid concentration of highly-skilled professional and technical workers in the south-east.
Service sector employment growth rate as a whole increases.	Continuing possibility for significant decentralisation of clerical work.
Consumer services – reduction in rate of growth in State services, increase in private sector.	Possibly some net negative effects on regional distribution of employment.

Kingdom, were showing through clearly now in the national industrial geography.

There was, however, renewed growth in services, and a continued possibility, therefore, of decentralisation of clerical jobs. The balance of employment change within services had also shifted, however. Producer services continued to grow though at a slightly lower rate, and they were proportionately less important. The office and computer boom was less evident. The balance in consumer services shifted dramatically from public to private, which in general would indicate a worsening of their regional distribution (see Chapter 4), but public-sector services nevertheless continued to grow and thus to retain some significance as a countervailing force in terms of the regional distribution of different types of employment. Putting all this together, and remembering its emphasis on manufacturing, it is evident that regional policy had less room for manoeuvre than during the previous decade.

*   *   *

This was reinforced by changes in the status of the policy itself. Indeed, once again, geographical unevenness and spatial policy were integral to the whole story. Between 1972 and 1979 spatial policy both changed in form and as a whole became less important in relation to national economic policy. In terms of regional policy, this subordination began with the increased sectoral emphasis of the Conservatives' Industry and Finance Acts and was continued under the Labour Government's Industrial Strategy (Johnstone, 1979). In the latter the decreasing importance of regional policy can be detected in the declining proportion of State financial aid to industry being awarded on regional grounds, in the relaxation of IDCs, the ending of REP, and in the actual spatial balance of some of the major sectoral policies, which favoured non-Development Areas (Cameron, 1979). This has often been interpreted as regional policy's being a primarily social and redistributive policy, and being traded-off against national economic imperatives. There is an element of truth in this, but there were also other threads to the story. We have already argued that regional policy itself had not up to this point anyway been playing a solely 'welfare' role. In fact two things seem to have been going on. First, the conditions within which regional policy had been playing its 'economic' role in aiding accumulation in parts of industry, for instance within restructuring, were themselves receding. Manufacturing employment was declining at an increased rate, but further, that decline was combined with low rates of investment and a fall-off, as we have seen, in the rate of growth of productivity. 'Potentially-mobile-manufacturing employment' is thus likely to have fallen even more than the simple employment numbers would suggest, for less of the employment decline seems to have been taking place in the context of investment in new techniques (Massey and Meegan, 1982). Under such circumstances regional policy would be less use to capital, either as simple aid or, perhaps more particularly, because the newly-available workforces of the Development Areas would no longer be relevant. These new workforces were on the whole more useful to big than little capital. But as we have seen, national industrial policy was now extended to significant sections of small capital, and these schemes were taken up by sectors both within and outside assisted areas. However for small capital, regional policy was unlikely to play much of a role in any process of restructuring. Take, for instance, the foundry and machine tool industries, for both of which sectoral schemes operated. Both are located primarily outside Development Areas, both are dominated by small companies and both are primarily male-employing. For precisely these reasons the incentives of regional policy would be largely irrelevant. Such small firms are less locationally mobile, and would be more likely to prefer investment *in situ*. Moreover in most cases in these industries new investment, even in more modern techniques, rarely led to in-creased employment of women, and therefore the reserves of female labour in the Development Areas were of little potential use. (And the attractions of a male workforce recently made redundant from the NCB or BSC are likely to have been minimal to the 'small businessman' of the west midlands.) In this context the easing of IDC controls must have been particularly welcome – indeed it seems to have reflected both this process and the reduced pressure on labour markets in the central areas. As would be expected given these arguments, regional policy became over the 1970s less effective in terms of job creation in the Development Areas (Moore, *et al.*, 1977; Massey and Meegan, 1982).

What was happening over this period, then, was certainly that regional policy was increasingly subordinate to national industrial policy, but also that the regional policy itself was in part a reflection of (or went hand in hand with) its own declining role as an arm of national industrial policy. There were also, of course, political conditions which enabled, or encouraged, a decline in emphasis on regional policy as a purely redistributive mechanism. In particular, unemployment in non-Development Areas was rising. They had no jobs 'to spare'. In the inner cities, equivalent problems of poverty and unemployment were beginning to take on serious political proportions. Under such circumstances, it was not inconvenient to let regional policy be blamed for decline elsewhere and difficult to continue it as such a major element of State policy towards industry.

In contrast to the modernisation period, therefore, when region-al policy had had an impact partly because of the strength of its operation and partly because the conditions existed in which it could succeed, in this later period it both had less room for manoeuvre economically and was subordinated politically.

The increasing geographical spread of high levels of unemployment exacerbated the specifically spatial competition for jobs, and workers in different parts of the country, *defining* themselves as workers from particular regions, were thrown into conflict for the few new jobs that were around. This was sharpened by the fact that much of the rhetoric of State policy was geared to an interpretation of regional or local unemployment as a result of the failings of the particular areas in question (a lack of skills, a lack of entrepreneurship, too much 'bureaucracy' on the part of local planners, too much militancy on the part of local workers). And in many cases, because of the immediacy of the local problems, the issue was taken on in those terms. For spatially separate interests are real; the high national level of unemployment *was* unevenly distributed between areas.[5] Regions are thus set in competition with each other. The example of Inmos in Figure 6.2, for which nearly 100 local authorities competed, was just one of many during this period. Merseyside workers demanded work for Merseyside, inner city groups complained that regional policy was responsible for their loss of jobs and there were rival claims to have the highest local rate of unemployment. Not only did this divide people in one region from those in another, and divert attention from the overall problem of unemployment, it also prepared the ground for local attacks on trade unions. It was the workers of Merseyside who drew most attention on this score, the decline of the area being frequently blamed on their lack of 'discipline'. In June 1978 a report drawn up for the Department of Industry recommended 'a charter for industrial relations which would commit Merseyside management and unions to improving the area's reputation with potential investors'. During this period it was primarily in this way that geography became a weapon in the hands of State and management, and here, as in so many other ways, this period laid the groundwork for the next. The election of 1979 was barely over when Mr Prior, the new Employment Secretary, was up on Merseyside: ' "Merseyside had had a reputation for industrial relations which were at the heart of Britain's malaise", Mr Prior said. And he called on the region's workers not to strike for two years. This would go a long way towards attracting industrial investors and creating the atmosphere that the Conservatives wanted' (*Guardian*, 26 May 1979).

Inmos offered nearly 100 sites for factory

BY MAX WILKINSON

NEARLY 100 local government bodies are competing to offer sites for the first UK factory of Inmos, the National Enterprise Board's micro-electronics subsidiary.

Local councils and regional development organisations are vying to produce a combination of attractive sites, financial inducements and political pressure. The prize is 1,000 jobs, which the factory is expected to create when it starts production in two-and-half years' time.

The company expects to be offered a choice of 150 possible sites in about 100 separate submissions. Interest and political feeling have been running so high that Inmos has been obliged to extend the deadline for receipt of submissions. The closing date set by its consultants. PA International, was originally February 10, but it has been extended by "up to two weeks".

Inmos was established by the NEB last year to mass-produce electronic micro-circuits for the international market. It is expected to concentrate in its earliest phase on high density components for computer memories and on micro-computers. In the longer term the company says it hopes to provide 4,000 jobs in four factories in the UK. The funding of Inmos is expected to reach a peak of £50m.

The latest submission is from Tyne and Wear County Council and the five metropolitan district councils in the area. The 200-page submission offers eight possible sites which are all said to be "tailored to the requirements of Inmos".

Tyne and Wear is also offering what it describes as a unique financial inducement, which could give Inmos a subsidy of about £9m, or about 30 per cent of the cost of setting up the factory. The Tyne and Year Act, 1976, allows the council to offer a factory rent-free for up to five years, with rate and interest relief and subsidies for land acquisition.

Mr. Michael Campbell, chairman of the council, says the submission makes an "irrefutable case for Inmos to locate its production units in this county".

Mr. Brian Stevens, Inmos's administration manger, however, took a cautious line yesterday on the selection. He said the 150 possible sites would have to be reduced to 10 or 20 for closer analysis. He expected a final choice between May and June.

The great interest shown in Inmos by local councils is in some ways surprising, because semi-conductor plants are highly automated and provide relatively few jobs for unskilled labour. The crucial requirement of Inmos will be for highly skilled scientists, technicians, and computer operators.

Such experts are in short supply in both the UK and the U.S. Inmos will therefore need to locate its plant in an area attractive to well qualified graduate scientists.

It has already announced that its UK headquarters and technology centre will be in Bristol. A site near Bristol for its first production unit would, therefore, be convenient.

The company's pilot production will start in Colorado, U.S., in about 15 months. Mass production will then be transferred to the UK.

FIGURE 6.2 *Competition between areas*

Source: *Financial Times*, 6 February 1979.

The effects of these economic and political conditions differentiate this period from the earlier one.[6] While on a number of indices the peripheral regions continued to perform reasonably well, by the middle of the period they were beginning to waver. It was the conurbations – Merseyside, Clydeside and Newcastle – which led the areas' accelerated job loss. It was what Townsend (1982) aptly calls the intersection of regional and urban problems, that is of the 'traditional' regional problem and the now accelerated decline of older manufacturing more generally – the intersection, in other words, of the impact of two shifts in the international division of labour.

The pattern of geographical differentiation in job type and occupational structure continued to be reproduced, though again with differences from the earlier period. Overall, the spatial centralisation of control, and the establishment and spatial concentration of managerial hierarchies in the south-east, continued, though at a slower rate. 'General management' remained over-represented in Greater London and the rest of the south-east (ROSE) throughout the period, and indeed increased its over-representation (Kirwan, 1981). Exactly the reverse was true for the north, and Wales and Scotland, where under-representation was reinforced. Moreover, 'assistant management' (which includes the whole gamut of professional support) showed exactly the same pattern.[7]

But if the picture was clear for management, that for professionals in science, technology and engineering was much more mixed. This could reflect the decline in importance of producer services, both as a proportion of employment change and in their own rate of growth (though the category also includes the more production-based engineering technologists – see Chapter 4). It would be interesting to explore these connections further. Certainly one can detect the declining emphasis on modernisation and technical change.

At the other end of the occupational structure, too, the character of the period left its imprint. Although there continued to be a shift within women's employment towards assembly work, there was an absolute overall decline in numbers, reflecting the declines in new means-of-production industries and in consumer goods. In all regions this kind of employment for women fell in importance, and the biggest losers included the Development Areas of the south-west, the north and Wales. The north actually moved into deficit over the period (New Earnings Survey). In other words, while, except for the north, all the Development Areas remained 'over-represented', the (net) process of movement of these jobs to peripheral regions did not continue in any consistent manner over this period.[8]

But while there was hesitation in the decentralisation of assembly jobs for women, the decentralisation of clerical jobs – as would be implied by the aggregate economic changes – continued throughout the period. Greater London, ROSE and East Anglia all decreased their representation. In contrast, the north of England, the south-west, Scotland and Wales all increased their relative proportions of these jobs – in the cases of the first three, very significantly (Kirwan, 1981).[9]

All these shifts in balance can thus be understood in relation to the national changes discussed earlier. Many of the trends of the previous period continued. Management continued its process of spatial centralisation, clerical work continued to decentralise. But the speed and balance of the different components changed. There was a less spectacular rate of concentration of male professional workers in the south-east of England, the balance of women's jobs decentralising (relatively) to the peripheral regions shifted more towards clerical work. The basic sectors continued to decline, but at a slower rate. Overall, the shift between spatial divisions of labour at the broad national level continued but, reflecting economic and political changes, it did so more haltingly and in a different form.

*   *   *

The Callaghan government was slowly shipwrecked on the contradictions of its own, and Wilsonian, politics. Both of them laid the basis for the politics of Margaret Thatcher. The kind of State intervention pursued in the sixties alienated the left and gave anything to do with 'the public sector' a bad name. The Labour government of the seventies did much the same for the unions. Coming to power on the rejection of Heath's challenge ('who runs the country?') it did much to improve the unions' legislative position (Hodgson, 1981; Coates, 1980). It was ironical that the notion of union power was boosted just as those very unions were knuckling under to year upon year of wage restraint. The rank-and-file pressure of the beginning of the period seemed completely burned out, but by 1979 it burst forth again, in a winter of discontent among the low-paid, and a series of rebellions against narrowing wage-differentials among the higher-income groups. Each in its different way was important in the Labour Party's loss of the election.

There were continuing conflicts, too, at the regional level. While there were pressures – in the national economy and in the cities – for a reduced emphasis on regional policy, there was a growing regional *problem*. In this context, stimulus for indigenous employment, however unlikely to succeed, was one of the few options available. It was also encouraged by a change, already mentioned, in the nature of regional politics themselves. In the context of claims for devolution in Scotland and Wales the high degree of external ownership, in part itself a result of regional policy, became an increasingly important component of the politics of regionalism (see, for an early example, Firn, 1973). The Communist Party in the north-west (Communist Party, undated), the Labour Party in Scotland (Labour Party, 1977), the Welsh and Scottish Nationalist Parties, and other organisations in 'the regions' raised this as a major issue of complaint. In the context of these shifts the Welsh and Scottish Development Agencies were established. They were thus both political and economic responses, and their brief focused, more than had the previous form of regional policy, on the generation of internal growth. The lack of a basis for such a strategy was apparent, however, and in fact all the regional IDAs spent more time continuing the policy of trying to attract new investment, frequently in acrimonious competition with each other, than on 'stimulating the existing local economy'. Symbolically perhaps, the government finally went down on the devolution issue.

Monetarism

The election of 1979 marked a break from the ever-shifting terms of the post-war consensus. Many of the actual economic policies of the new Thatcher government – the so-called new monetarism – were in fact not new. A concern about the public-sector borrowing requirement, the political formulation of the economic situation as being primarily a problem of inflation, and cuts in public expenditure all had their precursors under the previous Labour government.

But in political terms the victory of the Conservatives in 1979 did mark a shift. The advent of Margaret Thatcher as Prime Minister heralded a departure, particularly in rhetorical and ideological terms, from the post-war social-democratic tradition so manifestly in disarray. The failure of the policies of previous decades laid the basis for the victory of the right. Real disenchantment with undemocratic State intervention, brilliantly orchestrated in a populist 'individual freedom' campaign, agreement between Conservatives and the Labour right that public expenditure was 'too high' (but where that expenditure was inextricably associated with the policies of Labour) and years of attempts to stem the growth of wages (but apparently to no avail in terms of economic recovery) together produced an election victory for a Conservative Party newly-dominated by its right wing. It was a right wing prepared to break the old consensus, to break through the shifting stalemate that went with it. It was thus a very different tradition within the Tory party. It had more commitment to market ideology – at home now, as well as in international trade – than to the settled old terms of class rule. It could not have been further from the Conservative Party which, nearly twenty years before, had established the National Economic Development Office. But to pursue this new philosophy meant social reconstruction, and for real, not just as part of the rhetoric of the new vision. What was now popularly paraded as the monolith of the trade union movement had to be shaken up and weakened. While it might not provide much in the way of its own visions of an alternative future it was still strong enough in defence to prevent a way out of the crisis being found on other terms. But such a course meant also the reconstruction of many other aspects of British social life, including the entrenched and archaic institutions of the establishment, peopled in large part by members of the 'old' Tory party.

In many ways the terms of debate of the 'modernisation' period of the sixties were now reversed. This was not just in the most obvious senses, from Welfare State and public sector to cutback and privatisation. The attack on State expenditure and on public intervention was partly enabled by re-working the distinction between 'productive' and 'non-productive' parts of the economy.

In the sixties the productive sector was pre-eminently manufacturing; services were relegated to second place and politicians in both major parties, as well as managers in major (manufacturing) companies, attacked the 'speculators' of the property boom as parasitic and unproductive. A decade later the distinction had come to mean something completely different: it was the market (private) sector which was productive, the public which was the parasitic dead-weight. Both distinctions, in very different ways, had clear geographical repercussions. There were other such contrasts, too. Instead of Arnold Weinstock, efficient manager of big capital, the likes of Freddie Laker – paraded in the image of free-booting entrepreneur – were held up for public approbation, the kind of attitude that was needed if the British economy was to be rescued. Along with this went a parallel shift in relation to professionals, scientists and technologists. Clearly those in the State sector no longer held the key to recovery. But it was more than that; the idea of technological advance through the research laboratories of big capital was superseded by the notion of the scientist as entrepreneur. The periods of modernisation and of monetarism were not just different because the wider economic situation had changed so dramatically, because 'the requirements of accumulation' were different; they were also dramatically contrasting in the dominant political interpretations of what those requirements were.

But Thatcherism did not sweep the board. It was, again, an election victory with a definable social base and a clear geographical dimension. Its core was in the growing white-collar and middle strata alongside, within capital itself, those elements which identified ideologically with an 'entrepreneurial' label. The contrast with the sixties is again clear. Thus, in terms of the 'sci-tech' brigade: 'The Wilsonian seizure of science as the theme for the 1964 election . . . sought to define and capture a new stratum – that of scientists and technologists – and to insist that their interests lay with Labour. . . . A high proportion of scientists and technologists must have voted Labour in 1964. Almost certainly, a high proportion of the same group voted for Thatcher in 1979' (Rose and Rose, 1982). The white-collar strata were not to be disappointed, either ideologically or economically (in distributional terms), but small business, although approving ideologically, was soon to suffer rather than gain in purely economic terms. Support from big manufacturing industry was always more reserved, and occasionally oscillated quite dramatically, but a call early on by the head of the CBI for a 'bare-knuckle fight' was resisted. Party-political loyalties were hard to break. In spite of its patience being sorely tested, the CBI at its conference in 1982 found it hard to forget its long-term party allegiance. After numerous boardroom battles, reported in the Press, over possible transfer of support to the new Social Democrats, most companies retained their longer-term political and class loyalites above more immediate economic interests. And throughout, the Institute of Directors gave the new strategy total support. The election also saw the desertion of Labour by considerable sections of the skilled, male, manual working class, including significant numbers of union members,[10] lured by tax cuts and 'free collective bargaining' after a long erosion of relative wage-levels by the combination of incomes policies and inflation.

The Thatcher victory also had a very definite geographical base. The traditional electoral differentiation between the west and the north on the one hand and the south and the east on the other was reinforced. Labour on the whole retained its support in the former but saw it disintegrate in the latter. As an article in the *New Statesman* put it: 'Perhaps the most startling statistic of the election is that north of the Mersey–Humber line Labour did not do appreciably worse than in 1945, the year of Attlee's landslide. South of the line, however, a Labour lead of 100 seats has turned into a Conservative lead of 146' (Kellner, 1979, p. 704). To some extent this dichotomisation continued a statistical pattern in which 'a party which is losing votes nationally tends to lose more where its voting strength is relatively weak than it does where it is relatively strong, whereas a party which is winning votes nationally tends to win most (in relative terms) where it is already strong' (Johnston, 1981, p. 32). The question is why this happens and specifically why it happened in 1979. Indeed, the general dichotomy between north and south was further strengthened by the local elections in 1981. Such shifts may in part be a reflection of precisely that spatial recomposition of the class structure which has begun to emerge from the analyses in the Chapters 4 and 5. The concentration in the south and east of particular parts of the professional and 'scientific' strata, for instance, points in this direction. P. J. Taylor (1979) points to the backcloth of long-term urban decentralisation as part of the contrast between shire counties and conurbations, but there is more to it than that. Nationally, in social-class terms Labour lost out over the five year period (1974–9) among skilled (and semi-skilled and unskilled) workers, but 'held its own amongst professional and managerial classes' (Price, 1979). Had such results held evenly over the country as a whole Labour would have lost more in the north and retained more in the south. The actual results therefore indicate that among both skilled workers and 'the professional and managerial classes' there was a definite 'regional' bias. Skilled workers remained more with Labour in the north, were more tempted by tax cuts in the south. The traditional Labour base seems to have held in the former. 'The British working class sometimes continue[s] to vote Labour after the most appalling clobbering – as they did in 1950, and as they did to a great extent in the North and Scotland this time' (Price, 1979, p. 706). Similarly, those parts of the white-collar middle strata which, as was seen in Chapter 5, are an increasing element in the social structure of 'the north' seem to have been more disposed to vote Labour than those apparently holding a broadly similar place in the national social structure, but geographically located in the south-east. A study of the election commented that the evidence for what it called 'class de-alignment' was made all the more remarkable by the simultaneous strengthening of regional alignment (Penniman, 1981).

The implications of all this are interesting. It reinforces the indications in Chapter 4 and 5 that there are increasing geographical divisions within each of these broad social groups. The differences within the managerial and scientific–technical groups are particularly interesting. From Chapters 4 and 5 it is clear that within these broad groups social status and geographical location are related and, what is more, that they may also be mutually-reinforcing. In 1979 the autonomous influence of the regionally-based Labour alliances and strength, discussed in Chapter 5, continued to hold up. In other words, the within-class biases towards Labour in these areas, not only among 'lower middle and working' but also among 'middle' classes have been retained, if not reinforced, given the known changes going on in social structure.[11] Here we see again, then, a 'reverse effect', of regional individuality on national political structures, of the possible importance of 'spatial' characteristics in the formation of social characteristics.

*   *   *

In the first year after the election the geographical basis of the Government was mirrored in the cutbacks made in regional policy. There were a number of contributory reasons behind these cuts. First, the international economic situation, combined with the effects of the Government's own economic strategy, sent manufacturing employment into an unprecedented decline. That, together with lower investment in new building, left little opportunity for any spatial redistribution. Second, this Government had no political alliance with the unions and no political base in most of the regions which stood to gain from the existing pattern of regional incentives. There was therefore no major political pressure for regional policy. Third, the Government was proclaiming an ideological commitment to the market and to cuts in public expenditure. Economic conditions, political base and ideological predisposition thus all indicated at least some cuts in regional policy, and these indeed took place. The cuts themselves, moreover, indicated some change in the nature and potential role of regional policy. They did not simply make it even more of a means to underpin accumulation. The cutbacks in the automatic Regional Development Grants provoked outright attack from the CBI which, although agreeing it would not push for labour subsidies or IDCs, declared that it did 'favour regional assistance being concentrated on investment incentives' and supported factory building and infrastructure provision, and confirmed its 'strong support for the current Regional Development Grant system as a mechanism for assisting investment' (CBI, 1979). Overall, it declared 'the CBI's continued support for a strong regional policy based on positive incentives' (CBI, 1979). The detail of this is interesting. The lack of argument for labour subsidies might in part reflect the decline of labour-intensive mobile employment (and measures such as the Temporary Employment Subsidy, as well as selective regional assistance were still available). Much of the capital-intensive investment in Development Areas is based there in any case. But the overall message is clear, that in regional policy as more generally, the new politics was not entirely to the liking of important sections of big capital.

It soon became apparent, however, that this reaction was not typical of smaller companies. Sharp exchanges took place. A National Executive member of the Association of Independent Businesses wrote on the matter to the *Financial Weekly*

> there is a difference between large, established, powerful corporations and the up-and-coming enterprises from which will emerge the giants of tomorrow. The former are well-geared to seek government handouts – some have whole departments doing nothing else; the latter have neither the time nor the patience. As the pre-eminent representative body for smaller firms, we have shown that in spite of the fact that our sector employs two out of five members of the workforce, and pays much more corporation tax than big business (the tax which effectively pays for grants and subsidies), our members have done badly from handouts in the last decade. Little wonder that we support cuts in corporation tax and an end to State subsidies
> . . .
> The current debate on regional aid crystallises these deeply divergent points of view just as much as the most obvious division between businessmen who can and do receive the bounty of 'special development areas' and those elsewhere who merely foot the bill . . .
> We hope that the current debate will continue beyond the strict bounds of the impact of the welcome cuts which . . . Sir Keith Joseph has instituted (*Financial Weekly*, 27 July 1979).

Moreover, it was not only the cuts in incentives which did not work simply to the advantage of all sections of industry. The areas over which the incentives were to be available were also reduced, and in that reduction the basis of their definition changed. The previous, extremely broad, definition of Development Areas had covered whole regions, effectively allowed wide choice over location for capital in receipt of incentives and indeed had included a number of relatively healthy sub-areas. The redrawing of the boundaries in 1979 thus marked a switch to a more political and welfare basis. The prime criterion was now the *local* level of unemployment (Townsend, 1980). While the cutback in regional policy can thus be seen as its final subordination to 'economic imperatives', these imperatives were themselves interpreted through a particular political prism. The character of the policy itself underwent a change. It become *less* growth-oriented, less positively geared to play a direct economic role in accumulation. Selective assistance was still available, and this was important. But more generally, growth was to come through response to the rigours of the market and the kind of 'freedom from constraints' supposedly provided in the new 'Enterprise Zones'. These small areas of high subsidy and reduced controls were, again, scattered about the country in response to immediate difficulties. As with much else, the rhetoric was more *laissez-faire* than the actual policies, and this was clearly recognised, particularly by small firms in areas bordering the zones. Once again they were vocal in their response. A letter in the *Financial Times* (8 February 1982) expressed 'a deep sense of injustice felt by many businessmen who will now face unfair competition from competitors cushioned by 100-per-cent allowances on rates for a ten-year period. How does this new concept of "free trading" tie up with Sir Keith Joseph's thinking?' If the Wilson government's regional policy was part and parcel of its strategy for national economic growth, this exercise in enterprise zones was integral to the Thatcher government's pro-clamation of a new politics. Indeed, it may well turn out to be their major impact (Anderson, 1983; Labour Party, 1980; Massey, 1982). Even the changed conception of scientists and technologists was reflected in employment policy. 'Science parks' sprang up in the hope that the geniuses of the local academic institutions might turn their talents in an entrepreneurial direction, make money out of their PhDs, and the link between academic science and the pursuit of profit be strengthened. Finally, one arm of regional policy was abandoned entirely. This government, whose avowed aim of social reconstruction included, indeed necessitated, the modernisation of many institutions of 'the British establishment', gave way before the social power of higher-level civil servants and agreed to abandon plans to decentralise to 'the regions' offices of the central State. Regional, and more generally spatial, aspects of policy continued their downward slide in importance while at the same time their nature and role shifted yet again.

Moreover, this cutback in regional policy came at a time when other elements in the national strategy were hitting the declining peripheral regions particularly hard. The cutbacks in the national-ised industries, especially steel and coal, had a regionalised impact, as did public expenditure cuts. Local authority employment was one of the few parts of the job-structure not operating, in income and skill terms, dramatically against the peripheral regions (Chapter 4). Cutbacks were therefore in that sense bound to have the effect of increasing regional inequality. The situation was worse than this, however, for in spite of the losses of jobs in the nationalised industries, regions such as Wales, the north-east and Scotland remained the most dependent in the country on State activity of some sort, whether in expenditure per capita (where Northern Ireland and then Wales topped the list), or in terms of jobs. On the latter, the dependence of people in these regions on the public sector for relatively well paid white-collar jobs increased over the 1970s, and this was especially true for women (Kirwan, 1981). In these regions virtually the only source of higher-paid and/or professional employment which is available to women is the public sector. In all these ways, then, cuts in the public sector hit people in these regions hard. To some extent that in itself, and the strength of the labour movement there, may have reduced the level of reductions. Rumours of 'social unrest' and threats of action seem to have slowed for a while the eventually dramatic cuts at Llanwern and Port Talbot; and it was the lead by the Welsh miners which forced the government to back off in early 1981 on its financial stringency with the NCB. Later, there was political reluctance to close the Ravenscraig steelworks in Scotland, part of BSC's planned cutback. But overall the attempt to cut back on welfare provision and the public sector generally was regionalised in its impact.

Moreover there was little prospect, as there had been in the sixties, that these losses would be replaced by jobs in other industries. Regional policy had been cut back, and anyway the economic conditions for its operation were by now far less propitious, while public expenditure cuts removed that element of the earlier period's *quid pro quo*. Finally the deepening international recession, combined with the government's commitment to policies which led to high interest rates and high levels of exchange for sterling, provoked severe cutbacks in many of the industries which had decentralised in the sixties and seventies.[12] Unemployment in the Development Areas rose dramatically. By late 1982 the rate in Northern Ireland was 20 per cent, in the North and Wales over 16 per cent and in Scotland over 14 per cent. The 'regional issue' became once again a focus of discontent.

But this time it was not just the traditional regional-problem regions which saw major losses of jobs. The impact of the recession was very general; even the service industries were losing employment. But most of all, the combination of international recession, the United Kingdom's particularly weak position, and government strategy wreaked havoc on manufacturing industry. The economies of the older manufacturing regions, particularly the west midlands and the north-west, virtually collapsed (Townsend, 1982; Lloyd and Shutt, 1982). The rate of unemployment in each of these two regions was soon above that for Scotland. By the end of 1982, the figures were over 15 per cent in both the west midlands and the north-west. In what was dubbed 'the first combined statement of its kind' the chairpersons of the CBI's west midlands, north-west, and Yorkshire and Humberside regions issued a stern demand for relief for industry (Garnett, 1982). The *Financial Times* ran a serialised report on 'West Midlands in Recession' and the regional branch of the CBI was for a while particularly loud in its complaint, but at the same time evidence from innumerable plants and disputes indicated that the trade union movement in the region was rocking from the effect. 'West Midlands bosses find they have the upper hand' ran one headline, typical of many (Massey and Meegan, 1982), and in 1982 wages in the west midlands, which not so many years before had been only 1 per cent below average earnings in Greater London, were more than 13 per cent behind (Taylor, 1982).

The statistical result of all this, measured on the old bases of percentage differences in unemployment and the old definitions of centre and periphery, was that 'regional differentials' narrowed. 'Convergence' appeared to be under way again. This time, however, its meaning was different. It was more clearly convergence about a rising national average. Absolute differences increased. What was signalled mostly was the shift of the old dividing line between the relatively prosperous and the definitely peripheral and 'the periphery' in those terms now covered the bulk of the country. While the traditional regional problem continued to reassert itself, it was now matched by, and had in places superimposed upon it, a newer regional problem, that resulting from the deindustrialisation of Britain.

6.3 Changes in the geography of class relations

The geography of the ownership of production

Analyses of the United Kingdom's economy and society have long emphasised the divisions within British capital between internationally-orientated capital and 'the rest', the overwhelming political dominance of the former, and the significance of this for national social and economic structure and development. *If one thing is clear from the foregoing chapters it is that these characteristics of British capital are also of fundamental importance for the national geography.* The geography of accumulation in these two different parts of capital in the United Kingdom is quite distinct, and it is the geography of internationally-orientated capital which is increasingly dominant and which lies behind the emerging spatial division of labour and the structure of spatial inequality.

In this section we are concerned with the geography of ultimate control over the relations of ownership and possession. One thing is certain: that control is increasingly exercised from the south-east of England. However, the argument is more complicated than it looks at first sight. The most obvious fact is that the headquarters of British international capital is in the south-east, in and around London. This has been true of banking capital for centuries, and it is true of most big, internationalised British manufacturing capital. Each increase in the economic importance of such companies brings with it also an increase in the spatial concentration of control over the relations of production and over accumulation. It was true of the emergence of new manufacturing multinationals in the fifties. The merger boom of the late 1960s did the same. While the aspatial concentration and centralisation of capital has not brought in its train spatial concentration of production activities, it *has* brought with it geographical centralisation of the *relations* of production, of control over the relations of ownership and possession. Not only centralisation but also concentration has had this effect. On the whole, the larger the company the more likely it is to have a detached head office and the more likely it is that that office will be in the south-east region. On the whole, therefore, it is larger capital which is centralising the ownership of its production in that region.

But the formal criterion of absolute size alone is not sufficient.

For one thing, a number of very large UK companies *do* have their headquarters 'in the regions'. What is interesting is which companies they are. As Crum and Gudgin (1978) point out, they tend to be companies which are confined to one broad product-area and which are based within a region where there is a historical specialisation within that product-area. Thus 'Tootal remains in Manchester,[13] Pilkington Bros. in St. Helens, Coats Patons in Glasgow, Distillers in Edinburgh, and Joseph Lucas and Tube Investments in Birmingham' (p. 113). Certainly these companies are huge – and internationalised – but Crum and Gudgin are right to point to their relatively confined product bases.[14] It is something of what was referred to in Chapter 2 as a production rather than a financial orientation. There may, then, though this needs further investigation, be differences in type of company, in the social nature of capital, even within major, internationally-orientated capital, between that which congregates in London and the south and east and that which has more tendency to remain in its traditional and more peripheral fastnesses. Nonetheless it is true that the bulk of large, internationalised British capital has its headquarters in the south and east of England.

'Modernising' the British economy in the sense understood in the 1960s had contradictory effects, not only in that the newly-strengthened international companies went off and invested abroad (which itself had geographical effects – if only implicit – in removing existing or potential investment in the national economy – Singh, 1975) but also in that it reinforced this spatial concentration of control over the relations of production. At the same time it is these companies above all which have benefited from regional policy, and their differences with the rest of capital over regional policy have, as we have seen, been as marked as they have in the wider spectrum of economic strategy.

But there is more to the argument about the spatial centralisation of control over accumulation than plotting the headquarters of big firms. Nationalisation has also contributed to this trend. So, too, has the pattern of self-employment and very tiny firms, what Wright would classify as petit-bourgeois or as ambiguous between petit-bourgeois and fully capitalist. Although this social form of production is less important in the United Kingdom than in other, broadly comparable, societies it nevertheless reinforces the overall pattern. What our partial, but indicative, analyses show is that the very different social groups which make up this overall category have distinct geographical distributions. Chapter 4 looked at the service industries only, but these account for about three-quarters of the self-employed, many of the rest being in agriculture and construction. And what was evident from the analysis was that growth-orientation, indeed growth *possibility*, social status and geographical distribution were all related. Those with the higher social status and growth potential were far more congregated in the south-east. One other aspect, which we shall take up again later, is the importance of small firms in inner urban areas.

If self-employment and very tiny companies are relatively unimportant, there is another category of British industry which emerges as a more significant element in the structure of the economy. It is much of what is referred to in the term 'the rest of British industry'. Gamble (1981) writes of 'the growing division between the profitable and expanding international businesses of the City and the leading manufacturing companies in Britain, on the one side, and the rest of British industry on the other' (p. 118) and of their characteristics: 'Allied to the social conservatism of British institutions, the comparatively low status of industry in relation to the professions and public service, the lack of technical and business education, the proliferation of small family businesses, and the resulting poor quality of many British managers, what British industry clearly required after 1945 was a wholesale clear-out and reorganisation' (p. 119). This kind of capital is still relatively important in the British economy. It is still significant in engineering, textiles, clothing, printing, timber and some timber products: companies often with no more than a few hundred workers and based in old-established sectors of production.

Many of these sectors are precisely those which have historical regional bases, often outside the south-east. Textiles in Lancashire and Yorkshire, footwear in the east midlands and East Anglia, nuts, bolts and every possible variety of widget in the west midlands. Are such spatial concentrations of the ownership of capital then important centres of 'local control' over accumulation? Are they potential regional centres of indigenous growth? The evidence is not encouraging. None of these are major growth sectors. But more important than sectoral fortunes is the type of capital involved. The ownership of these firms *continues* to be old-fashioned and traditional in its ways, concerned more with survival than with expansion. It has already been seen that these characteristics are important in the clothing and footwear industries.[15] In terms of survival and employment, they have an ambiguous effect. On the one hand, the very smallness of the companies, the associated lack of flexibility and their often old-fashioned methods, make them vulnerable to closure in adverse economic conditions. Examples of this have already been cited. On the other hand, their sectoral rigidity and their concern with survival rather than maximum profit on capital invested (otherwise they would have got out of the sector years ago), their very *lack* of concern with accumulation in the full sense of the word, enables them to survive in the teeth of what often look like insuperable difficulties. Boswell (1973) reports on a number of examples of firms with up to 500 workers. First, 'the extreme, almost limiting case: that of the Lancashire cotton textile industry ... a story of smaller firms: of their obsolescence and decay, their dogged resistance to outside pressures, their persistent refusal either to adapt or [to] go under' (p. 114). In an attempt at rationalisation, and given that market forces did not seem sufficient to induce closure, the State stepped in. Indeed, it did so on a number of occasions. The worsening of the competitive position during the fifties led to the Cotton Industry Act in 1959. Much public-sector money was made available for restructuring and re-equipment. The idea was that firms would take advantage of the opportunity either to leave the industry, or to scale down production by scrapping some of their plant, or to modernise and re-equip. 'But on all three of these fronts the outcome was disappointing, particularly from the small firms whose response was felt to be critical. Well under a quarter left the industry, rather over a quarter scrapped some of their plant and only a few re-equipped. As many as one-half of the small firms didn't participate in the scheme at all' (Boswell, p. 115). In 1969 the Textile Council pointed to exactly the same inertia and rigidity, and commented on this apparently inexplicable form of behaviour 'but the question still remains as to how and why so many high-cost firms have survived'.

Just across the Pennines, in the West Riding of Yorkshire, is the wool textile industry, which has already figured in our analyses. Here again, as late as the early seventies it was true that 'many of the industry's small firms are inefficient and traditionalist, and are also deeply entrenched' (Boswell, p. 116). The same author reported on a 'comprehensive survey of the industry in 1969, whilst praising its frequent good human relations and other features, strongly criticised many small firms in the industry for their inadequate marketing, their failure to innovate, their neglect of proper training and management controls, and their "inbred and generally unimaginative management".' And yet, it continues: 'with this conventional syllabus of errors went a recognition of the remarkable ability of such firms to survive' (p. 116).

There never has been that 'wholesale clear-out and reorganisation'. At different periods, as we have seen, different political strategies have been adopted towards this part of the economy. During the modernisation period it was marginal, largely given up as irrelevant, even as lost. In comparison, the Wool Textile Scheme introduced by the Conservatives in the early seventies, and the subsequent Labour Government's Accelerated Projects Scheme and Selective Investment Scheme were remarkably successful in terms of reorganisation, though leading to considerable losses of jobs in the regions affected. In the serious decline in competitiveness from the late seventies these kinds of company were very vulnerable, either directly, as through increased competition from imports, or because of decline in demand from consumer industries (for examples see Massey and Meegan, 1982; Martin, 1982).

But as employers of a significant section of the workforce, in manufacturing at least, they still survive. How, then, should they be characterised? They include a range of different labour processes and crop up in a number of parts of the economy. What they have in common is a certain set of characteristics to do with the organisational structure of capital. These include size (measured in employment terms, or by assets or turnover), but size alone is insufficient. What they essentially have in common is a certain social nature. As we have seen they are concerned with survival and perhaps succession. They are not overwhelmingly concerned with expansion, the essential ingredient of capitalist accumulation. They retain, in other words, many of the behavioural characteristics of the classical petit-bourgeoisie. In Wright's framework, presented in Chapter 2, there is a dimension of contradictory locations between petit-bourgeoisie and bourgeoisie. It is a classification adopted by Wright only for extremely small firms – he gives a range of upper limits of employment, from ten to fifty employees. This is a definition based, like the distinction between working class and capital, on the nature of the underlying social relations of value-production: 'When a petit-bourgeois producer employs a single helper, there is an immediate change in the social relations of production, for the labour of a worker can now be exploited. Still, the surplus-value appropriated from a single employee is likely to be very small' (p. 35). As the number of employees increases, however, the proportion of surplus product generated as surplus value by workers increases, and the proportion generated by the owner (and the unpaid labour of her/his family) declines. 'At some point [the latter] becomes less than half of the total surplus product, and eventually becomes a small fraction of the total surplus. At that point, the petit-bourgeois producer becomes firmly a small capitalist' (pp. 35–6). As Wright says, there is no *a priori* basis for saying how many employees turns an employer into a capitalist in those terms. It will depend for instance on technology, and it will change over time. But what is clear is that, on this criterion, the companies being discussed here are plainly capitalist. The non-accumulative characteristics which they share with the classical petit-bourgeoisie are the result of social behaviour rather than of an underlying structure of value relations. It is not that this part of production is conducted within the formal value relations of petit-bourgeois production. It is that in the United Kingdom a significant section of capital conducts its business in a singularly undynamic, even 'uncapitalist', fashion.

Why is this important to the analysis here? Because it is this kind of company which represents much of what remains in the United Kingdom today of 'local capital', much, in other words, of what remains in regions other than the south and east of locally-controlled industry, and quite a bit of what is in that region too. The very reasons for the survival of such companies often express their characteristics. Three factors stand out from Boswell's survey of British firms of up to 500 employees. The first has been reliance on cheap labour, in the case of cotton and wool textiles usually female, and often Asian. The lack of regional policy incentives in the home areas of these industries, and the existing higher female activity rates, may also have meant that there was less in-migrant competition for such workers. In these cases the labour is cheap because of its wider characteristics (sex, race) and the discrimination associated with them. In other parts of the small- and medium firm sector this kind of labour is not employed but the 'small firm sector' as a whole is notorious for its low degree of unionisation and low pay, in part a result of the nature of the companies themselves and the difficulties of organising within them. Second, in some industries, and particularly cotton and wool textiles (Boswell, 1973) and footwear (Mounfield, Unwin and Guy, 1982) geographical characteristics themselves may have been significant. The frequent location of plants in these industries in isolated communities where labour has had little bargaining power (Boswell, p. 115) has been a factor in keeping wages down, while the coincidence within a very local geographical area of the whole package of workforce, management and ownership (the latter two often the same) has seemed to provide some sort of focus for a common front between workers and owners, the one in defence of their jobs, the other in defence of their companies. (It is not being suggested that 'geography' itself has a necessary effect here. The mining villages discussed in Chapter 5 were very similar in their purely descriptive spatial aspects, yet their history is of much greater conflict. It is the combination of this particular kind of capital and a particular segment of the labour force (in this case mainly women) – in other words *of a particular set of social relations in a particular geographical structure* – which is significant (see Urry, 1980). But the shifts which we have analysed in other sections of capital seem likely to threaten both of these 'advantages'. On the one hand, and over the long term, there is the increasing employment of women in 'more modern' sectors – we have already seen the impact of that on the clothing and footwear industry. And on the other hand, there is the relative decentralisation of 'more attractive' jobs, especially in services, from conurbations to smaller towns and from the south-east of England to the regions beyond – as again we saw in the case of footwear. In other words, the new geography of *production* (as opposed to control) in some sections of big capital may well pose a threat to the survival of some of these remaining strongholds of local ownership.

The third, and the main, factor in the survival of this type of firm is simple rigidity – the very fact that the owner either cannot, or simply does not want to, transfer either the invested cash, or him or herself to another, more lucrative, sector of production (Boswell, 1973). This is not the flexible capital of big intersectoral companies, searching for maximum profit. It is commitment to the family business. It is not the dynamism and entrepreneurship invoked in much political rhetoric about small companies. In fact, as in the cases described here, it has often been the very lack of a drive to accumulate which has preserved small and medium-sized firms in such large numbers. It is not then surprising that over and over again area-based analyses point to the fact that local ownership is concentrated in slower-growing sectors.

It is perhaps worth noting that much the same general point (the lack of ability to form a new independent dynamic of accumulation) applies to other kinds of small and medium capital even where it is not of this very traditional character. Thus in many sectors such firms are completely dependent on the dynamic of the large companies which they serve. The form may vary: from small firms producing consumer goods, which are often tied to, or dominated by, major retail outlets (see the discussion of clothing in Chapter 4) to component manufacturers, as in the car industry. But in most cases, although the small firms may be significant as employers, and may even be, immediately, 'responsible' for the creation of numerous jobs, their position in the overall structure of the economy means that the real dynamic of accumulation lies elsewhere, with the large capital of the retail companies or the big car firms.

There are, however, some small companies which do have those much-referred-to characteristics – entrepreneurship, growth-potential and enterprise. Such firms exist, as we have seen, in electronics, in instrument engineering, in producer services. They are not always, by any means, independent of big firms, but they may be real foci of growth. They tend to be not only small, but relatively new. They are also, in most cases, internationally-oriented. What characterises them geographically is their concentration is that 'sunbelt' stretch from East Anglia to Southampton and Bristol. Not only are the sectors in which they are most frequent located mainly in the south-east (see the examples in Chapter 4), but so is that stratum of the population which has the highest propensity to start new firms – graduates, and those with other forms of higher education (Gudgin, Brunskill and Fothergill, 1979). This is much the same kind of duality, then, as in self-employment in services, with the old and declining elements hanging on in varying degrees over the country as a whole but with the new and growing parts, with high status and high income, being overwhelmingly concentrated in the south-east, plus a recent tendency to migrate to neighbouring regions.[16] When one considers the factors which lie behind both the ease of starting up new firms and the potential for success, this regional distribution is understandable. Storey's (1982) research indicates two main conditions underlying the propensity to start up new businesses: previous and dominant industry, and finance – particularly personal savings and second mortgages. We have already noted how the industrial structure of the heavy-industry Development Areas worked against new-firm indigenous growth (Chapter 5). In contrast, the distributions of personal savings, of owner-occupation and of high house prices are all biased towards the central regions. The background reasons for success – previous management experience, educational level and local markets – push in the same direction. Of all the new companies established in 1980, 35 per cent were based in the south-east (Department of Industry). It does seem indisputable that, were there ever to be a 'small-firm strategy' which actually worked but which was undifferentiated spatially, it would provide most benefit in employment terms to the south and east of England (Storey, 1982). The real social and economic distinctions which exist within both the small-firm and self-employment sections of the economy are thus important spatially. Not only do the distinct elements have different geographical distributions, they also have different implications for future growth.

So it is not just that the geography of ownership is increasingly concentrated in the south and east. The contrasts in dynamism between the different parts of capital, together with their different geographical distributions, means that control over *accumulation* is even more concentrated in that corner of the country than is formal ownership. This picture is massively reinforced when we bring back into the picture banking capital, still operating to a large extent from its old home-base in the City of London, and from here controlling not just the financial sector itself but also, to varying degrees, other parts of the economy. In a variety of ways, then, spatial centralisation of real control over production, over the process of accumulation, is occurring to an extent far greater than that which would be indicated by the simple tallying-up of headquarters, weighted, say, by employment. For it is precisely in those parts of the economy which lead the process of accumulation that the south and east is increasingly important as the location of control. In counterposition to this, the rest of the country is subject to external control (that is, the more strategic functions in the overall relations of ownership and possession are absent) to a degree greater than is evident in the figures for legal ownership.

The divisions within, and characteristics of, British capital which are important to an economic and political analysis of the United Kingdom and its rise and decline as a capitalist power, are fundamental also to its industrial geography. Conversely the broad divisions of the economy which are appropriate to a geographical analysis reflect that long economic and political history. The whole structure is dominated by relatively dynamic and internationally-orientated financial and industrial companies (and much of the accumulation which is controlled from the south and east is, of course, abroad – not in the United Kingdom at all). The 'rest of British industry' is very much what remains, in terms of geographically-local control, in 'the rest of Britain'. And, of course, the national geography is also marked by the long-lingering inheritance of Empire and of commitment to an international role. The importance of internationally-orientated capital is one aspect of this but in other ways too British industrial geography bears the marks of the national role of more than a century ago, just as much as do the economy and the class structure. While in the Development Areas the decline of the old production-bases of Empire continues to create poverty and unemployment, the financial side of the international role, based in the south-east, continues to flourish.

*   *   *

So far we have looked only at a very broad sketch, and considered only the distribution of ownership. Looking below that, and considering also wider questions of spatial organisation, the geography of direct production, there is a more complex picture. There are subdivisions within each of the major groups. Within big industrial capital in the dynamic parts of the economy, for instance, electronics majors are not like chemical giants, nor yet again like multinational clothing companies. Here, technology and labour process in particular are important, though not on their own a defining characteristic. The great differences in spatial structure are related to contrasts in labour process, to the long-term nature of technological development, and to the related social patterns of the workforce.

There are also clear divides within that group of middle-sized and small companies still attempting to tick over quietly in the regions where they have long been based.[17] First, there are the small-scale firms involved in the production of basic goods and means of production: the firms which turn out nuts, bolts, fasteners, iron-castings, small-batch-production machine tools and so on. They tend to have heavy, non-standardised labour processes in terms of the work involved and, overwhelmingly, they employ men. The dominant unions are the AUEW and the TGWU. The companies are located, geographically, largely in the heartlands of manufacturing industry, the West Midlands most obviously, but also in other areas. The market is often local, the companies are often deeply integrated into their regional economies, and often dependent on one or two of the larger producers in those economies. There is increasing international trade in some of these goods, and some firms in these industries are beginning to feel the impact of foreign competition, but most of all these firms are suffering from the general rundown of the British economy and in particular its manufacturing sector. Because of their place in the economy, they are *victims* of deindustrialisation as well as part of it. Their appeal for aid is often in terms of being vital to recovery, to argue that their disappearance would hinder any national economic reconstruction. The machine tool industry was the focus of this attention in the 1960s and a whole series of others have followed. In late 1982, the fastener industry representatives (the British Industrial Fasteners' Federation) argued that theirs was a strategic sector. A number of the industries have undergone co-ordinated rundown; their decline is an element in the general decline of skilled and semi-skilled manual jobs for men in manufacturing.

In complete contrast is that group of companies engaged in the production of what might be called old-fashioned consumer goods and related industries – clothing, textiles, footwear, cutlery and hosiery. Because of their different place in the economy, and also in many cases the greater transportability of their products, these industries are not so much *threatened by* the deindustrialisation of Britain, they are one of the most dramatic elements *of* it.

Production in the United Kingdom in these industries is under severe threat in the context directly of the changing international division of labour. The decline in these industries leads the decline of others. Textile machinery has been a recent victim. In these industries the claim on the State is usually in terms of demands for import controls. In further contrast to the nuts-and-bolts group, this part of the economy has historically employed a much more important element of female labour. This is particularly true of the clothing–footwear–hosiery group. Others, though, such as cutlery, have been sources mainly of jobs for men. Again in contrast with the big cross-sector unions typical of the means-of-production industries, many of these sectors have industry-specific unions; as we saw in Chapter 4, in clothing and footwear there was anxiety on the part of management to keep it that way. Historically, these industries pre-date the Industrial Revolution, their products are basic consumer goods, and their production in the United Kingdom has often slowly evolved through a series of stages to fully-capitalist and factory production. Their geography is different, too, from the nuts-and-bolts industries. Interestingly, for these are consumer-goods industries, they are probably *less* market-orientated. A surprising number of them have developed over the last couple of centuries very particular local and regional bases – as we saw in the case of footwear in Chapter 4. And many of the medium-sized and smaller companies are still there.

*   *   *

Economic, social and geographical contrasts within 'British capital' are integrally bound up with each other. These are just a few examples. What they show is that each of the 'criteria' discussed in Chapter 2 is important: their significance has been seen a number of times in the foregoing chapters. At different points and in different ways they cross-cut and are interwoven with each other and in that guise are part of the analysis of the complex, and particular, picture of the social economy and geography of British capital.

White-collar hierarchies

The centralisation of control over relations of economic ownership and of possession in the south-east feeds down through management hierarchies to sites of production throughout the country. Through the spatial extension of these relations of production a variety of 'interregional relations' of control are established. Different places in these tentacular forms of organisation are occupied by different kinds and levels of management, and this structure in turn is related to social differentiation. The higher the social status, the more likely to be in the south-east; the further removed from direct production in a functional sense, the further removed also in many cases in a spatial sense. In terms of the framework of social structure discussed in Chapter 2, this is the dimension between bourgeoisie (which includes a fair slice of top management) and working class. And we have seen from the studies in Chapters 4 and 5 how increasingly in a number of important parts of the British economy this dimension of social structure has a definite and systematic geographical form.

We have seen also that much the same is true of the spectrum of production engineers, technicians, technologists and scientists. Both between different kinds of production and within particular segments of the economy there is a developing relation between social position and spatial location. Industries in which 'scientific input' came from engineers in the old sense, highly qualified but with a close relation to production, both functionally and geographically, are becoming proportionately less important. The old 'engineering universities' were in the regions of engineering *production*. We saw in Chapter 4 some elements of the decline of the industrial-social structure which has been going on at least since the fifties (with the introduction into old firms of electronics-based scientists), but the precipitate collapse of engineering and engineering-related industries since the late seventies has accelerated the process. In contrast, industries where there is a far longer and more highly-differentiated division of labour on the technical and scientific side, and where the upper echelons of that hierarchy may be quite removed in an immediate functional sense from direct production have grown in relative importance, and grew in absolute terms very strongly in the sixties and parts of the seventies. Once again, functional distance from production has often gone along with geographical distance. In terms of the social framework introduced in Chapter 2 this spectrum of people is best characterised along the dimension between petit-bourgeoisie and working class, and as the social status gets 'higher' (greater degrees of autonomy, greater distance from the working class) so does the likelihood of living in the south and east of England. It is ironic that the long-time calls for a raising of the low status of 'engineers', a low status which itself was part and parcel of the low status in general accorded to production within the social structure of Britain, have only found an answer with the functional distancing of engineering, in the scientific sense, from production. In this aspect of industry as in management the development of the division of labour has extended the range of social strata involved and increased their social separation. It has also increased their geographical separation.

There is, as we have seen, some difference in Britain between the geography of higher-status scientists and technologists on the one hand and of higher managerial groups on the other. It is a difference, again, which reflects their contrasting functions within the overall relations of production. Management is more conurbation-oriented, and specifically London-based. Research and development staff can more often be found in the comparative seclusion of a secondhand country mansion somewhere in the crescent of country stretching from Bristol through the Home Counties and into East Anglia – the 'British sunbelt'. It is this latter distribution in particular which is shared with the new entrepreneurs, the dynamic end of the small-firm sector. It is around these groups that the 'sunbelt' has developed. To the extent that there has been any significant movement in recent years, it has been the decentralisation of headquarters, and therefore of upper management to the area. Financial companies moving lock, stock and barrel from London to Bristol, for instance. Such shifts reinforce both the decline of London as a centre of employment and the dominance and social character of the sunbelt. Finally, this general pattern, of the concentration of high-status jobs in this crescent of country, is stimulated and reinforced by the geographical structure of certain elements of State employment. This is, as we saw in Chapter 4, particularly true of the central State. Local State sectors are one of the few sources of professional jobs in 'the regions', and this is true particularly for women.

Southern and eastern stretches of England, then, are home to a variety of different elements of the higher reaches of white-collar strata. The increasing importance of each over the long term

reflects a number of historical developments within British capitalism: the concentration of ownership, the changing division of
labour in society as a whole, the increasing divorce between
mental and manual labour in production, and the growth of the
State apparatus. The group includes the top end of management
hierarchies of multiregional firms, the more rarified parts of
research and development in science-based industries, the professionals of the growing service sectors, the City, the upper-level
civil servants of the central State, the centres of the old professions, and the graduate entrepreneurs. Performing different functions within society as a whole, they nonetheless share much in
common socially. This is not, of course, the only part of the
country in which such people are to be found. In earlier chapters
we have noted 'research outliers', in northern Cheshire for instance and around Edinburgh, and there are the more environmentally minded elements of small-business entrepreneurship
which have taken up residence in places such as Cornwall. But as
a generalisation of the overall pattern, this broad picture is not
unfair.

We have seen in Chapter 4 a number of the detailed reasons
which lie behind this pattern, both the fact of concentration and its
location in the south and east. Reasons of contact and linkage,
ordering patterns, the community of scientists, the community of
class, the functioning of labour markets, and social and residential
preferences. Over the longer span of history the pattern has much
to do, of course, simply with the fact that London is the capital and
that the State and all its central demands in terms of goods and
services emanated from there. It was from here too that the
financial sector played such a part in organising international
trade. Once established, such a centre can generate its own
momentum. Over the last half century the location of the central
State has been very important to the electronics industry, for
instance, much of which developed through, and often still is
closely related to, the military and defence establishment.

So the fact that the headquarters of State and Empire have been
in the south-east has been an important starter-motor for this
process of concentration. And we have seen that even the most
iron of prime ministers failed to move them. But why *not* move the
Foreign Office, say, or the Ministry of Defence, to Longbenton,
Newcastle-upon-Tyne? The clerical jobs in social security were

decentralised there. There are of course many reasons of 'linkage' and 'contact' which might militate against such a move, or call for some thoughtful reorganisation. But there are other reasons, too, and most of them revolve around social power.

Between them, indeed, the upper echelons of these white-collar social strata more or less 'control' the geography of employment in Britain. This is obvious in a simple way of management in the larger firms – they make the 'location decisions' – and they do so, as we have argued, in the context of wider economic conditions. But there is also an element, as we have seen, of more purely social power. The spatial immobility of upper-echelon civil servants is part of this, and so is what seems to be the presently-increasing social and spatial power of the upper end of the spectrum of technologists and scientists. Ever since the end of the Second World War this group has been centrally important both economically and politically. Scientists and technologists emerged from the war and into reconstruction with greatly enhanced prestige: 'the sense of élite status which derived from membership of the new technological club, played no small part in the decision of many concerns to invest in development laboratories' (Burns and Stalker, 1966, p. 43). The defence programme reinforced that position. In the sixties, as we have seen, science and technology were regarded as the central elements in modernising and thereby rescuing the British economy. At that point it was primarily scientists in the laboratories of large companies who were the focus of attention and the locational form in which they were embedded was often the kind of hierarchical structure described in Chapter 4 for electronics. By the late seventies and early eighties it was the scientist-as-entrepreneur who held centre stage and the terms of the locational emphasis had shifted to things such as science parks. Some individuals moved between groups. In the later period there were management buy-outs and various company-promoted schemes of going solo, where former employees turned themselves into self-employed subcontractors. But whatever the nature of their economic or ideological significance it carried with it locational power. Such people have considerable freedom to decide where they want to work. They do not want to go to the industrial north, they *do* want to be distanced from production, virtually every advertising brochure for every local authority in the country now panders to their social and residential tastes, science parks are designed to attract them: 'We recognise that these parks employ a disproportionately large number of qualified technicians and professional staff who seek an attractive parkland environment in which to work, close to major centres of technical research and well served by air and road ... An essential part of the scheme, apart from proper landscaping, will be associated retail and leisure facilities which will enhance a community atmosphere' (director of Multinational Management Group, quoted in *Financial Times*, 5 October 1982). Some of the same cultural and social considerations enter into location decisions even about headquarters of major companies, where the requirements of upper management have to be met. Most of these people, as we have said, are male, but the difficulty of decentralising them is exacerbated by the even greater lack of professional job opportunities for women 'in the regions' – the 'professional couple' might find it very difficult for both partners to get jobs outside the south-east and its surrounding area. And public expenditure cuts, since it is the public sector which provides most professional jobs for women in the regions, only make the problem worse: the concentration in the 'sunbelt' is therefore reinforced.

This is the top end of the spectrum of this multifarious white-collar group: the various hierarchies which they head are being stretched and increasingly differentiated both socially and spatially. Important issues arise about what kind of social divisions exist along these hierarchies. How much difference is there, socially and politically, between the white-collar middle strata of the north-east, say, and those of the 'sunbelt'? It is clear that within white-collar hierarchies social and geographical differences are mutually reinforcing. We have seen how place in the relations of production changes, how social status changes, how voting patterns vary geographically for these groups, and along the same dimensions, so how much has the spatial extension of these hierarchies had an independent effect on their social form? How much does the fact of spatial distance and the fact of being based in regions very different in overall class structure and culture lead to an even greater social divorce between the top and the bottom of these hierarchies? It is not possible to answer the question here, and indications could be pointed to in either direction. Perhaps the short-stay nature (or hoped-for-short-stay nature) of their residence outside the south-east nullifies such an effect. On the other hand, voting patterns and a number of recent cases where management in the regions has fought alongside workers against closure (feeling itself just as much as the rest of the workforce 'on the receiving end' of central decisions) may indicate a potential social and political polarisation in alignment within these groups. The social status of the 'sunbelt' itself would seem to point in that direction. To the extent that such contrasts are increasingly important, then 'geography' in all its meanings will have played an active role.

Social and spatial restructuring in the working class

This has been a period of major recomposition for the working class also, and a recomposition in which geographical reorganisation has again been integral. Indeed, one of the central stakes at issue for the whole of this period has been the shape, organisation and strength of labour. 'Geography', as we have seen, has not merely reflected that battle; it has been one of the cards in the game.

Over and above everything else which has happened since the 1960s has been the erosion of some of the central bastions of working-class trade union strength, the old heartlands of the labour movement. The old sectoral union bases, in mining for instance, have continued, and often accelerated, their steep numerical decline, and what that has threatened to take with it has been the geographical cores of labourism. There have been other equally distinctive and equally major losses: the result of deindustrialisation. It has been the cities and the midlands and the north-west which have been most caught up in this decline, and general and craft, rather than sectoral, unions; unions like the TGWU and the AUEW. It has been part of the recomposition of the working class away from male manual workers. It has affected, too, many a smaller town with an old industrial base – Swindon, for example, a railway town once, but now with jobs for the male manual working class contracting as the high-tech industry and executive housing sprouts up all around. The 'sunbelt' was not empty before the arrival of the middle class. Deindustrialisation has also humbled even the more-recently developed centres of militancy. The devastation of Merseyside, including the attack on the car industry there, is the most obvious example. There are many other parts of the economy losing jobs (the fall in employment for women in industries such as clothing has been massive), but in terms of that old defensive strength and straightforward economic militancy, the ones just listed are probably the most crucial losses. What stands out is how much has gone. This is not a simple rerun of the 1930s: this time the concatenation of events is taking with it not one but two or three generations of union strength.

Within the working class also, the geography of functions, of individual job control, of autonomy, is changing. This is particularly evident in the decline of skilled manual jobs. We saw in Chapter 5 how the old skills and customs of individual job control have actually proved problematical to industries newly-arriving in peripheral regions, employing redundant miners but having no demand for such human assets. The skills of which such jobs have been shorn are concentrated in other parts of the country. The same is true too of a significant proportion of the new jobs for women in these regions. In regions such as these, the old coalfields, a curious double and contradictory process is under way. At the same time and by the same process as local cohesiveness within the workforce has been undermined, by an increase in the variety of industries, employers, and so on, so the monofunctionality of work, and the lack of control over the individual work-process, has increased. Functions and places within the relations of production have been separated out, allocated to different social groups, and geographically removed.

All these spatial changes have been part and parcel of the shifting national composition of the working class. The period as a whole has seen more than job loss and unemployment. Within that, as we have seen, there have also been major changes in skill and gender composition. Increasing numbers of women have been drafted into the labour force, public-sector and white-collar clerical jobs have, over the period as a whole, expanded, non-manual jobs have expanded at the expense of manual, and older craft-related skills have continued to be diluted.

It is, moreover, not just that the recomposition of working-class jobs, and of unemployment, has had a geographical form, it is also that geographical form and spatial mobility has been integral to recomposition. The combination of a previously economically-inactive reserve and high unemployment, together at times with the changing demands of the dominant production processes, have enabled capital within Britain to cut costs and increase its control by shifting location to less organised workers. At the same time, it has left unemployed those whose participation in the previous century's pattern of production enabled them to become stronger and more organised. What increase in employment there was for working-class people during this period on the whole *avoided* the newly-unemployed workforce, both in the cities and in the Development Areas, and instead sought out new reserves of labour in smaller towns and among the women of the older industrial (but non-conurbation) areas. And the distinctiveness of those areas was often important; we saw in Chapter 5 how the particular characteristics of the mining areas were important to the preservation there of a pool of female labour. The growth of the female labour force and the spatial mobility of capital were also interlinked in more complex ways. When some of the older consumer-goods industries in the cities, particularly in London, had their young female labour forces poached by the growing service sector they frequently decentralised, changing not only location but also the part of the female labour force they employed. In the new locations many of the jobs went to older, married women. And when clerical services, too, started to decentralise they either found brand new workforces or, as we saw in the case of footwear, outcompeted older-established local industries, which in turn were forced, if they did not die, to decentralise even further. While some of the newer female-employing industries (electronics for example) went straight to decentralised locations for their labour force, in those cases where the growth industries have at least initially gone for more central locations (as in the case of services) they have pushed older industries out to the periphery. The internal composition, and the geography, of women's employment has been transformed over this period, and the two have gone hand in hand. The same is true of white-collar, non-manual employment. It is not just that this has expanded as an element of the workforce, and more specifically also of the working class, but that in the process it has been spatially sorted.

Geography has been important in more particular ways, too. The concentration of capital, the creation of larger firms, might in some ways be expected to provide easier conditions for building labour solidarity. But together with increasing size of firm has gone not increasing size of individual plant but fragmentation into a multiplicity of different and separate locations. Where this is a cloning structure, instead of the preconditions for solidarity it provides an easy way to play off one group of workers against others in another plant. Where the multi-plant organisation is in a part-process structure there are other difficulties too, for here the workers are not only separated into different locations, but they also do different jobs, have different working conditions, face different day-to-day problems, perhaps belong to different unions. They are also probably scattered between areas with different labour-movement traditions to draw on. Meanwhile in each there are the increased negotiating difficulties which go with the distancing of ownership and control.

In many ways this story seems one of unremitting gloom, and it is often presented as such. It is certainly true that both the decline of the old and the form of the new composition and geography of the working class present difficulties to the construction of a coherent workforce organisation. The solid old bastions, and some of the newer foci of militancy, *have* been weakened. Conditions in the cities, the fact of that kind of geographical environment, the density of the social network, the links between plants, the kinds of (manufacturing) industry which were dominant, provided propitious conditions for building solidarity (Lane, 1982). What remains today of the private sector in the cities – small firms and the service sector – is notoriously difficult to organise. The scattering of more isolated plants in smaller towns, and in rural and semi-rural areas, particularly given the kind of labour they employ, seems to be a much less helpful starting point. Indeed, we have seen that spatial isolation can at times be an explicit element of managerial location strategy. Once again social and spatial recomposition of the workforce reinforce each other. Put this together with the socially-orientated location strategy of managements and technicians and one gets a vision of a future geography of industry: management acting out its dreams of a rural idyll, workforce obligingly docile in widely-scattered factories, or clustered in small groups on trading estates. In present terms, a trade union organiser's nightmare.

However, that *is* to look at it in present terms. Industrial restructuring and reorganisation only provide new preconditions:

they do not determine the outcome. Even the present 'bastions of strength', 'heartlands of the labour movement' etc., had to be built, consciously constructed. It will certainly be difficult for trade unions to rebuild former kinds of organisational strength, but that is not an unmitigated disaster: those forms had their own problems of defensiveness, labourism and social conservativeness. Their sexism was part of what now makes possible their own undermining through the employment of women at such low wages. There was an asymmetry in the situation. While it was clearly important to British capital to undermine the defensive strength and economic militancy of the dominant unions it was far less clear that such unions could provide a way out of the impasse in a new political direction. Nor is it clear now that, in spite of carefully chosen workforces and carefully selected locations, the new recruits to the economically-active working class will remain forever docile. Some of the fiercest battles of the early 1980s were fought by women in the old 'male' industrial areas. The break-down of 'geographical coherence' in some of the older regions may not be entirely detrimental to working-class organisation either: the other side of intraregional coherence can be (though it is not always) interregional division. Also it is not the case that in all parts of the country such coherence is being dismantled. In some regions – for example, Cornwall, the south-west more generally, East Anglia – an industrial waged-labour-force of any size is only just being constructed. The national aggregate decline has been accompanied in certain parts of the period and in certain parts of the country by the *extension* of capitalist wage-relations.

And not all the new kinds of employment growth are impossible to build on. Multi-locational companies certainly increase the danger of dividing workers within companies, but they also form a basis for different forms of organisation – combines, for instance – and hold out some potential for networks of linkages spanning the country. The long-term growth of employment in public sector services holds out possibilities both of links between workers in different parts of the country and of connections between employ-ment and service provision at a more local community level. It is sometimes argued that the newly-emerging geography of employ-ment is in itself essentially negative ground for trade union organisation. The contrast is posed between highly integrated industrial cities and regions and rural isolation, individual labour markets dominated by individual plants (Lane, 1982). But even between these extremes the issue is not entirely clear. Certainly in the studies in earlier chapters (in footwear, for instance, and the Lancashire textile industry) there have been cases in which such locality-structures have been one element in a situation more generally inimical to organisation. But only one element. It was the combination of particular social relations in a particular geographical structure which was really decisive. The evidence from Lockwood (1958), from Sayles (1958) and from the mining villages of south Wales shows that a different combination of social relations, but in a similar spatial structure, can produce a very different result. Geography matters, but it does not in itself determine any particular social outcome.

The present major geographical reorganisation of the British working class represents, not some final defeat, but new problems and new preconditions. Indeed, precisely as the economic strength of our largest cities is under attack, so those cities have become important foci for resistance, new alliances are being constructed out of the wreckage, determined that it shall go no further, and that reconstruction might be on other terms. The response varies also by region. A reassertion of defensive solidarity in the old regions of the industrial periphery, an unbelieving clinging to individualistic consumerism in parts of the midlands. Different periods and forms of past economic development have created the conditions for very different labour movements, and the legacy they leave as industrial decline sets in is correspondingly distinct. It is true that the greater mobility of capital gives it the advantage in setting the terms of the conflict. Indeed its high and increasing spatial mobility may prove the hardest problem to overcome, greater than the characteristics of any particular new locational pattern. The changes going on at the moment can be conceptualised in terms of a shift between dominant spatial divisions of labour. But that is to talk of a social process, involving disruption, change, and conflict: as such the outcome is always uncertain.

Postscript   The Reproduction of Inequality: A Question of Politics

The period we have been looking at has been a crucial one for British society. Economically, socially and politically it has undergone enormous changes. It has also been transformed geographically.

The old spatial division of labour based on sector, on contrasts between industries, has gone into accelerated decline and in its place has arisen to dominance a spatial division of labour in which a more important component is the interregional spatial structuring of production within individual industries. Relations between economic activity in different parts of the country are now a function rather less of market relations between firms and rather more of planned relations within them. Relations of production are increasingly centralised in the south and east of the country. There is a growing geographical, as well as social, division between conception and execution. The continuing elements of sectoral differentiation only serve to reinforce this dichotomy. The growth of new 'hi-tech' industries – biotechnology is a prime example – is largely in the already-favoured areas. This is the new spatial division of labour, and it brings with it a new north–south divide. This time it is between the 'sunbelt' and the rest, where 'the rest' consists of relatively decentralised employment and great pools of unemployment where production used to be. This is, of course, a simplification. The detail, as we have stressed and shall stress, is more complex, but the old form of the regional problem was always caricatured too. And the broad picture is undeniable.

Spatial inequality has dramatically changed its form. The indices, the social structure and the map itself: all have been transformed. The new kinds of spatial organisation of production no longer lead to problems of excessive dependence of particular areas on particular industries. Instead they bring with them all the problems of the cloning, part-process, subcontracting and other spatial structures discussed in previous chapters. There is also another major difference. The spatial division of labour which was based around industrial differentiation and specialisation only produced a 'regional problem' when the sector in which the area was specialised went into decline or moved away. In the case of the newer spatial structures, and most particularly in the case of the part-process structure, this correspondence between industrial and regional decline no longer holds. Increasingly, the ways in which companies are being organised over space mean that geographical inequality is actually inherent in the spatial structure itself. In a way which is true neither of sectoral specialisation and local control nor of simple branch-plant structures, this kind of use of space is actually predicated upon spatial inequality; it requires it and necessarily reproduces it. Companies operating production hierarchies both depend on and reproduce inequality while they are healthy and growing. We have stressed a number of times in the course of this analysis that spatial inequality does not simply increase with the historical development of capitalist society; that the process is more complex, involving changes in form and nature as well as degree. That is true, but what does need to be said about the new form and nature of geographical inequality in Britain is that it is integral not to decline but to growth – or, at least, growth in any of the terms which have been tried since the 1960s. It becomes even more apposite to ask 'a regional problem for whom?'

The term 'regional' is here, as throughout, being used generically for 'spatial', or subnational. For it is clear that even the shape of the map has been refashioned. The contours of the new spatial division of labour are different from those of the old. The 'sunbelt' crosses south-west, south-east, east midlands and East Anglia. Regions only recently 'central' in terms of prosperity have joined the economic periphery. And the geography we are actually faced with, the result of the combination of an emergent spatial division of labour with the declining but still present form of the old, is highly intricate. No longer is there really a 'regional' problem in the old sense. No longer is there a fairly straightforward twofold division, along a single line between central, prosperous areas and a decaying periphery. The map of unemployment itself has undergone a change, the persistent decline of the periphery now being added to by collapse in manufacturing regions and urban areas. Every one of the 'standard regions', prosperous or otherwise, includes within it enormous variation, is in particular plunged through by the dereliction of the inner cities.

Within the broad-brush picture presented earlier, then, there is a complex mosaic of great variety. The 'British spatial problem' of the last quarter of the twentieth century reflects both the continued reproduction of the problems and inequalities of previous spatial divisions of labour and also, superimposed upon it, a new layer of disparities, those of the presently emerging spatial division of labour. It is precisely *because* this is not a simple process of deepening inequality but the superimposition of different structures that different regions go through different kinds (even different directions) of change. The dynamic of social reproduction varies geographically and so do its effects on social composition. In the coalfields the old homogeneity of the working class is being broken down and the starkness of its distinction from other classes being blurred. In many rural areas there is an increase in the importance of a working-class element in the social structure, and a decline of some other components. In the south-east a process of social dichotomisation appears to be under way. While professional and managerial strata increase in importance, manual workers face a loss of manufacturing jobs and a decline in conditions of employment as casual work, the service sector, and work within small firms grow in relative importance. Different parts of the country have different relationships with the international economy, some functioning as the production outposts of multinational capital, some as more self-contained or nationally-orientated economies, others as themselves bases for international empires. When one puts all this together with the fact that the 'regions' and 'localities' are themselves constantly being formed and re-formed, constructed and disintegrated, the complexity of the mosaic that is British industrial geography is evident.

So, too, should be the importance of recognising that complexity in analysis. Local uniqueness matters. Capitalist society, it is well-recognised, develops unevenly. The implications are twofold. It is necessary to unearth the common processes, the dynamic of capitalist society, beneath the unevenness, but it is also necessary to recognise, analyse and understand the complexity of the unevenness itself. Spatial differentiation, geographical variety, is not just an outcome: it is integral to the reproduction of society and its dominant social relations. The challenge is to hold the two sides together; to understand the general underlying causes while at the same time recognising and appreciating the importance of the specific and the unique.

So a new social and industrial geography is in the making, and a new set of disparities is coming on to the agenda. An outcome of changing international and national class relations, this new spatial division of labour also had the ground prepared for it by the preceding one: the social reproduction of inequality, one form of spatial organisation being a precondition for the next. In Chapter 5, we saw this process in operation in the coalfields. The present lack of 'indigenous growth' in these regions is now frequently blamed, by academics and politicians alike, on their 'lack of entrepreneurship'. But to talk of a lack of entrepreneurship is to comment upon one aspect of class structure, and, as we have seen, in these regions the lack of a significant element of small capital is to an important extent due to their previous industrial history – through both the dominance of oligopolistic structures and the lack of development of those white-collar and technical strata from which 'entrepreneurs' typically emerge. Further, the non-generation of any real 'middle-class' strata under the previous division of labour produced a lack of their associated 'culture and society' (Morgan, 1979, pp. 31–2). This combines with another inheritance of the old industries – the despoliation of the natural and built environment – to reinforce the difficulties of attracting the upper echelons of technical and managerial staff in the new spatial structures. Finally, the existence and the nature of the reserve of female labour has provided one of the most important attractions to the incoming industries. It was not only the existence of a reserve of labour which was important, but also the fact of its low levels of organisation. And these characteristics – the lack of previous experience of wage relations, the masculinity and sexism of the local culture – owe not a little to the preconditions established under the dominance of the previous spatial division of labour.

What we see here are some of the mechanisms of the reproduction of the spatial structures of dominance and subordination and their associated effects. The process by which one use of space lays the preconditions for another is a complex one, and depends on the political and organisational response of the classes and social groups involved. What has happened in these areas is that both the social dimensions of interregional differentiation and the underlying economic structures on which they are based have undergone a transformation. The subordination of these regions continues, but the form of that subordination and its social effects are changing.

Again, at the other end of the country the initial location of the machinery of the State, and the concentration of 'high status people', in the south-east of England has been an important reason for the latter's increasing concentration there. This is, again, not just an 'economic' mechanism but a mechanism of social class. Residential preferences, and more particularly the differential ability to operate them, are a social means by which this stratum, increasingly important in absolute terms as a result of changes in production, has become so spatially concentrated. It is in a sense a class process of cumulative causation and a dynamic which is very different from that found in other parts of the social structure and in other parts of the country. Here too the new spatial division of labour is being built on the past.

If the old spatial division of labour laid the basis for the further reproduction of geographical inequality, what about the new one? What are its dynamics; what does it hold in store? It seems all too clear that it too contains within it the basis for the further reproduction of inequality. In the old industrial Development Areas, and in other regions of the country, the high levels of external control, the low levels of linkage, the redundancy of the old skills of the workforce and the lack of new ones provide little basis for indigenous private-sector growth. In the 'sunbelt' of the south and east the cumulative causation which is under way will be difficult to stop by any of the presently accepted policies of individual firm incentives. There are some signs of change; a few headquarters have been decentralised from London, though often only to the south-east, and some companies are making efforts to reunite research and production. This is particularly true of non-British capital and it is there, too, that higher levels of management are to be found in peripheral regions (once again the social character of capital is all-important). From Silicon Valley comes a story which indicates that the process of cumulative causation might one day burn itself out. The competition for electronics engineers in that area is now so fierce that some companies are deliberately locating 'their most important research and development projects well away from Silicon Valley – where their top engineers will be less likely to be tempted by competitors' (Kehoe, 1982). But overall, the signs are that the dynamics inherent in the presently-emerging spatial division of labour in the UK look set to entrench the country into a highly unequal geography.

What kind of policy intervention might halt these trends, enable a more equal geographical future? One thing which is fascinating about the period since the early sixties is the variety of political strategies which have been adopted. A couple of versions of social democracy and a bold attempt to break out of the mould in a rightwards direction. None of them have solved the problems of the economy, nor is it yet clear that any of them have broken the political log-jam. What *is* abundantly clear is that each of these strategies for social and economic reorganisation, each attempt to 'do something about the British economy' has not only, by not facing them, been undermined by structural social and economic contradictions, each has also, as part and parcel of the same process, produced different patterns of uneven development. There is certainly a long-term shift under way in the national spatial division of labour, but the various components of it have been pushed forward differentially and unevenly with each economic and political conjuncture. Strategies of technocratic reforming modernisation, epitomised by the White Heat of Wilsonism, reproduced 'the old regional problem' with a vengeance. The decline of employment in the old imperial bases of the peripheral regions, especially coal, was at its fastest. But at the same time, this strategy, operated in a period when the world economy was still relative buoyant, produced also the fastest growth of the new spatial structures, of decentralisation of production to less urban areas and to 'the regions'. It was, moreover, an economic strategy combined with an active regional policy and important growth in local State employment. All this together looked for a moment really like renovation: new jobs for the regions, convergence of unemployment rates. In reality it was the emergence of one aspect of a new form of geographical inequality. In the mid-seventies a combination of prevarication on both economic and regional fronts led to less dramatic changes in the old Development Areas. But in the more recent industrial heartlands and in the inner cities the decline of manufacturing was heralding new 'problem areas'. With the advent of Thatcherism the balance of processes changed again. The loss of jobs in the old Development Areas was accelerated once more and this time not just in the old basic industries but also in some of those decentralised as recently as a decade before. Nor was there any new wave of decentralisation to plug the gap, not even new jobs in the local State sectors. The emergence of that element of the new spatial division of labour seemed to have gone into reverse, or at least to have slowed down. But other elements of change continued apace. Britain's manufacturing role in the international economy continued its dramatic decline, taking with it wide, and previously relatively prosperous, areas of the country. Both politically and economically the room for manoeuvre for 'doing something about the regional problem' was dramatically narrowed.

What all these contrasts show is that the changing form of 'the regional problem', and of spatial inequality more generally, is not inevitable, inexorable, or uniquely a question of economics. It is also political. In order to understand geographical shifts at any particular time it is necessary to understand the economic, and the political, characteristics of the period. These three periods with their different politics and their contrasting economic backdrops and pressures, produced very different movements in the industrial and social geography of the country. These outcomes could not be read off at this level from the state of the economy.

But on the other hand and at a deeper level, all of these political strategies were themselves bound by the ultimate constraint: the dominance of capitalist relations of production.

One of the main burdens of this book has been to produce an interpretation of spatial patterns of employment in terms of the geographical organisation of the social relations of capitalist economic activity. We have seen that when the issue of spatial form is considered in this way and not just as a question of the geographical distribution of jobs, then even the nature of the problem changes. The issue of external control is not simply a matter of the geography of ownership, as most current arguments imply. Any real solution would have to tackle also the question of the *social* location of control and the deeper organisation of production itself. As happened earlier this century in the north-east of England (see Chapter 5) and is to some extent happening in the north-west now (Lloyd and Shutt, 1983), when a region becomes relatively unprofitable, capital – even 'local' capital – will diversify its investments to pastures new. It is true the growing size and sectoral and geographical spread of individual companies increases the flexibility of their investment. It is also true, there-fore, that the expansion of multiregional capital, and therefore of external control, will increase the problems for some regions – but only for those regions which are relatively unprofitable (Swales, 1979). To this extent, demands that regional policy should be designed to restructure local economies towards more locally-owned, *but still capitalist*, growth amounts to a demand that capital should decrease again its geographical and intersectoral flexibility – hardly a move which is in the long term likely to provide the basis for dynamic accumulation. Instead of retaining the profit-motive and requiring it to operate suboptimally it would be better to question the implications of that motive itself. It is the same with the differential spatial distribution of occupational groups and social strata. The new spatial division of labour depends on a particular form of technology, one in which some do all the strategic thinkwork and others all the assembly or whatever. The kind of growth we see now in the outer south and east of England depends on there being other areas where only unskilled work is available. It depends on the division of society into those contrast-ing types of work in the first place. But there is not just one type of 'new technology': technology is designed not discovered. Nothing did more to establish the new forms of spatial inequality than that Wilsonian mix of a 'modernisation' policy which believed in the social and political neutrality of technology and a regional policy which considered only the numbers of jobs and paid no attention to their quality. These, in other words, are not just problems of geographical distribution – spatial issues to be tackled by simply spatial reorganisation – they are also, necessarily and integrally, issues which pose questions of the wider organisation of social relations. *Really* tackling 'the regional problem' or 'the urban problem' means tackling those underlying relations. This conclu-sion is inescapable. No amount of tinkering around with spatial policies without in any way challenging the nature of the relations of production has the slightest hope of doing more than marginally mitigating a few symptoms. It cannot eradicate the cause.

Nor is it only 'capitalist relations of production' in some general sense which must be challenged. It is also the specific class form which they take, for which they are the basis, in the United Kingdom. Attacking geographical inequality in the United Kingdom, just as much as facing up to the problems of the national economy, means attacking the dominance – political, economic and spatial – of international capital. It also means challenging the social power of certain strata in British society, in particular the upper echelons of white-collar hierarchies, managerial, professional and technical, and those who occupy and maintain the archaic structure of the British establishment in its broadest sense. None of the political strategies examined here have attempted, let alone achieved, such a change. All have refused to face up to the contradictions inherent in the political dominance of international capital; all in various ways have lionised the new professional strata; none of them – neither Labour nor Conservative 'modernisers' – have faced up to the entrenched establishment. The result in all cases has been that it has been working people who have had to bear the brunt of the strategies. Questions of geography in the United Kingdom reflect, not just the formal relations of production, but wider questions of politics, power and social class.

Yet they are not *simply* a reflection. The geographical organisation of society is integral to its social reproduction and to politics in the widest sense. For decades now the battle over labourism, and to some extent over trade union power itself, has been fought in and over particular regions. The recomposition of national social structure could not have taken place without the geographical changes we have been documenting here. The formation of the characteristics of certain classes, and subgroups within classes, is bound up with geographical form. The old heart of the labour movement would not have been the same without geographical concentration, nor the shop stewards' movement in engineering – nor trades councils – without the varied social infrastructure of the big cities. Today certain social strata have their status reinforced by the fact of their location. The battles may now be over new bases of the left – the big cities maybe. 'Thinking geographically' is part of thinking about society more generally, and recognition and understanding of geographical variation is essential for any strategy of national political change.

Notes and References

Chapter 2: Social Relations and Spatial Organisation

1. On this debate see Keeble (1977, 1978, 1980); Hudson (1978); Massey (1979) and Sayer (1982).
2. Timpanaro (1974) produces a ringing critique of this easy, and incorrect, association of free will with indeterminacy:

    It is astonishing to note that even serious philosophers calmly identify *freedom* (which, if it is not understood mythologically, means a capacity for planning, and subordinating means to ends) with *indeterminacy*, merely because both are commonly counterposed to causal determinism. 'Me-ti said: physics has just declared that the fundamental particles are unpredictable; their movements cannot be foreseen. They seem to be individuals, endowed with free wills. But individuals are not endowed with free will. Their movements are difficult to predict, or cannot be predicted, only because there are too many determinations, not because there are none'. Brecht, *Me-Ti: Buch der Wendungen* (Frankfurt, 1965 p. 11, n6).

3. Which does not mean to say they will be successful. The probability of any manufacturing firm formed in the present period in the United Kingdom having 100 employees ten years after start-up is extremely low.
4. There are other reasons, too, which we shall come to, why such an 'explanation' is adequate.
5. It is only the *individual* worker's freedom to organise her or his own work process which is at issue here. Control in the wider sense of power on the shop floor is a different matter; it is certainly not a simple function of technology or the overall organisation of the labour process.
6. It is important to stress that none of these kinds of change actually operate historically as a simple and immutable progression. They are introduced here as a conceptual tool for looking at the empirical situation in the United Kingdom, not as processes implying laws. For discussions which provide a useful corrective to the 'tendency-as-iron-law-under-the-control-of capital' approach, see Elger (1979) and

Brighton Labour Process Group (1977), Burawoy (1979) and Wood (1982). There are also other aspects of these processes, some of which will be taken up later. One evident parallel to those discussed here is the distinction between mental and manual work, though, again, this is a distinction which has to be treated with some caution (Brighton Labour Process Group, 1977). The frequent classification of routine clerical work as 'mental labour' is one example. In this study clerical workers in general are counted as part of the working class.

7. This is the term coined by Wright, and for convenience we continue its use, but the analysis here does not follow the whole of Wright's position. His framework is used as a starting point because our own starting point, given that we are looking at industry, must be production and the social relations of production, and Wright's analysis of these relations provides a good framework. For Wright, contradictory class locations are contradictory in the sense that 'if classes are understood as social relations, not things ... certain positions have a contradictory character within those social relations. On certain dimensions of class relations they share the characteristics of one class, on others they share the characteristics of another' (1976, p. 23). For our purpose this is a useful initial formulation. But it is not meant here to carry with it the implication, implicit in some of Wright's arguments, that while for contradictory strata the contradictory nature of their position within the social relations of production gives them an indeterminate political orientation, open to ideological influence, groups which occupy determinate positions within the relations of production are correspondingly 'determinate' in their political orientation.

8. This integral relation is beginning to be recognised, by Urry (1981) and Giddens (1979) in sociology, for instance, and by Duncan (1979), Sack (1980) and Sayer (1981) in geography.

Chapter 3: Uneven Development and Spatial Structures

1. Obviously 'regions' do not interrelate as regions. What is referred to here by this term are the relations between plants in different localities.

2. This applies, of course, to differentiation within the labour market *in general*. The differences do not have to be geographical, but that is our focus here.

3. The level of spatial disaggregation being defined as relevant to the particular questions being asked.

4. In fact, such (small-batch) production is itself now becoming in-

308 *Notes and References*

creasingly automatable through, in particular, forms of numerical control. The *Financial Times* 'Technical Page' gives a good indication of the emphasis being put on reducing labour content and increasing labour-force control in production processes of this sort.

5. We are here considering only the case where the whole of this process takes place within a single firm. In many cases subcontracting arrangements operate even for major components, though this varies significantly from country to country. Its effects will also be different. The technical division of labour described here may also in part itself be a response to 'spatial opportunities' – as the Italian example in the next paragraph demonstrates.

6. This discussion, because of the comparison with Fiat, is mainly on an intracompany basis. In fact, as Friedman's argument implies, inter-company geographical differentiation in wages survived. The ten week strike in 1971 by Ford workers was for parity with the Midlands plants of other companies in the industry, primarily BLMC (see Beynon, 1973, ch. 11).

7. Geographical differentials within the industry as a whole continued even when those within individual firms had been successfully broken down.

8. The quotation marks are here deliberately used as scare-quotes. Given that the geography of inequality can change, so can the regionalisation of a country. It is also possible that in many cases the notion of a role within the national economy is irrelevant. Given the comments made earlier, it is just as likely that the role of a particular region can only be established internationally. Similarly, the term 'interregional relations' is being used as a shorthand term for relations between economic activities in different regions.

9. The discussion here is confined to relations between industries organised on a capitalist basis.

10. It is important to stress again that this discussion is of intranational regional issues. At international level this issue has far wider, and more real, political implications.

11. All this raises a number of issues concerning the definition of a division of labour. Friedman puts it like this:

> Marx distinguished between the social division of labour and the manufacturing [technical] division of labour. In the social division of labour the collection of different employments producing distinct commodities is divided among different producers. In the manufacturing division of labour the work process for producing a single commodity is subdivided among different workers. (Friedman, 1977, pp. 92–3)

Here the social division of labour is defined not in terms of physical units of the labour process, but in terms of the production of *commodities*. The definition is related to the production of profit and the process of accumulation. It is *not* a function of some supposedly natural division into product areas. The notion of social division of labour under capitalism is based, not on some ahistorical notion of production, but on the specifically capitalist aspects of it. Although, as Marx pointed out, a social form of division of labour may exist in many different kinds of economic formation, it will be a product of, and defined by, different social processes in different cases. Under capitalism, this division will be marked by the exchange of commodities (on this see *Capital*, vol. 1, pp. 351–2 and, especially, p. 359). Whether or not component production and assembly are separate branches of production in this sense will depend, therefore, not on some external characteristics of the two processes, but on their relation to the structure of capital ownership and the structure of accumulation.

It should be said that there has been considerable debate about the meaning of 'social division of labour'. The discussion here is based on *Capital*, vol. 1 ch. XIV, section 4. Marx is here making an assumption: 'one commodity per capitalist', which is empirically untenable today. But neither this, nor the dispute over the term 'social division of labour' matters here. What concerns the present argument is the difference between market relations and corporately-planned relations. This, again, marks them out as definitions specific to a capitalist economy. It is worth quoting Marx again, if only for his wry political comments:

Division of labour within the workshop implies the undisputed authority of the capitalist over men [*sic*], that are but parts of a mechanism that belongs to him. The division of labour within the society brings into contact independent commodity-producers, who acknowledge no other authority but that of competition, of the coercion exerted by the pressure of their mutual interests; just as in the animal kingdom, the *bellum omnium contra omnes* more or less preserves the conditions of existence of every species. The same bourgeois mind which praises division of labour in the workshop, life-long annexation of the labourer to a partial operation, and his complete subjection to capital, as being an organisation of labour that increases its productiveness – that same bourgeois mind denounces with equal vigour every conscious attempt to socially control and regulate the process of production, as an inroad upon such sacred things as the rights of property, freedom and unrestricted play for the bent of the individual capitalist. It is very characteristic that the enthusiastic apologists of the factory system have nothing more damning to urge against a general organisation of the labour of society, than that it would turn all society into one immense factory (p. 356).

12. Here there is obviously a distinction to be made between some of the work on corporate organisation and what might be called more straightforward statistical analyses. It is the latter to which this point most clearly applies. For the former, what is being suggested is more a way of conceptualising some of the detailed results into a wider framework. Many of the ideas are similar to those in Dicken (1976), for instance, though it would not be suggested here that the approach should be confined to the level of the individual firm, or that the prime cause should be seen as managerial strategy.

Chapter 4: Some Changing Spatial Structures in the United Kingdom

1. The interaction of all these factors is discussed in Chapters 5 and 6. For the moment they are taken for granted – as the 'location surface' facing industry. In fact, as will be seen, this surface was being formed at precisely the same time. Both sides of these new location factors were being constituted together.
2. This, of course, is pre-eminently the case in the Free Production Zones of the Third World, the zones precisely functioning as areas in which, unlike the rest of the country, other conditions are available to make it possible to use the cheap labour of surrounding areas (see Froebel, Heinrichs and Kreye, 1980).
3. This process of changeover is really an intersectoral phenomenon. 'Old means of production industries' – which would include these middle stages – were declining fast at this time (see also Chapter 6).
4. Even if they were, their effects, precisely because of intranationality, would be different.
5. This argument applies both to electronics and to instruments. Like the rest of electronics, mlh 354 has as a whole traditionally been heavily concentrated in the South East, with an outlying centre in the North West. While much decentralisation to Development Areas has occurred in the sector as a whole, the difficulties for small firms in this process are, as we shall argue, enormous. Oakey in fact argues this for mlh 354 as a whole, but, as ever, there are differences within the mlh.

His arguments seem to apply *a fortiori* to the small firms in the high-technology-based part of the sector – i.e. those being discussed here. In a number of ways, larger firms may behave differently. In particular, they are more likely to introduce changes in technology, and the adoption of NC, and neo-Fordist labour processes, may well reduce skill requirements sufficiently to enable decentralisation (Massey and Meegan, 1979; Perrons, 1979). Although such techniques are applicable to small-batch production, their installation may require significant investment and therefore at present be ruled out for many small firms. Interestingly, one of Oakey's case studies which involved movement to a Development Area (the south-west) was of a larger firm (over 1000 workers) and one which did have a significant demand for semi-skilled labour power. This demand was easily satisfied, and it was mainly women who were employed (p. 279). The difficulties arose as a result of an attempt to relocate the headquarters. Thus, while 'the aim of employing a large number of semi-skilled predominantly female, staff from the local area has been achieved', 'criticism was made of the "lack of intellectual, artistic and cultural entertainments and lack of high-class shopping and civic amenities" (questionnaire response)' (p. 279). Even more forcefully, the major advantage and disadvantage of the (St Austell) location reflected this dichotomised labour demand: 'The major advantage gained from the new location was attested to be a "cheaper and more stable labour force" (questionnaire response). However, the main disadvantage was described as "a period of sustained production and supply difficulties which resulted from inadequate training and knowledge of new staff, which so badly affected sales, it was exceptionally difficult to recover" (questionnaire response)' (pp. 279–80). (It is perhaps necessary to stress that it is *changes* in location that are being discussed. There are locally-owned firms in advanced electronics in both the north-east of England and parts of Scotland, both established bases for such activity. The trends, however, are not in their favour.)

6. Some of the causes of this stem precisely from measures adopted by the Government 'to make British industry more competitive'. Thus, the use of incomes policies to hold down wages also means that people have less to spend, and some consumer-goods industries, such as clothing, may suffer. This can happen both because people spend less overall on clothing and because, with what they do spend, they may put a higher premium on cheapness, and thus further encourage low-cost imports (NEDO, 1976).

7. The next section discusses the service industry. The decentralisation of this industry to the regions around the south-east has also been an important phenomenon and may have affected competition for labour

in regions such as the east midlands. Certainly the shoe industry in that region suffered from increased competition for women workers over the sixties and seventies, in a few cases prompting a shift to Development Areas such as the Northern Region (see Massey and Meegan, 1982; and Mounfield, Unwin and Guy, 1982, p. 192).

8. This difference relates to the sexual division of labour in the industry and the particular relevance of PBR systems in machining, which is mainly done by women. While of all employees in the industry about 50 per cent are on some form of payment-by-results (PBR) system, this proportion rises to between 55 and 60 per cent for women (Clothing EDC, 1972). The importance of PBR relates to the nature of the labour process in the industry. Technologically, the speed of production can still be controlled by the individual worker, especially in machining, and speed has therefore to be maintained by a mixture of exhortation, incentive and threat (see Massey and Meegan, 1982).

9. 'Unfortunately managements' efforts to deskill operations bring other problems, related to job-satisfaction and the need for adequate compensation . . . which are likely to cause increasing concern in the next few years' (NEDO, 1974a, p. 48).

10. The NEDO Review to 1977 refers to this practice, and to some of the 'difficulties' it can cause

> Migratory labour, particularly from those countries which have special links with the EEC, may provide a new source of employees for the UK clothing industry as they already have in Germany. Such labour, particularly if employed by smaller establishments, would pose problems with regard to adequate supervision of their social and working conditions (NEDO, 1974a, p. 48).

11. There was also, of course, an even larger reserve of cheap labour in the Third World and a number of the largest companies switched investment abroad, thus further accelerating the problem of imports (NEDO, 1977, p. 54).

12. The aggregate figures show a high percentage of male employees in London, but such figures conceal too many other differences to allow of confident inference.

13. Care must be taken before generalising or extrapolating this point. Not all small firms in these sectors are in competition with larger. They often serve different markets. What is being described here is the clear partition into two groups rather than the start of a process of extinction of small capital. Indeed, there is evidence in the 1970s of higher closure rates among multiples (*medium* sized) firms.

14. Or from 68.6 per cent to 72.9 per cent if Transport and Communica-

tion are excluded as being more properly classified as production industries.

15. Some of whom also – those in legal services, for example – have their pre-capitalist bases, of course (see Lipietz, 1978), but who are not at present threatened by 'more capitalist' forms of organisation.

16. See also 'Small firms ... in the South East of England' by Brimson, Massey, Meegan, Minns and Whitfield (1980).

17. The same applies to wholesale distribution.

18. We are dealing here with employment, i.e. the production of the services rather than the level of their provision. Data on the latter are produced e.g. in *Social Trends* (CSO), although in examining levels of provision the regional level is probably not the most – or the only – appropriate one.

19. The employment effects of these parts of the public sector are very different from those of the central State. The latter is not only primarily concentrated on London but in its recent moves, now curtailed, towards geographical decentralisation it has reproduced and thus reinforced the pattern of regional social differentiation. It has been most importantly the lower level functions, and especially routine clerical jobs, which have been decentralised. These central State functions, of course, include also some consumer services.

20. This is the point made by Mills and Lav (1964) in their critique of Lösch, for assuming *both* private capitalist ownership *and* total coverage of the area/population. Marquand writes

    Although consumer services are widely dispersed, there is considerable variation between MELAs in their endowment with them. The variations are sufficiently wide to make it clear that it is unjustifiable to assume that the market will operate to distribute consumer services (relatively) evenly in relation to population, or population and size of urban centre (para. 4.64).

21. Cuts in public expenditure have in fact been reducing the *rate of growth* in these sectors since 1975 (Marquand, 1979, para. 1.18).

22. The same authors point out elsewhere that these factors are reinforced by State intervention in industry.

23. This, of course, is the corollary of the lack of service links from branch plants, noted by Marquand (1979).

24. One very important aspect of this process is the relative decline of London and the relative gains in the rest of the south-east.

Chapter 5: The Effects on Local Areas: Class and Gender Relations

1. This coherence and simplicity of economic structure was not confined to mining towns. Humphrys (1972) writes of the tinplate towns of south Wales: 'In all these towns there was a direct and simple relationship between industry and community' (p. 23).

2. All this is comparative, with other industries and other kinds of community. There certainly are bases for sectionalism within mining. There are winding-enginemen, colliers, craftsmen and so on, and the history of union organisation within the industry has often revolved about their interrelation (Francis and Smith, 1980; Unofficial Reform Committee, 1912). But the relative homogeneity of the coal industry is nonetheless clear, even in comparison with the other basic industries – such as steel – in the wider regions (Cooke, 1981b).

3. Carney, Lewis and Hudson (1977) refer to this history in the north-east, and Francis and Smith (1980) document the history of the miners' union in south Wales in the twentieth century. There have been considerable differences between regions, however; south Wales and Scotland have historically been far more militant than the north-east.

4. Even this process has not been smooth. By the end of the 1970s, deepening recession was causing losses of jobs in the new industries too. Chapter 6 looks at this variation over the period.

5. Which is not to deny that the geographical location of control has effects – see Chapter 3, and later in this chapter.

6. These kinds of changes apply not just to the range of incoming sectors which are being mainly considered here, but also to others, such as the car industry.

7. External orientation is not new to these areas, of course. The export of coal involved precisely that. But the direction of orientation, the functions it performed and the markets it served, and the degree of intraregional linkage it allowed, have all changed.

8. This sorting-process has, of course, also been commented on by others in relation to the new towns of the South East.

9. Neither is it without its parallels in the coal-field regions. There the sources of alternative income are State transfer payments of various sorts – including redundancy pay, miners' pensions and forms of EEC and ECSC income maintenance (mostly in steel areas). These are all temporary. Longer-lasting but at lower levels is unemployment benefit, a form of State transfer which, in a 'standard married couple' situation, is far more likely to cheapen female wages than male (since more men are eligible for unemployment benefit). These factors are

small, but not insignificant. Similar situations occur on a rather larger scale in Ireland (Stanton, 1979, and Southern Italy (Wade, 1979).

10. Much of the information here is drawn from the County Structure Plan and associated documents – Cornwall County Council, (1976a and 1976b).

11. If there is any wider connection here, it would reinforce the point made in Chapter 4 that it might be easier for R and D workers and related professionals to operate their residential preferences than it is for managers and owners of capital.

12. The study also implies, of course, that although a pleasant environment may have helped, it would not have been sufficient to rescue the coal-fields. Of course, all that is being referred to here is physical environment. Cornwall still lacks the range of cultural amenities which seem to be a necessary condition for attracting top management, R and D personnel, etc. (see Chapter 3).

Chapter 6: Class, Politics and the Geography of Employment

1. Regional policy is by no means, obviously, the only arm of policy to have a regional dimension. Almost all policies have spatially-differentiated effects, and some sectoral ones very much so.

2. This difference was to become very obvious from their contrasting responses to cuts in regional policy.

3. The repercussions of this period were felt throughout the 1970s. In 1977 at C. A. Parsons on Tyneside the power engineering workers prevented the completion of the restructuring of power engineering begun under the IRC, fighting off a combination of the NEB, much of the Labour Government – and Arnold Weinstock (see Coventry, Liverpool, Newcastle and North Tyneside Trades Councils, 1980).

4. The exception in the United Kingdom to this general decline was of course North Sea oil, where again the regional effects were significant. Moore, Rhodes and Tyler (1977) estimated it had generated some 20 000 jobs in Scotland by 1976.

5. The criticism of location theory for being concerned only with geographical distribution does not mean that the problem of distribution, at a political as well as theoretical level, does not exist, but that it cannot be adequately explained, nor adequately attacked, without relating it to prior quotations about production.

6. Data for these individual periods is inevitably all rather sparse. The ten-year census period bears no relation to a politico-economic periodisation.

7. In all cases except one (General Management in Wales) the overall

deficits in these occupational groups in the North, in Scotland and in Wales were greater than could be 'accounted for' by sectoral changes within the regions and occupational change nationally within the sectors (Kirwan, 1981) – a clear indication of the possible existence of hierarchical spatial structures.

8. What would be interesting would be to investigate the components of this relative loss. Kirwan's (1981) analysis indicates that while national changes in occupational structure by industry would have indicated an increase in female assembly work in the Development Areas, the areas' own changes in industrial structure would imply a considerable decline. The specifically regional residual component, though small, did not show such big losses and in Scotland it actually increased. Such an analysis of numerical components cannot lead to an explanation in terms of process. But the pattern to which it points, and which could be investigated, is that there was a greater closure rate of 'cloned' branch plants – such as in clothing – than of branches at the bottom ends of production hierarchies. Certainly, in all the industrial Development Areas the regional component of the 1980 distribution remains firmly positive.

9. In all cases, moreover, this increase was indicated by both industrial structure and regional factors. Again, this was a contrast with the regions of the south and east where in each case while industrial structure indicated an increase, the residual regional component was negative.

10. These electoral characteristics are drawn from an analysis of both opinion polls and election results in Kellner, 1979. Analysis of the 1983 election reveals many of the same trends (Massey, 1983).

11. Examination even of simple patterns of voting behaviour makes the point clearly. For the whole period from the sixties to the eighties voting behaviour in general elections varied noticeably by region. In some elections, such as that of 1964, the 'influence' of region on social-class voting patterns was greater than variations due to interregional differences in class structure (Butler and Stokes, 1974). For the 1970 election Butler and Stokes (1974) compared precisely the two kinds of areas examined in Chapter 5 – mining seats and resort areas. Table A.1 reproduces their breakdown of class composition, by occupational grade, in the two kinds of constituencies, and the results of their inquiry as to 'class self-image'. The difference between the two kinds of area on both counts – and on the relation between the two – is clear. There is a wide difference in social structure between the two kinds of constituency, but this is not enough to account for voting differences: 'the much more spectacular difference has to do with the behaviour of the classes. The Conservatives actually outran

TABLE A.1 *Class composition and class self-image of mining and resort areas, 1970 (in percentages)*

	Mining areas	Resorts
Class composition		
Occupational Grades I–IV	19	55
Occupational Grades V–VI	81	45
	100	100
Class self-image		
Middle class	23	51
Working class	77	49
	100	100

Source: Butler and Stokes (1974, table 6.6).

Labour among the working class of resort areas ... In the mining seats, however, the picture is almost reversed. The Labour Party received fully 50% of the middle-class vote and lost only one fifth of the vote of the working class' (pp. 131–2). Actual Party support is given in Table A.2. While in the mining seats the advantage to Labour of this pattern of cross-support was 29 per cent (50 per cent minus 21 per cent), in the resort areas the advantage was to the Conservatives by a proportion of 32 per cent (52 per cent minus 20 per cent). As Butler and Stokes argue, 'the role of class composition in regional variations [in voting behaviour] may be larger than is at first

TABLE A.2 *Partisan self-image by class in mining areas and resorts, 1970 (in percentages)*

	Mining seats		Resorts	
	Class self-image		Class self-image	
	Middle class	Working class	Middle class	Working class
Conservative	50	21	80	52
Labour	50	79	20	48
	100	100	100	100

Source: Butler and Stokes (1974, table 6.7).

apparent'. The influence may be that of the overall regionally-specific and geographically-differentiated class structures on the character of their individual elements.

12. In all these cases, of course, the rhetoric was again tougher than the action. Subsidies to nationalised industries (the NCB, BSC and BL in particular) continued, and the Cabinet backed off from a confrontation with the regional core of the labour movement – the miners.

13. This is no longer the case for all of Tootals – it was announced in May 1982 that the headquarters of the threadmaking section had been transferred, not to south-east England but to the United States!

14. It should be added that NEI has been trying to diversify, for instance through a takeover of Extel (Duffy, 1982).

15. It is not being suggested that these characteristics are universal. There are exceptions even in the 'traditional sectors'. Boswell (1973) reports on the comparative dynamism of small capital in hosiery and knit-wear, for instance (p. 206).

16. This is not to imply that all small firms and self-employment in the South East are of the 'modern' variety. Both traditional and modern elements are found in that region and there is a distinct division between them (Brimson et al., 1981).

17. In all the industries discussed here there are also major companies, often multinationals, involved.

Bibliography

Aglietta, M., *A Theory of Capitalist Regulation – The US Experience* (London: New Left Books, 1979).

Allen, V., 'The differentiation of the working class', in Hunt A. (ed.), *Class and Class Structure* (London: Lawrence and Wishart, 1977) pp. 61–79.

Allen, V., *The Militancy of British Miners* (Shipley: The Moor Press, 1982).

Anderson, J., 'Geography as ideology and the politics of crisis: the enterprise zone experiment', in Anderson, J., Duncan, S. and Hudson, R. (eds), *Redundant Spaces in Cities and Regions: Studies in Industrial Decline and Social Change* (London: Academic Press, 1983).

Beacham, A., 'The coal industry', in Burn, D. (ed.), *The Structure of British Industry: A Symposium*, vol. I (Cambridge University Press, 1958) pp. 108–55.

Bennison, D. and Davies, R. L., 'Retail changes in North East England', in *North Eastern Studies*, Institute of British Geographers Annual Conference, Department of Geography, University of Newcastle upon Tyne (January 1977) pp. 9–18.

Benwell Community Project, *The Making of a Ruling Class: Two Centuries of Capital Development on Tyneside* (1978a).

Benwell CDP, *Women, Work and Wages: Clothing Workers in West Newcastle* (1978b).

Beynon, H., *Working for Ford* (Harmondsworth: Penguin, 1973).

Birnbaum, B., 'Women, skill and automation: a study of women's employment in the clothing industry 1946–1972' (mimeo, undated).

Bleitrach, D. and Chenu, A., 'Amenagement: régulation ou aggravation des contradictions sociales? Un example: Fos-sur-mer et l'aire métropolitaine marseillaise', *Environment and Planning A*, vol. VII, no. 4 (1975) pp. 367–91.

Blondel, J., *Voters, Parties and Leaders: The Social Fabric of British Politics* (Harmondsworth: Penguin, 1977).

Board of Trade, Second report of the Select Committee on Estimates: Session 1955–6, *The Development Areas* (London: HMSO, 1955–6) p. viii.

Bolton Committee, Bolton Report: *Report of the Committee of Inquiry on Small Firms*, Cmnd 4811 (London: HMSO, 1971).

Boswell J., *The Rise and Decline of Small Firms* (London: George Allen and Unwin, 1973).

Braverman, Harry, *Labor and Monopoly Capital: The Degradation of Work in the Twentieth Century* (New York and London: Monthly Review Press, 1974).

Brett, M., Brody, M. and Stobart, C., 'The City and Industry', *Investors Chronicle Inquiry* (1975).

Brighton Labour Process Group, 'The capitalist labour process', *Capital and Class*, 1 (Spring 1977) pp. 3–42.

Brimson, P., Massey, D., Meegan, R., Minns, R. and Whitfield, S., South East Regional Trades Union Congress (1981), 'Small firms: the solution to unemployment? An examination of employment in small firms in the South East of England' (South East Regional Trades Union Congress, Discussion Paper, December 1980).

Burawoy, M., *Manufacturing Consent: Changes in the Labour Process Under Monopoly Capitalism* (Chicago: University of Chicago Press, 1979).

Burns, T. and Stalker, G. M., *The Management of Innovation* (London: Tavistock, 1961).

Buswell, R. J. and Lewis, E. W., 'The Geographical Distribution of Industrial Research Activity in the United Kingdom', *Regional Studies*, vol. IV (1970) pp. 297–306.

Cameron, G. C., 'The national Industrial Strategy and regional policy', in MacLennan, D. and Parr, J. B. (eds), *Regional Policy: Past Experience and New Directions*, Glasgow Social and Economic Research Studies 6 (Oxford: Martin Robertson, 1979).

Carney, J., Lewis, J. and Hudson, R., 'Coal combines and interregional uneven development in the UK', in Massey, D. B. and Batey, P. W. J. (eds), *Alternative Frameworks for Analysis* (London: Pion, 1977).

Castells M. and Godard F., *Monopolville: l'entreprise, l'état, l'urbain* (Paris and the Hague: Mouton, 1974).

CBI 'Government aid to regions still vital – support for industry needed until profitability improves, says CBI', Press Release, 15 July, on CBI Memorandum (E 706 79) to the Government on regional policy (1979).

Churchill, D., 'Sharp fall in number of grocery outlets', *Financial Times* 21 January 1981a.

Churchill, D., 'Toy industry scrutinised', *Financial Times* 2 February 1981b.

Coates, D., *Labour in Power? A Study of the Labour Government, 1974–1979* (London: Longman, 1980).

Communist Party, *The North West: Technological Relic or Modern Industrial Region?* (statement, undated).

Cooke, P. N., 'Local class structure in Wales', UWIST Papers in Planning Research, no. 31 (Cardiff: 1981a).

Cooke, P. N., 'Inter-regional class relations and the redevelopment process', UWIST Papers in Planning Research, no. 36 (Cardiff: 1981b).

Cooke, P. N. and Rees G., 'The industrial restructuring of South Wales: the career of a State-managed region', UWIST Papers in Planning Research, No. 25 (Cardiff: 1981).

Cornwall County Council, *County Structure Plan*: Policy Choice Consultation Document (1976a).

Cornwall County Council, *County Structure Plan: Topic Report: Employment, Income and Industry* (1976b).

Cornwall Industrial Development Association, *The Economy of Cornwall: a discussion document prepared with particular reference to the Cornwall Structure Plan*; 2nd edn (1977).

Courlet, C., 'Capitalisme et différenciation régionale: analyse de la differenciation régionale Nord-Sud en Italie 1950–1975', Thèse de Doctorat de Troisième Cycle, Institut de Recherche Economique et de Planification, Université des Sciences Sociales, Grenoble II (1977).

Coventry, Liverpool, Newcastle and North Tyneside Trades Councils, *State Intervention in Industry: A Workers' Inquiry* (Newcastle upon Tyne: 1980).

Cowper, R., 'Carpet trade taking a beating', *Financial Times* 2 March 1979.

Crum, R. E. and Gudgin, G., 'Non-production activities in UK manufacturing industry', Commission of the European Communities, Regional Policy Series, no. 3 (Brussels: 1977).

David, R., 'Britain's downtrodden carpet industry', *Financial Times* 15 April 1980.

Davies, G. and Thomas, I., 'Overseas investment in Wales: the welcome invasion', published for the Development Corporation for Wales (Christopher Davies Ltd, 1976).

Deaglio, E., *La Fiat com 'è* (Feltrinelli, 1975).

Deane, P. and Cole, W. A., *British Economic Growth: 1688–1959* (2nd edn) (Cambridge: Cambridge University Press, 1967).

Department of Employment and Productivity, 'Ryhope: a pit closes. A study in redeployment' (London: HMSO, 1970).

Department of Industry, 'Towards a strategy for the plastics-processing industry: a study based in a survey of plastics-processing companies in south Wales' (London: HMSO, 1978).

Department of Trade and Industry, *Memorandum on the Inquiry into Location Attitudes and Experience*, Minutes of Evidence, Trade and Industry Sub-Committee of the House of Commons Expenditure Committee, Wednesday 4 July, Session 1972–3 (London: HMSO, 1973) pp. 525–668.

Dicken, P., 'The Multi-plant enterprise and Geographic Space', *Regional Studies*, vol. x, no. 4 (1976) pp. 401–12.

Dicken, P. and Lloyd, P. E., 'Geographical perspectives on United States investment in the United Kingdom', *Environment and Planning A*, vol. VIII, pp. 685–705.

Disher, M., 'Bespoke figuration by computer', *Manufacturing Clothier* (July 1980).

Drummond, in *Financial Times*, 30 June 1978.

Duffy, H., 'NEI: a proud engineering giant in need of more drive', *Financial Times* 19 February 1982.

Duncan, S. S., 'Qualitative change in human geography – an introduction', *Geoforum*, vol. x, no. 1 (1979) pp. 1–4.

Dunford, M. F., Geddes, M. and Perrons, D., 'Regional policy and the crisis in the UK: a long-run perspective', *International Journal of Urban and Regional Research*, vol. v, no. 3 (1981) pp. 377–410.

Dury, G. H., *The British Isles: a systematic and regional geography* (2nd edn) (London: Heinemann, 1963).

Economists Advisory Group, *British Footwear – The Future, Volume II: The Industry* (A report prepared for the Department of Industry) (London: Economists Advisory Group Ltd, undated).

Elger, T., 'Valorisation and "deskilling": a critique of Braverman', *Capital and Class*, 7 (Spring, 1979).

Evans, A. W., 'The location of the headquarters of industrial companies', *Urban Studies*, vol. x (1973) pp. 387–96.

Firn, J., Memorandum submitted to the Expenditure Committee (Trade and Industry Sub-Committee), Minutes of Evidence (1973) pp. 694–712.

Firn, J., 'External control and regional development: the case of Scotland', *Environment and Planning A*, vol. VII, no. 4 (1975) pp. 393–414.

Foster, J., *Class Struggle and the Industrial Revolution: Early Industrial Capitalism in Three English Towns* (London: Methuen, 1974).

Fothergill, S. and Gudgin, G., 'Regional employment change: a sub-regional explanation', *Progress in Planning* 12 (3) (1979) pp. 155–219.

Francis, H. and Smith, D., *The Fed: A History of the South Wales Miners in the Twentieth Century* (London: Lawrence and Wishart, 1980).

Friedman A., *Industry and Labour: Class Struggle at Work and Monopoly Capitalism* (London: Macmillan, 1977).

Froebel, F., Heinrichs, J. and Kreye, O., *The New International Division of Labour: Structural Unemployment in Industrialised Countries and Industrialisation in Developing Countries* (Cambridge University Press; Editions de la Maison des Sciences de l'Homme, 1980).

Gamble, A., *Britain in Decline: Economic Policy, Political Strategy and the British State* (London: Macmillan, 1981).

Garnett, N., 'Budget relief for industry vital, CBI regions warn', *Financial Times*, 3 March 1982.

Giddens, A., *Central Problems in Social Theory* (London: Macmillan, 1979).

Goddard, J. B. and Smith, I. J., 'Changes in corporate control in the British urban system, 1972–1977', *Environment and Planning A*, vol. x (1978) pp. 1073–84.

Gooding, K., 'Ford imports exceed exports', *Financial Times*, 27 April 1982.

Goodman, J. F. B., Armstrong E. G. A., Davis J. E. and Wagner A., *Rule-making and industrial peace* (London: Croom-Helm, 1976).

Gough, T. J., 'The diversionary effects of institutional property investment', *Estates Gazette*, vol. ccxxxv, 19 July 1975 pp. 199–201.

Gramsci, A., 'The historical role of the cities', in *Selections from Political Writings, 1910–1920* (1977 edn) (London: Lawrence and Wishart).

Gray, R., 'Left holding the flag', *Marxism Today* (November 1982) pp. 22–7.

Groves, R. E. V., Samuels, J. M. and Goddard, C. S., 'Company Finance in Europe', The Institute of Chartered Accountants in England and Wales (1975).

Gudgin, G., Brunskill, I. and Fothergill, S., 'New manufacturing firms in regional employment growth', Centre for Environmental Studies, Research Series, no. 39 (1979).

Hall, S., 'The "political" and the "economic" in Marx's theory of classes', in Hunt, A. (ed.), *Class and Class Structure* (London: Lawrence and Wishart, 1977) pp. 15–60.

HMSO, National Plan (Cmnd 2764, 1965).

Hodgson, G., *Labour at the Crossroads: The Political and Economic Challenge to the Labour Party in the 1980s* (Oxford: Martin Robertson, 1981).

Holland, S., *Capital vs the Regions* (London: Macmillan, 1976).

Hoogstraten, P. van, 'On relations between economic and physical planning: remarks on recent tendencies in the Netherlands.' Paper presented to the European Conference of the Regional Science Association, London (1979).

Hudson, R., 'New towns and spatial policy: the case of Washington New Town' (mimeo, 1979).

Hudson, R., 'The paradoxes of State intervention: the impact of nationalised industry policies and regional policy on employment in the northern region in the post-war period' (mimeo, University of Durham, 1982).

Hughes, J., 'Democracy and planning: Britain 1968', in Coates, K. (ed.), *Can the Workers Run Industry?* (London: Sphere, 1968) p. 81.

Humphrys, G., *South Wales* (Newton Abbott: David and Charles, 1972).

Hunsicker, J. Q., 'The matrix in retreat' *Financial Times*, 1982.

Hu, Yao-su, 'National attitudes and the financing of industry', PEP, vol. XLI, Broadsheet No. 559 (December 1975).

Hymer, S., 'The multinational corporation and the law of uneven development', in J. N. Bhagwati (ed.), *Economics and World Order* (London: Collier-Macmillan, 1972) pp. 113–140.

Institute for Workers Control Motors Group, *A workers' enquiry into the motor industry* (CSE Books, 1978).

Jessop, B., 'The transformation of the State in post-war Britain', mimeo, 1979, subsequently published in Scase, R. (ed.), *The State in Western Europe* (Later: Croom Helm, 1980).

Johnston, R. J., 'Regional variations in British voting trends – 1966–79: tests of an ecological model', *Regional Studies*, vol. xv (1981) pp. 23–32.

Johnstone, W. D., 'The National Industrial Strategy', *Town and Country Planning* (January 1979) pp. 23–5.

Keeble, D., *Industrial Location and Planning in the United Kingdom* (London: Methuen, 1976).

Keeble, D., 'Spatial policy in Britain: regional or urban?', *Area*, vol. IX, no. 1 (1977) pp. 3–8.

Keeble, D., 'Spatial policy in Britain: regional or urban? a reply to Hudson's comment', *Area*, vol. x, no. 2 (1978) pp. 123–5.

Keeble, D., 'Industrial decline, regional policy and the urban-rural manufacturing shift in the United Kingdom', *Environment and Planning A*, vol. XII (1980) pp. 945–62.

Keegan, V., 'A land where they still believe in the phoenix', *Guardian*; 22 July 1980, p. 15.

Kehoe, L., 'A case of the biter bit down in Silicon Valley', *Financial Times*, 1 September 1982a.

Kehoe, L., 'Silicon Valley bursts its seams', *Financial Times*, 2 December, 1982b.

Kellner, P. 'Not a defeat, a disaster: how voters became Tories by experience', *New Statesman*, 18 May 1979, pp. 704–5

King, S. A., 'The clothing industry: women employed and technology' (mimeo, Department of Geography, London School of Economics, 1981).

Kirwan, R. M., 'A note on regional economic structure and occupational change in Britain, 1973–1980' (mimeo, Department of Land Economy, University of Cambridge, 1981).

Labour Party Scottish Council, *An Industrial Strategy for Scotland* (Glasgow, 1977).

Labour Party, 'Enterprise Zones – NEC Statement' (1980).

Laclau, E. and Mouffe, C., 'Socialist strategy: where next?', *Marxism Today* (January 1981) pp. 17–22.

Lane, T., 'The Unions: caught on an ebb tide', *Marxism Today*, (September 1982) pp. 6–13.

Läpple, D., Urban structures and territorial socialization: a theoretical approach for the analysis of urbanization in the context of uneven spatial development', MS of English translation of an article appearing in Mayer, M. *et al.*, *Stadtkrise und Soziale Bewegung – Texte Zur Internationalen Entwicklung* (Frankfurt, 1978).

Läpple, D. and van Hoogstraten, P., 'The spatial structure of capitalist development: the case of the Netherlands', in Carney, J., Hudson, R. and Lewis, J. (eds), *Regions in Crisis* (London: Croom Helm, 1979).

Laurençin, J.P., Monateri, J.C., Palloix, C., Tiberghien, R. and Vernet, P., 'The regional effects of the crisis on the forms of organisation of production and location of industry in the Mediterranean Basin', in Massey, D. B. and Batey, P. W. J. (eds), *Alternative Frameworks for Analysis* (London: Pion, 1977).

Leigh, R., 'A profile of acquisitions in the clothing sector in 1973'. Industrial location research project, Working Paper no. 6 (Middlesex Polytechnic (Geography and Planning Group), The Burroughs, Hendon, London NW4 4BT 1975).

Lipietz, A., *Le Capital et Son Espace* (Maspero: Economie et socialisme, 34, 1977).

Lloyd, P. E. and Shutt, J., 'Recession and restructuring in the north west region: some preliminary thoughts on the policy implications of recent events', paper presented to Regional Studies Association Enquiry on Regional Policy (London: RSA, 1982).

Lockwood, D., *The Black-coated Worker* (London: Allen and Unwin, 1958).

Lojkine, J., 'Big firms' strategies, urban policy and urban social movements' in Harloe, M. (ed), *Captive Cities* (London: J. Wiley and Sons, 1977) pp. 141–56.

Lorenz, C., 'Inescapable Problems of the Electronic Revolution', *Financial Times*, 13 May 1976.

Lovering, J., 'The theory of the "internal colony" and the political economy of Wales' (mimeo, 1979).

Mandel, E., 'The dialectic of class and region in Belgium', *New Left Review*, vol. xx (1963) pp. 5–31.

Marglin, S., 'What do bosses do?', *Review of Radical Political Economy* (Summer 1974).

Marks, S., 'South monopolises microchips: decision to build at Bristol is bad news for depressed regions', *New Statesman*, 25 January 1980.

Markusen, A. R., 'Regionalism and the Capitalist State: the case of the United States', *Kapitalistate*, vol. vii (Winter 1979).

Marquand, J., *The Service Sector and Regional Policy in the United*

Kingdom, Centre for Environmental Studies Research Series No. 29 (1979).

Martin, R., 'Britain's slump: the regional anatomy of job loss', *Area*, vol. XIV, no. 4 (1982) pp. 257–64.

Marx, K., *Capital* (Moore and Aveling translation) (London: Lawrence and Wishart, 1970–72).

Massey, D. B., *Industrial location theory reconsidered* (Open University, 1976).

Massey, D. B., 'Regionalism: some current issues', *Capital and Class*, no. 6 (1978) pp. 106–25.

Massey, D. B., 'In what sense a regional problem?', *Regional Studies* 13 (1979) pp. 233–43.

Massey, D. B., 'Enterprise zones: a political issue', *International Journal of Urban and Regional Research* vol. VI, no. 3 (1982) pp. 429–34.

Massey, D. B. 'Contours of victory, Dimensions of defeat', *Maxism Today*, July 1983, pp. 16–19.

Massey, D. B. and Catalano, A., *Capital and Land: Landownership by Capital in Great Britain* (London: Edward Arnold, 1978).

Massey, D. B. and Meegan, R. A., 'The Geography of Industrial Reorganisation: the spatial effects of the restructuring of the electrical engineering sector under the Industrial Reorganisation Corporation', *Progress in Planning*, vol. X part 3 (1979).

Massey, D. B. and Meegan, R. A., *The Anatomy of Job Loss: the How, Why and Where of Employment Decline* (London: Methuen, 1982).

McClelland, W. G., 'The Industrial Reorganisation Corporation 1966/71: an experimental prod', *Three Banks Review* (June 1972) pp. 23–42.

McCrone, G., *Regional Policy in Britain* University of Glasgow: social and economic studies, 15 (George Allen and Unwin, Unwin University Books, 1969).

Michon-Savarit, C., 'La place des régions françaises dans la division internationale du travail: deux scénarios contrastés', *Environment and Planning A*, vol. VII, no. 4 (1975) pp. 449–54.

Moore, B., Rhodes, J. and Tyler, P., 'The impact of regional policy in the 1970s', *Centre for Environmental Studies Review*, 1 (1977) pp. 67–77.

Morgan, K., 'Regional inequality and the Tory Government' (mimeo, University of Sussex, 1980).

Morgan, K., 'Restructuring steel: the crises of labour and locality in Britain', Working Paper in Urban and Regional Studies, no. 30 (University of Sussex, 1982).

Moseley, M. J. and Sant, M., *Industrial Development in East Anglia* (Norwich, Geo Abstracts Ltd, 1977).

Mounfield, P. R., Unwin, D. J. and Guy, K., 'Processes of change in the footwear industry in the East Midlands', Final Report on SSRC Project HR 5819/1 (SSRC, 1 Temple Avenue, London, 1982).

Myrdal, G., *Economic theory and underdeveloped regions* (London: Duckworth, 1957).

Nairn, T., 'The crisis of the British state', *New Left Review*, no. 130 (1981) pp. 37–44.

NALGO, 'Public expenditure: the role of the public sector in a depressed region' (London: National and Local Government Officers Association, 1978).

NEDO, 'Labour turnover' (Clothing Industry Economic Development Council, 1967).

NEDO, 'Industrial Review to 1977: Clothing' (London, 1974a).

NEDO, 'Low-cost work aids for the clothing and garment industries' (London, 1974c).

NEDO, 'Finance for investment' (London: 1976).

NEDO, 'People make clothing', Clothing Industry EDC (London: 1980).

National Union of Tailors and Garment Workers, *Employment in Clothing: A Struggle for Survival* (Milton Keynes: NUTGWU, undated).

Oakey, R., 'The British scientific and industrial instruments industry: a study in industrial geography', Ph.D. (University of London, 1978).

Parlanti, 'Da Valletta a Piazza Statuto', *Primo Maggio*, no. 9 (undated).

Parsons, G. F., 'The giant manufacturing corporations and balanced regional growth in Britain', *Area*, vol. iv, no. 2 (1972) pp. 99–103.

Partridge, H., 'Italy's FIAT in Turin in the 1950's', in Nichols T. (ed), *Capital and Labour: A Marxist Primer* (London: Fontana, 1980).

Pederson, P. O., 'Interaction between short- and long-run development in regions – the case of Denmark', *Regional Studies*, vol. xii, no. 6 (1978) pp. 683–700.

Penniman, H. R. (ed), *Britain at the Polls, 1979: A Study of the General Election*, American Enterprise Institute, distributed by Transatlantic Books Service (1981).

Perrons, D., 'the role of Ireland in the new international division of labour: a proposed framework for analysis', *Regional Studies*, vol. xv, no. 2 (1981) pp. 81–100.

Perry, R., 'A summary of studies of the Cornish economy based on surveys carried out 1974–78' (Cornwall Industrial Development Association, 1979).

Phillips, A. and Taylor, B., 'Notes towards a feminist economics', *Feminist Review*, vol. vi (1980) pp. 79–88.

Pollard S., *The development of the British economy, 1914–1967* 2nd edn (London: Edward Arnold, 1969).

Price, C., 'Recovering the doorstep vote: three-dimensional socialism is now needed', *New Statesman*, 18 May 1979, p. 706.

Purdy, D. and Prior, M., *Out of the ghetto: a path to socialist rewards* (Nottingham: Spokesman, 1979).

Rees, G. and Lambert, J., 'Urban development in a 'peripheral' region: some issues from South Wales' (mimeo, 1979).

Rees, G. and Rees, T., 'Migration, industrial restructuring and class relations: the case of South Wales', UWIST Papers in Planning Research, no. 22 (Cardiff: 1981).

Rose, H. and Rose, S., 'The 1964–70 Labour Government and science and technology policy' (Notes for the Group for Alternative Science and Technology Strategy, 1982).

Rubery, J., 'Structured labour markets, worker organisation and low pay', Cambridge Journal of Economics, vol. II (1978) pp. 17–36.

Sack, R., *Conceptions of Space in Social Thought* (London: Macmillan, 1980).

Salvati, M., 'The impasse of Italian capitalism', *New Left Review*, no. 76 (1972) pp. 3–33.

Saxenian, A., 'Industrial restructuring: a case study of the electronics industry in Santa Clara County, California' (unpublished paper, 1979).

Sayer, A., 'Epistemology and conceptions of people and nature in geography', *Geoforum*, vol. X, no. 1 (1979) pp. 19–43.

Sayer, A., 'Conceptions of space in social thought: a critique'. Research Papers in Geography, no. 7 (University of Sussex, 1981).

Sayer, R. A., 'Explaining manufacturing shift: a reply to Keeble', *Environment and Planning A*, vol. XIV (1982) pp. 119–25.

Sayles, L. R., *The behaviour of the industrial work group: production and control* (London: Wiley, 1958).

Scott, P. A., *Electronics and Electrical Engineering: A Survey* (London: Joseph Sebag and Co., 1974).

Secchi, B., *Squilibri regionali e sviluppo economico* (Padua: Marsilio Editori, 1974).

Secchi, B., 'Central and Peripheral Regions in a process of economic development: the Italian case', in Massey D. B. and Batey P. W. J. (eds), *Alternative Frameworks for Analysis* (London: Pion, 1977).

Segal, N., 'The limits and means of 'self-reliant' regional economic growth', in Maclennan, D. and Parr, J. B. (eds), *Regional Policy: Past Experience and New Directions*, Glasgow Social and Economic Research Studies, 6 (Oxford: Martin Robertson, 1979) pp. 212–24.

Singh, A., 'Take-overs, economic natural selection and the theory of the firm: evidence from the postwar UK experience', *Economic Journal*, 85 (1975) pp. 497–515.

Singh, A., 'UK industry and the world economy: a case of de-industrialisation?', *Cambridge Journal of Economics*, 1 (1977) pp. 113–36.

Smith, D., 'What IRC wrought', *Management Today* (October 1969).

Southwark Trades Council and Roberts, J. C. (Southwark CDP), 'Employment in Southwark: a strategy for the future'. Southwark Trades

Council and Southwark Community Development Project, London (1976).

Spooner, D. J., 'Industrial movement and the rural periphery: the case of Devon and Cornwall', *Regional Studies*, vol. vi, no. 2 (1972) pp. 197–215.

Stanton, R., 'Foreign investment and host country politics: the Irish case', in Seers, D., Schaffer, B. and Kiljunen, M.-L. (eds), *Underdeveloped Europe: Studies in Core-Periphery Relations* (Brighton: Harvester, 1979).

Steuer, M. D., Abell, P., Gennard, J., Perlman, M., Rees, R., Scott, B. and Wallis, K., 'The impact of foreign direct investment on the United Kingdom' (HMSO, 1973).

Storey D., *'Enterpreneurship and the New Firm'* (London: Croom Helm, 1982).

Swales, J. K., 'Entrepreneurship and regional development: implications for regional policy' in Maclennan, D. and Parr, J. B. (eds) *Regional Policy: Past Experiences and new Directions* (Oxford: Martin Robertson, 1979).

Taylor, G., 'The restructuring of capital in the Teesside chemical and steel industries', Centre for Urban and Regional Studies, University of Birmingham. Paper presented to the Regionalism Working Group of the Conference of Socialist Economists, University of Durham, 8 December 1979.

Taylor, P. J., 'The changing geography of representation in Britain', *Area*, vol. xi, no. 4 (1979) pp. 289–94.

Taylor, R., *Workers and the New Depression* (London: Macmillan, 1982).

Thomas, D. E., 'Mother Wales, get off me back?', *Marxism Today* (March 1982) pp. 34–5.

Timpanaro, S., 'Considerations on Materialism', *New Left Review*, no. 85 (1974) pp. 3–22.

Townsend, A. R., 'Unemployment and the new government's "regional" aid', *Area*, vol. xii, no. 1 (1980) pp. 9–18.

Townsend, A. R., *The Impact of Recession* (London: Croom Helm, 1982).

Treasury, 'Trends in UK manufacturing industry', *Economic Progress Report*, no. 71 (London: HMSO, February 1976).

Unofficial Reform Committee, *The Miners' Next Step: Being A Suggested Scheme for the Reorganisation of the Federation, Tonypandy*. Reprinted in *Reprints in Labour History*, no. 4. (London: Pluto Press, 1973).

Urry, J., 'Paternalism, management and localities'. Lancaster Regionalism Group, Working Paper 2 (Lancaster University, 1980).

Urry, J., 'Localities, regions and social class', *International Journal of Urban and Regional Research*, vol. v, no. 4 (1981a) pp. 455–74.

Wade, R., 'Fast growth and slow development in Southern Italy', in Seers

D., Schaffer B. and Kiljunen M.-L. (eds), *Underdeveloped Europe: Studies in Core-periphery Relations*, (Brighton: Harvester, 1979).

Walker, D. and Storper, M., 'The spatial division of labour: labour and the location of industries' (mimeo, University of California), forthcoming in Tabb, W. and Sowers, L. (eds), *Sunbelt-Snowbelt: The Political Economy of Urban Development and Regional Restructuring* (New York: Oxford University Press, 1982).

Wells, F. A., *The British Hosiery and Knitwear Industry: Its History and Organisation* (revised edition) (Newton Abbott: David and Charles, 1972).

Westaway, J., 'The spatial hierarchy of business organisations and its implications for the British urban system', *Regional Studies*, vol. VIII (1974) pp. 145–55.

Westergaard, J. and Resler, H., *Class in Capitalist Society: A Study of Contemporary Britain* (Harmondsworth: Penguin, 1975).

Whittington, G., 'Changes in the top 100 quoted manufacturing companies in the United Kingdom 1948 to 1968', *Journal of Industrial Economics* (November 1972).

Wight, I., 'Territory versus function in regional development; the case of Cornwall', paper presented at the 6th International Marginal Regions Seminar (Norway, 1981).

Williams, G., 'Mother Wales, get off me back?', *Marxism Today* (December 1981) pp. 14–20.

Williams, R., 'Problems of materialism', *New Left Review*, no. 109 (1978) pp. 3–17.

Wilson, H., 'The Labour government 1964–1970 (Harmondsworth: Penguin, 1974).

Winyard S., 'From rags to rags', *Low Pay Unit*, Pamphlet no. 7 (1977).

Wood, S., *The degradation of work?* (London: Hutchinson, 1982).

Wright, E. O., 'Class boundaries in advanced capitalist societies', *New Left Review*, 98 (1976) pp. 3–41.

Wright, E. O., *Class, Crisis, State* (London: New Left Books, 1978).

Author Index

Subject Index

31, 32, 41, 42, 43, 53, 54, 63,
73, 85, 99, 130, 134, 148, 150,
153, 173, 175, 201, 213, 214,
243, 278, 283–4
labourism 222–3, 291, 295, 305
layers, combination of 117, 118,
121, 195, 204–23, 226–33, 236
linkages 106, 107, 108, 171, 191,
192, 204, 288, 301
material 108
service 108, 192
local control/ownership 83, 100,
102–5, 107, 169, 180, 181, 189,
199, 200, 206, 209, 218, 226,
228, 231, 233, 276, 279, 280,
283, 298
locality 6, 60, 105, 107, 109,
116, 120, 123, 196, 296, 299
location factor 9, 12, 14, 32, 47,
74, 121, 139–45, 172, 173, 174,
191
locational considerations 73, 74
flexibility 19, 24, 32, 56, 57,
102, 172, 304
requirements 13, 14, 19, 24,
81, 129, 147
strategies 63
London 57, 60, 93, 94, 103, 128,
135, 137, 138, 154, 158, 159,
161, 163, 164, 166, 186, 187,
189, 190, 191, 193, 208, 263,
274, 275, 287, 288, 293, 301

managerial function 2, 55, 74,
86
structure 28, 38, 69, 76, 82,
286
market forces 3, 45, 104, 107,
277
relations 20, 27, 48, 100, 103,
157, 185, 297
Marx, Karl 46, 212
Marxism 5, 6, 46–50, 70
mode of production 30, 44, 46,
49, 85
monetarism 235, 254, 264–73
monopoly, spatial 54, 144, 162–
3, 164

motorways 220, 222
multinationals 19, 22, 54, 55,
79, 92, 104, 164, 206, 208, 218,
254, 274, 283
multipliers 104, 232

NALGO 2, 211
nationalisation 84, 107, 130,
131, 197, 201, 218–19, 231, 275
nationalised industries/State
ownership 18, 64, 84, 182–3,
201, 202, 209, 226, 255, 271,
272
neo-classical school 3, 4, 46, 123
Northampton 93–9, 119
NUGMW 130
NUM 2, 198, 202
NUTGW 162, 163

occupational structure 1, 7, 9,
112, 200, 262
ownership 26, 35, 36–7, 38, 55,
71, 72, 76, 85, 107, 109, 110,
131, 153, 175, 181, 184, 209,
274–85, 294
real 76, 100, 169, 207
relations of 26, 31, 101–5,
156, 164, 184, 190, 191, 274,
283, 285

particularity (*see also* uniqueness)
6, 8
part-process spatial structure
75, 83, 86, 92, 101, 108, 113,
150, 165–6, 168, 294, 298
plants 78
periodisation 64
periodising 22
peripheral regions 1, 2, 24, 49,
60, 90, 92, 110, 112, 114, 117,
168, 170, 171, 173, 194, 243,
245, 256, 262, 271, 272, 301,
302
petit-bourgeoisie (*see also* class
structure) 61, 111, 113, 114,
153, 177, 199–200, 206–7, 227,
228, 232, 278–9, 286
petrochemicals 27, 81, 85